VIRAGO
CLASSIC NON-FICTION

Janina Bauman was born in 1926. The elder of two daughters, she and her family lived a comfortable life in Warsaw, surrounded by uncles, aunts, cousins and grandparents. With the outbreak of war and the siege and surrender of Warsaw, this life was destroyed. Her father disappeared in 1939 and was killed in the Katyn Massacre of 1940.

Janina Bauman was awarded her BA in 1950 from the Academy of Social and Political Sciences in Warsaw, and her MA in Aesthetics in 1959 from the University of Warsaw. She worked in Polish film for twenty years as a translator, researcher and script editor. She and her husband and three children had to leave Poland in 1968. After three years in Israel they came to Britain and they now live in Leeds. Until 1979 Janina Bauman was assistant librarian in a comprehensive school. After taking early retirement she began to write *Winter in the Morning*, which was later followed by its sequel, *A Dream of Belonging: My Years in Postwar Poland*.

V V

The author, aged 11. Drawing from a photograph, by Lydia Bauman, Janina Bauman's daughter

WINTER IN THE MORNING

A Young Girl's Life in the
Warsaw Ghetto and Beyond
1939–1945

Janina Bauman

Author Note

I have changed the names of some of the people in my
book; with some other names I have replaced the capital
W with V, the Polish Wala sounds like Vala. I have kept
the Polish street names in Warsaw with one exception:
Ulica Graniczna is referred to in English as Border Street.

J.B.

A *Virago* Book

Published by Virago Press 1991

Reprinted 1997

First published in Great Britain by Virago Press Ltd 1986

Copyright © Janina Bauman 1986

A CIP catalogue record for this book is available
from the British Library

ISBN 0 86068 652 3

Printed and bound in Great Britain by
Clays Ltd, St Ives plc

Virago
A Division of
Little, Brown and Company (UK)
Brettenham House
Lancaster Place
London WC2E 7EN

Contents

Why? And Why Now?   vii

1 The Peaceful Years   1
2 Border Street   16
3 Behind the Walls   37
4 The Walls Tighten Around Us   65
5 Beyond the Walls   98
6 On the Run   113
7 Out of Hiding   155
8 Winter into Spring   170

Postscript   191

Chronology   194

To the memory
of my Mother and Sister

I want to thank very warmly my dear friend Maria Hirszowicz who, for years, kept urging me to write down my memories. I am glad I surrendered.

I am also deeply grateful to Reverend Hugh Bishop, Molly Gaunt, Margaret Gothelf, Dorothy and Alan Griffiths, Łukasz Hirszowicz, Griselda Pollock and Janet Wolf who gave me courage when I needed it most. And to my keen, friendly editors and publishers, Ruthie Petrie, Julia Vellacott, Fenella Gentleman, and all the other members of Virago Press, who shine to me as an example of insight, enthusiasm and efficiency, I feel infinitely grateful, too.

Last but not least, I thank Zygmunt, my husband, who had to put up with my 'absence' when, for almost two years, I dwelled in the world of my youth that was not his world.

Why? And Why Now?

It took me about forty years to feel ready to write this book. All these years I hardly ever thought about the past. Never talked about it with my mother or sister. Never told my husband and daughters the full story of my survival. I preferred to forget. The horrifying images would return only in my dreams. Neither have I ever tried to publish my diaries and short stories written during the war: for years they lay forgotten in my private drawer in Warsaw. I reread them only after my mother died and, among her keepsakes, I found some of my diary pages and stories carefully copied by herself in her neat handwriting. Only then, in the early eighties, in Leeds, did I feel I should start writing.

I dived deep into the past, forgetting my present age and becoming this young girl again. Amazing how much one can recall when one decides to revive the past, year after year, month after month, experience after experience. I made an effort to be faithful not only to the facts but also to my own thoughts and feelings at the time. I tried hard not to let my present knowledge, my present mature reflection interfere with my memories. I wanted to re-enter the life, the places, the episodes as I lived them then. Yet mine was the small, limited world of a teenage girl living in fear, in seclusion, in ignorance of very many important facts and occurrences. That is why my account is not and does not pretend to be a historical document. (For the sake of younger readers, who might feel 'historically confused' while reading it, I have included a brief chronology of the relevant historical events, of which, at the time, I was not always aware myself.)

My book is meant as a tribute to those innumerable people who helped me, my mother and my sister to survive the war. The majority of them were women of different social backgrounds, ages and occupations. The motives of risking their lives to help us were as varied as their characters.

During the war I learned the truth we usually choose to leave unsaid: that the cruellest thing about cruelty is that it dehumanises its victims before it destroys them. And that the hardest of struggles is to remain human in inhuman conditions.

Janina Bauman, Leeds, 1985

1 The Peaceful Years

A patch of early morning sunshine on the pinewood floor, the squeak of a tram fading away around the corner, the monotonous clatter of horse's hooves late at night – these are the most distant memories of my life. The twenties were just turning into the thirties. We lived in Warsaw at 10 Senatorska Street, not far from the district where most Jews lived. Later, when my father became well enough known to start his private surgery, and when my sister Sophie was born, we moved to the centre of the city and lived in a large apartment house at 5 Sienna Street. In its place there now stands the Palace of Culture and Science, the monumental gift of the Soviets to the Polish capital.

I was growing up in a happy family. My father was a doctor and surgeon, dealing with people's kidneys and bladders. My mother's father, Grandad Aleksander, was a doctor too, his fame well established in Warsaw before I was born. My paternal grandfather, whose name was Maks, ran a music shop in the most elegant part of the city, until he went bankrupt. I remember him as a modest old man with plenty of time and warm feelings for myself. Somehow I knew that he and Grandma Viera were poor and dependent on my father, while the other grandparents, who lived in Border Street, were rich. They were rich not only because Grandad Aleksander was a gifted doctor and surgeon but also because Grannie Eva's family was well off. Grannie Eva's family was also the *crème de la crème* of society, great-grandfather serving for years as both head of the Jewish Council and councillor of the City of Warsaw. There were lots of uncles, aunts and cousins on both sides of the family, most of them doctors, others lawyers, engineers or suchlike. Except for my great-grandfather, who died before I was born, no one in my large family spoke Yiddish, wore beards, skullcaps or traditional Jewish gaberdines. Nobody was religious. We were all Polish, born on Polish soil, brought up in the Polish tradition, permeated with the spirit of Polish history and literature. Yet – Jewish at the same time, conscious of being Jewish every minute of our lives.

I asked my father what 'Jew' meant when I was five years old. I don't remember exactly what he answered, but I believe it was very hard for him to explain this, not only to his young child, but also to himself. What I clearly remember, though, is a kind of litany: 'I am a Jew, you see, Mama is a Jewess, you are yourself and your little sister; Uncle Julian is a Jew' . . . 'And Auntie Maria is a Jewess . . .' 'No,' he said, slightly embarrassed, 'Auntie Maria is not, she is a Christian.' Auntie Maria, my favourite aunt, was not in fact my aunt. She had been my mother's and her two younger brothers' nanny when they were children. Now she lived with my grandparents at Border Street, being their housekeeper and a close member of the family.

In our vast flat in Sienna Street, which included father's private surgery, I lived with my parents, Sophie and a maid and a cook. There was always a nanny, or a governess and later a French teacher too. These women came and went, and I loathed them because they stood like an impenetrable wall between myself and my mother. Mother was always busy rushing somewhere, coping with patients, shopping, answering telephone calls, instructing the cook, or in between simply resting, locked in her room. I longed for her incessantly, for a full day spent together, to sleep in her bed, which happened only when I was ill. Of father I saw even less. He worked very hard, leaving for hospital when I was still asleep, receiving his private patients throughout the afternoon, making home calls in the evenings, sometimes late into the night. As far back as I can remember, I lived in terror that my parents might suddenly die. When they spent an evening out, dining at Border Street or going to the cinema, I could never get to sleep, imagining they were already dead and would never come back. Glued to the nursery window, I would watch the quiet, half-lit street until the two familiar shapes emerged from around the corner. Only then could I go back to bed. I never told anybody about my fears or night watches. It was my secret.

For some strange reason I was not sent to school until I was eleven. I was taught at home with six or seven other children by private teacher – at my own house or theirs. Early in May, Sophie and I were sent off 'to the country', as we called the fashionable suburb, Konstancin. In the early thirties Grandad Aleksander had had a large modern villa built there for all the family. Grannie Eva spent all summer at the villa, and other members of the family joined us for days or weeks. Under the loving care of Auntie Maria, who was the heart and soul of the house, Sophie and I would stay there till late September, in accordance with the common belief that the country was good for children. Perhaps this was why we were educated at home, so as not to be bound to the school calendar.

So more than a third of my early life was spent in the big garden bursting with fruit and flowers, in thick woods full of mushrooms, and in the vast fertile fields of the surrounding countryside. Later in life, trapped inside the ghetto walls, hiding in strange, stifling places, or even living as a free adult in postwar Warsaw, I dreamed and daydreamed about all this.

Sometimes Auntie Maria would take me shopping with her to the nearest village. It was a very poor, dirty place inhabited mainly by Jews. I can still remember little children sitting in the dusty road in front of their shabby cottages, playing with used flypapers black with dead flies. Live flies buzzed in their curly black hair, crawled on their filthy arms and legs. The children did not seem to mind. Their fathers were pedlars or poor craftsmen. They had long beards and wore black gaberdines. Their mothers wore untidy wigs. They all spoke a foreign language I could not understand. Their Polish was funny.

The queerness, the strangeness of those people who were Jews like us had puzzled me as long as I could remember. I used to see many of them in the park in Warsaw, but I saw them first of all in my father's surgery. Some of them looked very poor, but some did not. Still, they were all strangers and I felt frightened whenever I had to pass the corridor where they would sit and talk very loudly while waiting for my father to see them.

I feared them, perhaps I slightly despised them as sometimes children do when they meet people who speak in a broken language and look different. But most of all I wondered and wondered how they and we were Jews while other people, as sweet and familiar as Auntie Maria, for example, were not. Obviously it had nothing to do with being poor or rich. There were poor Jews in the village, well off Jews like my family, and Jews far, far richer than us – my uncle Jerzy's in-laws, for instance, who were bankers and wore diamond rings and gold chains when visiting my grandparents.

I learned somehow that Jews could be recognised simply by their looks – dark curly hair, black eyes, high-bridged noses. But this did not work, either. Uncle Józef was blond, my own eyes were pale green and there were many straight noses in the family. What then?

Maybe it had something to do with the church and religion. Jews did not go to church; we never did. Jews went to synagogue; but we never did, either. Like non-Jewish people we had always had a Christmas tree at home. But unlike them we also had those gorgeous celebrations at my great-grandmother's twice a year. It was called Pesach (Passover) in the spring and Rosh Hashana (Jewish New Year) in the autumn. We all sat at an endless table laid the length of two large rooms, my great-grandmother, half-deaf and cantankerous, at the top, and I – the youngest, since Sophie was too young to take part – next to her. We ate hard-boiled eggs in salt water and matzos if it was Pesach, fish, broth with noodles and lots of sweets. There were candles in the silver candlesticks on the table. I was allowed to drink sweet wine. It was my duty to reassure great-grandmother that the fish was delicious, which was a real ordeal because she could not hear me anyhow. The young uncles and aunts made a lot of commotion, throwing walnuts at each other. That is all I remember.

Were those lovely dinner parties that stopped for ever once great-grandma had died the only reason why we were Jews? And if so, was it worth being Jewish? If I had not been I would have been allowed to walk round the village with a Corpus Christi procession in the summer, wearing a white dress and a wreath. This would certainly have made me far more happy than our 'long table' celebrations.

I knew it was better not to be a Jew. There were posters on the walls in Warsaw saying, 'Don't buy in Jewish shops'. Once in the street I heard a stranger calling another stranger 'you filthy Jew'. When I told my mother about it, she said some people did not like Jews at all. They were anti-Semites, she said. I personally did not know any of them, everybody liked me, I was sure. To be quite certain I asked our Christian maid whether she did or not. She said yes, of course, she liked me very much. 'Do you like Jews?' I insisted. She seemed taken aback. 'No, not really.' 'Why not?' 'Jews are evil,' she said, 'they murdered our Lord Jesus.' This puzzled and worried me for a while. Jesus was goodness itself – I knew that. Who would have wanted him dead? Certainly not us. Nor would those noisy, dark strangers in my father's waiting room: that was impossible – Jesus lived ages ago when the years were still passing in the opposite direction.

Soon I learnt that it was possible to stop being Jewish. My father had three younger brothers. Vładek was a journalist, Julian a doctor, and Józef, the blond one, an engineer. I was about nine when Vładek was converted to Catholicism, changed his surname and married a Christian girl. The event was widely discussed amongst the relatives. Strangely enough, everybody whispered. I do not remember seeing Vładek often after that, and it was more than two years before we paid our first visit to his little flat where he lived with his non-Jewish wife, Halina, and their new-born son, Jurek.

Lying in bed in my room one night, soon after Vładek was converted, I overheard a sharp argument between my father and Uncle Józef who had come to supper. Father, whom I knew as a quiet, softly spoken man, raised his voice, scolding his brother with unusual fervour.

'Never, never in my life!' I heard him shout. 'Where is your self-respect? Do as you like, but don't come to me for my blessing!'

'And what about Vładek's self-respect?' asked Uncle Józef angrily. 'You went along with his decision, didn't you?'

'I neither approved it nor condemned it. His case is different. He fell in love with Halina, and he didn't want to antagonise her family.'

'Why can't you see *my* reason?' shouted Uncle Józef. 'I am suffocating, I can't carry on like this any longer. Just think how far I could get in life if I were not . . . '

'That's exactly what I hate and despise,' roared my father. 'Decking oneself in borrowed plumes, denying one's own identity, even one's name, just to make things easier, to get further, to carve out for oneself a brilliant career . . . *that's* what I call lack of dignity!'

That night, young as I was, I learned a crucial lesson. Be what you are, never pretend to be somebody else. Be Jewish if you were born a Jew, even if you don't quite understand what it means. Be dignified, don't deny your identity. Eight years later I did. It was not my choice. My life was at stake.

Uncle Józef never became a convert. He died, however, not because he was a Jew but because he was a Polish officer, killed   in the Katyń Massacre* together with my father.

In trying to put down the events and feelings of my early life, I do not

---

*On 13 April 1943 the Germans announced that they had discovered the mass graves of Polish officers in the Katyń forest near Smolensk, western Russia. The Germans identified the corpses as the officers who had been interned by the Russians at the Kozielsk prison camp before April 1940. Subsequent investigation by the International Committee of the Red Cross confirmed that about 14,500 Polish war prisoners – mainly officers of the Polish army – were executed in Katyń in the spring of 1940.

wish to suggest that I spent my childhood thinking about matters as broad and controversial as what it meant to belong to a large minority within a Catholic nation. I remember those years as a bright, warm time of sensual and emotional exploration, vivid imagination, a growing love for anything of beauty around me; as a time when I read my first books and made my first friendships.

It was my Grandma Viera who patiently taught me to read when I was five. I must confess I did not like her. She was a cool, ungiving person, not half as caring for me as Grandad Maks or Grannie Eva. Yet she did make me read and I shall always be grateful to her for that.

So I had already read many books when I first joined the little circle of boys and girls learning at home, and there I met my first two friends: Renata and Zula. Renata was a quiet, soft girl with dreamy eyes and gentle manners. She lived in the shadow of her elder sister, Joanna, who was a beauty and had a lot of friends. Renata, on the contrary, did not mix easily with other children and stayed rather aloof. Since I was shy too, we somehow stuck to each other from the very beginning. We were both fond of reading, so we swapped books and talked about them. We often stayed behind after classes to do our homework together. With Zula it was a different story. She joined the circle much later, when I was no longer shy. Ginger-haired, lively, joyful, she was a perfect mate to giggle with, talk rubbish with or pull a boy's leg. Keenly interested in matters of sex, she told me all sorts of strange stories about grown-ups, which I neither understood nor believed. But it was good fun and I enjoyed Zula's airy company. I kept in touch with both her and Renata for a long time after leaving our home circle.

In September 1937, being eleven, I was finally sent to school. I went into the sixth form, the last year of primary education, in a private school. 'Our School' as it was called, was run by a Jewish headmistress, all the teachers were Jewish and so were the pupils. Yet it could hardly have been called a Jewish school, since apart from the Jewish history lessons, everything was strictly Polish, even Christian holidays were observed. I was very happy in 'Our School', proved to be a good pupil, and made a few friends. The most important of them was Hanka, a serious girl of bright mind and judgement far beyond her age. I thought highly of her and felt proud to be her friend. We were close for many years after. She was not the only one, however, whose company I enjoyed in 'Our School'. After lessons, I would walk with the other girls and boys and discuss serious problems. They were all my age but they seemed far more mature and knew things I had not the slightest notion about, because they had spent half their lives at school while I was still stuck in my childish circle. I tried hard to make up for that and showered my parents with questions about what I heard, but still did not quite understand. Sometimes instead of going home, I went to Border Street to hear my grandparents' opinions on International Communism, or confirm the unbelievable latest news that women, like hens, laid eggs once a month.

Once one of my new friends, Jola, who was a rich businessman's daughter and the most politically conscious person in our group, asked me whether I was for or against the nationalist rebels in Spain. I thought a while, and as I only knew that there was a civil war going on in Spain and nothing else, said I wanted the rebels to win. My conclusion was based on the strong belief that any rebels fighting against any government were always right; they were true patriots and heroes – and I knew that from Polish history. But Jola said I was a reactionary, and she would not speak to me again until the following day. Soon I learned that the rebels were fascists, which was evil of course, and that the others were communists of a kind. Whether it was right or wrong to be communist, I was not sure. My new friends claimed it was right, while my grandparents sounded far less enthusiastic. As for Jola, who boasted she was 'red as blood', she was taken away by her parents to New York at the start of the war and lived there happily ever after.

About Fascism and Hitler I knew quite a lot. The subject was often discussed by my parents and relatives. In the summer of 1937, a great-aunt from Berlin came to visit and stayed in the villa for a month or so. She was very distressed and sad and always sighed heavily when she spoke about what was going on in Germany. She would lower her voice and give frightened, furtive glances around every time she was about to say 'Hitler'. I developed a sense that 'Hitler' was a rude, shameful word and I never used it. Whenever conversation in the sitting room touched upon the future – next holidays, for example, or plans for another family get-together – Aunt Eugenia would sigh, 'First let's survive.' I sensed that nobody really believed what she was telling us. Her frightened glances and whispers they would explain away as an obsession of old age or the first symptoms of paranoia. I think we all felt relieved when she went home to Berlin. None of us ever saw her again. She died in a German concentration camp before the war even began.

This vague feeling of menace, once planted in my soul, persisted and grew stronger all the time. The press and radio roared about Hitler's audacious moves, people talked anxiously about them and I was already old enough to listen and dread. When in March 1938 German troops entered and annexed Austria, war seemed for a while to be on the doorstep.

However, none of this affected my day-to-day life. I was still very happy in 'Our School', with the sad awareness that my bliss would not last for ever: my primary education was coming to an end and examinations for secondary school were approaching.

It had been decided since I was born that I would follow in my father's and grandfather's footsteps and become a doctor. I had taken this for granted as long as I could remember. There was, however, a major obstacle to this family daydream. At that time, it was hard for anyone to get into medical studies at Warsaw University – for a Jewish boy or girl it was almost impossible. Though total exclusion had never been introduced in Polish universities, there was none the less a clear unofficial restriction on the number of Jews admitted for studies, particularly those leading to professional degrees, such as medicine. Practically the only way a Jew could get in was to gain a good certificate from a state high school. But there the same obstacle lurked again: there were severe restrictions on the number of Jewish children admitted to state secondary schools. One had to be truly brilliant and pass the qualifying exams with top marks to be accepted. My father, obsessed with the idea of my becoming a doctor, decided to give me this chance.

So, in June 1938, I sat the state-controlled exams, perhaps the most difficult exams of my life, wishing I could fail and thus escape the ordeal I anticipated. Strangely enough, I passed with the highest marks and was admitted to a state high school for girls in the city.

The summer holidays that year dragged by, bleak and gloomy. I dreaded the autumn. In August, my mother took Sophie and me to Sopot, a seaside spa near Gdańsk. It was my first experience of the sea and I enjoyed it enormously, trying not to think about the future. One day we went to Gdańsk to see this beautiful ancient town which I knew so well from literature and history. To our dismay, all we saw were huge red banners with black swastikas entirely covering the ancient walls. Hundreds and thousands of Nazis in black uniforms and red armbands with swastikas marched up and down the city in time to deafening brass band music, singing their fascist songs. The town roared with the ribald mirth of the future conquerors, while Polish passers-by stared on with awe and hatred. We ran away back to Sopot and never went to Gdańsk again. Yet, the nauseating, sticky feeling of awe and hatred remained.

September came, warm and bright, and there I was in the new school which I had already feared and hated in advance. It was even worse than I had anticipated. I was the only Jewish girl – not just in my form but in the whole gymnasium (the first four years of secondary school). There was another Jewish girl in the lyceum but she was nearly at the end of school. From the very first morning I felt deeply uneasy and throughout the following ten months was more often unhappy than not.

I may be wrong after all these years, but it seems to me now that most of my suffering came from my own mind. The bitter awareness of being unwanted in my form, in the whole school, of being seen by others as different, perhaps worse, and being the only one like that – nobody else in the same situation to be friends with – all this was quite enough to make me feel insecure and profoundly unhappy, even without any open manifestations of hostility.

It was an ordeal to stand still in silence among my classmates – forty-three girls – when they said their prayers at the beginning and end of every school day and crossed themselves after 'amen'. It was agony to stay away from the classroom during religion lessons and have to explain time and again to passing teachers why you were reading a book in the hall instead of toiling together with your classmates. The priest who taught religion was young and kind. He always smiled to me gently if he met me on my way out of the classroom when he was coming in. Once I plucked up my courage and asked him whether I could stay and listen. He said of course I could and seemed rather pleased. After that, I stayed and found the lessons interesting. The Christian faith with all its earthly attributes was an entirely new realm for me, after all. I learnt a lot by just listening and it proved very useful later.

I do not remember having any trouble with the teachers. I was a quiet girl and a good pupil. I believe they rather liked me. Even the maths teacher, a good-looking, vigorous person in her mid-thirties, seemed to be friendly to me, in spite of the fact that I hated maths and was terribly slow at it, often almost giving up. She was our form tutor and met us once or twice a week to talk about matters other than fractions or equations. On one such an occasion, she made a fiery speech to make clear to us that we should not buy our stationery or anything else in Jewish shops. And that we should attend only Christian cinemas instead of pouring money into the pockets of Jewish owners. She even gave us a list with the addresses of cinemas belonging to Christians; to be honest, there were only a few in Warsaw. After that, I could never go to my tutor with any personal problems, though she was still friendly to me.

More than anything and anybody else at school, I loved Polish lessons and the Polish teacher. Mrs Kwaskowska, an elderly woman – or so she seemed to me, though she was only about fifty – was the ideal old-fashioned teacher: very strict, very fair, rarely smiling, highly qualified and experienced both as a scholar and a pedagogue. She would seldom praise her pupils or easily give them high marks. Yet I knew she thought highly of me. She openly praised my essays and often read them aloud to the class. My knowledge of literature, too, was far more advanced than that of any other pupil in my form. I expected a 'very good' mark at the end of the first term. To my bitter disappointment I got only 'good', exactly like eight or ten other girls. Nobody got 'very good', which was not much consolation to me since I knew for certain that in Polish I was better than any of those 'good' girls.

I could not and I still cannot explain this strange incident other than by my being Jewish. I think it went against nationalist feelings to admit that the Polish language and Polish literature could have been mastered by a Jewish child better than by forty-three children with pure Polish blood in their veins. I don't think that Mrs Kwaskowska was simply careful not to antagonise the school or the state educational authorities. I suspect she believed herself that it would be unfair to praise me higher than others. For the first time in my life, I felt myself a victim of real injustice from a person I particularly respected.

But on the whole, my relationships with teachers were of far less importance than those with my classmates. Nearly all of them slipped out of my life and memory entirely after this single year in the state high school. I do not remember their names or faces. I do remember, however, my enemies, my friends and 'the elite' group which was neither hostile nor friendly to me.

Two of my three enemies were big, strong girls, a couple of years older, who sat at the very back of the class. Lacking any abilities or interest in learning, they were now spending their third year in the first form. Later, at the beginning of the war, one of them gave up her education and enjoyed life, going out with German soldiers. For the time being, though, these two blockheads were a nuisance to everybody, but particularly to me, as they took great pleasure in making loud insulting remarks about Jews in my presence. This went on day after day. Some other girls would giggle. Nobody intervened, not even myself. I pretended not to hear. The third enemy was big and strong too. This was only her second year in the first form. She was rather intelligent but wild and unpredictable. She chose me as her main victim and sat just behind me, teasing me during lessons. Her methods were physical rather than verbal. She would pull my plaits, pinch my arms, kick my ankles, tear up my exercise books, brazenly take my small possessions like pens, pencils and rubbers. Physically weak and with no will whatsoever to fight back in the same way, too proud to complain or ask teachers for help, I assumed an air of indifference, pretending – as with the two blockheads – that I did not notice or care. It made her furious. The other girls, at least those sitting near, knew very well what was going on, but neither backed her nor helped me.

The open hostility of my three enemies was far less painful to me, however, than the aloofness of the bright, serious girls that I would have liked to be my friends. They formed a distinct group and were the leaders of the class, respected by the silent majority as well as by the teachers. Their little circle was closed to me, perhaps because they did not want me to be one of them, or perhaps because I was too proud to make an effort to join them. Our relationships were correct but cool.

I would have been very unhappy indeed had it not been for a number of friendly but very dull girls who toiled over their essays and exercises with little hope of getting even middling marks. As a rule, they would come to me, not to anybody else, to ask for help with their homework. I was only too pleased to offer them this help. And they liked me, really and truly, not just because they needed me. So at least I had somebody to talk to and to spend the breaks with. I was always surrounded by five or six of them. Nobody knew how lonely I really felt.

I can see now that being Jewish was only one reason for my estrangement. I belonged to a well-off professional family while most of my forty-three classmates were workers' or craftsmen's children, some of them very poor. The state high school with its low fees was meant for them, not for me. So I was a double stranger in this school, and deep in my heart I still bear some resentment towards my parents for having sent me there.

At twelve, nearly thirteen, I led a double life. There was the misery of the weekday mornings and afternoons at school, and the happy evenings and the blissful Sundays away from school. Once a week I attended an evening class in religion which was compulsory for all Jewish children learning in the state secondary schools. There were about fifteen of us – Jewish girls of all ages, all from state girls' schools in Warsaw. It was some relief to me to talk to them and learn that my experience was shared. One of them was my old mate from 'Our School', Irena. We would meet before each lesson and travel by tram together. She had never been a close friend before, but now we had much in common.

Strangely enough, though, Irena seemed to cope with her plight much better than I did. Not half as shy and self-conscious as myself, belonging to a rather less prosperous family, she was not unhappy in her school. The religion lessons themselves were dull – the history of Jews rather than religion, not half as stirring as the Christian religion classes at school. But I learned a lot from them, and was now in a position to choose between the two faiths. Nevertheless, I remained equally remote from and indifferent to both of them.

There were quiet, happy evenings at home. When once my homework and French lessons were over, I could play with Sophie or read. Sophie was about nine by then and a very good partner to play with. We camped in tents built from chairs and blankets, visited an enchanted world inhabited by fairies with whom we were on first-name terms, kept a Bank of Sweets, ran a medical laboratory (later in her life Sophie became a microbiologist), published our own weekly paper entitled *Common Wanderer* for our parents, grandparents and anybody else who might be interested. Sometimes we marched up and down our large flat sporting home-made banners in protest against the woollen pants we were forced to wear.

I was a keen reader, too, and already owned a large collection of books and a little lamp on my bedside table. Nobody objected to my reading as long as I wished, so I devoured books one after another. But apart from classics, they were just children's books. The first 'normal' book I ever read was *The Citadel* by A. J. Cronin in Polish. I read it in September 1939, in the cellar, in short breaks between air raids.

I loved my grandparents' home at Border Street, and since I was old enough to go out on my own, I would often pay them a surprise visit when I was free. There was something special about the place which always enthralled me; a special smell, a subdued light, a touch of the past century. The house was old, the vast flat full of mysterious nooks, cupboards and boxrooms which I was sometimes allowed to explore. I found there the old-fashioned toys that had once belonged to my mother and her brothers, Jerzy and Stefan, huge plushy elephants and tigers smelling of dust, rocking horses, celluloid dolls and dolls' houses. The furniture in the flat was even older, inherited from Grannie Eva's ancestors and said to be antique and valuable. The rich shapes of the heavy armchairs, the carved chests of drawers, sewing tables and sideboards were nothing like our own furniture at Sienna Street, which was light, glossy and smelled of fresh wood. There were old silver plates and bowls scattered all over grandparents' house, old porcelain vases, old etchings on the walls. One of the seven rooms, which used to be called 'the salon', housed a powerful piano, and when my mother was still at home, was played at big dancing parties. Later, when the daughter of the house had married and left, and grandfather Aleksander had grown too tired to enjoy this kind of social event, the salon was turned into a small gallery, its walls tightly covered with pictures by famous Polish painters of the turn of the century: Malczewski, Chełmoński, Fałat. I would wander from wall to wall and gaze at those pictures each time I visited the house. They all enchanted me: the landscape with a peasant and two horses ploughing the dark soil under the broad, heavily clouded sky; the self-portrait of the bald, rough artist at work; the bewildered face of a blonde girl horrified by the dead bird she cautiously held in her fingers. Two paintings were my favourites. One was three centuries old and did not belong to the rest. It was a tiny little Dutch painting in a thick black frame showing a hunting party resting in a forest. The small bright figures of men, dogs and horses seemed to spring out from the dark background as if they were alive. The other picture, painted by Malczewski, was big and featured a priest and a rabbi engaged in heated discussion. Their faces were sharp, their eyes gleaming, their hands animated. I would stare and stare at them, musing upon the great enigma of being or not being Jewish.

There was only one place in my grandparents' flat which did not look ancient: Uncle Stefan's room. It was furnished with smart modern stuff and housed a superb foreign radio. My youngest uncle was just back from England where he had studied economics. He was in his late twenties, not married and not yet working. Handsome, unusually bright and witty, he had a girl friend who was no less marvellous than himself. Jadwiga was about twenty-three, very beautiful with green eyes and auburn hair, very elegant too. Stefan and she were passionately in love and I was passionately fond of them. They were my idols. I could not understand why they were not getting married and why Jadwiga seldom came to Border Street. Once I overheard some relatives whisper that grandfather Aleksander was not very keen on her becoming Stefan's wife because she belonged to an inferior Jewish family: less prosperous perhaps, or with less education. Against this I silently rebelled. Jadwiga was obviously very clever, well-read and well-informed. She was much better, far more charming than Uncle Jerzy's wife, who was the daughter of a rich banker.

On my casual visits at Border Street, I rarely met grandfather Aleksander. He worked in his own clinic till late or rested in his study.

Usually I sat with Grannie telling her all about school and my worries. She was a perfect listener. I remember her, tall, well-dressed, very noble with her white hair and young face, listening intently to my confessions. Somehow she knew how to comfort me when I complained about my day-to-day ordeals. She always said that, instead of feeling pity for myself, it would be better to think about people whose lives were far less happy than mine, about children born in squalor who were deprived of everything I enjoyed. She was right, I felt ashamed and stopped grumbling for a while. When we talked, Auntie Maria kept trotting around, neat and cheerful, rustling in her starched apron, spreading the table with my favourite dishes. I loved to be with Grannie and her, I knew they cared for me and were never short of time when I wanted to sit and talk.

My Sundays were blissful, too. Father at home relaxed and ready to answer my questions, explain things, tell stories. Sometimes he would take Mother, Sophie and myself and drive us in his big black Chevrolet into 'the Unknown', which usually proved to be a lovely spot at the outskirts of the city. The trip ended, as a rule, with impressive cups of vanilla ice-cream or, if it was cold, lovely cookies in a cafeteria. Back home, we all had a meal together, which never happened on weekdays, since from Monday to Saturday children were served separately.

On Sunday evenings I attended dance classes. It was a social rather than educational enterprise launched by Renata's sister, Joanna, who was fifteen by then. Thanks to Renata's backing, I was admitted to this wonderful world of 'almost grown-ups' who would meet in private houses and dance till night under the care of a professional teacher who also played the piano. Socially, I counted for little, child as I still was, yet I always had a male partner to dance with and to look up at, both literally and metaphorically. One of them, a kind, intelligent boy called Jan, would see me home after each dancing party. We walked arm in arm along the darkened streets and I felt infinitely delighted. I imagined Jan was in love with me, and probably I was in love with him, if the vague, tender feeling of a twelve-year-old can be called love. Anyway, for the first time I realised I was pretty and began to care about my appearance and male glances.

The spring of 1939 brought gloom not only to my country but also to my private life. In March, as a result of the agreement signed in Munich six months earlier, Hitler finally annexed Czechoslovakia and Poland was to some extent a partner in the game. On the other hand, he renewed with added force his claims to the free city of Gdańsk, which

Poland sternly rejected. The swelling menace of war hung over the country and aroused strong nationalist feelings. These often degenerated into chauvinism. Anti-Semitic slogans, speeches, articles became a staple diet. The common unrest could easily result in anti-Jewish riots. Jews were expecting them, fearing them. The ominous word 'pogrom' entered my vocabulary.

In April Grandfather Aleksander suddenly died from a heart attack. This was my first experience of the departure of somebody I took for granted. My beloved Grannie Eva was seriously ill. Nobody ever told me what was wrong with her, but I suspected it was cancer and grieved bitterly for her.

The uneasy school year finally came to an end and the last summer holidays of my childhood began. Feeling greatly relieved – for the time being, at least – I was not in a hurry to do my holiday homework for the following September. There was not much to do, anyway. Only the Latin teacher wanted his pupils to work over the summer. I was supposed to learn a Latin poem by heart. The poem was particularly long and unusual. In fact it was a popular Polish song about gypsies enjoying freedom around a camp in the forest, which the teacher himself had translated into Latin. I still remember the first lines, the only ones I bothered to learn:

> *Ohe sub silva quid longe splendet:*
> *Velitum manus ignem incendit*
> (At the edge of the forest something shines from afàr:
> A handful of gypsies start lighting a fire)

My parents decided I was old enough to spend a part of my holidays with them and at the beginning of August took me to a famous spa in Galizia, the south-eastern part of Poland, near Lwów. The events that followed have almost entirely erased the memories of this trip from my mind. I do not remember how I spent my days in the spa or whether I enjoyed them or not. I can only put down on paper the bits I remember and shall never forget.

I decided not to wear plaits any longer, and copying Walt Disney's *Snow White* wore my long hair loose with a ribbon fastened around my head. Apparently because of this change, somebody told me I was a pretty girl, somebody else addressed me as 'Miss'. All this and nature itself brought home to me that I was no longer a child. There, in the spa, I celebrated my thirteenth birthday on 18 August.

With striking clarity, as though it were an unforgettable painting, I remember a small crowd of Galizian Jews sunk in their sunset prayers at the riverside. Their black silhouettes with long beards and huge round fur caps rocked to and fro against the background of the fiery sky; their ominous wailing filled my heart with anxiety and a vague premonition of disaster.

We were going somewhere in somebody's car – it must have been on 24 August – when from the car radio we suddenly heard news of the non-aggression pact between Hitler and Stalin. The next news was that, because of growing tension and the possibility of war, the beginning of the new school year was to be postponed from 1 September till a later date. 'So perhaps I shan't need to learn that damned Latin verse, after all,' I thought with slight relief.

2 *Border Street*

At 12.40 p.m. on August 31 1939, Hitler ordered hostilities
against Poland to start at 4.45 the next morning. Great Britain
and France declared war on Germany on September 3 . . .

For their invasion of Poland, the Germans employed some 40
normal infantry divisions, together with 14 mechanised . . .
divisions. Their rapid victory was to be effected by high-speed
armoured warfare . . . Poland lay patently open to such attack.
For their defence, the Poles had available roughly as many
infantry divisions as the Germans; but against the German
armour they had merely 12 cavalry brigades (one of them
armoured) and a sprinkling of light tanks . . .

By September 8 one of the German armoured corps was in
the outskirts of Warsaw, having advanced 140 miles in the first
week of war . . .

On September 10 the Polish commander in chief, Marshal
Edward Śmigły-Rydz, ordered a general retreat to the south-
east. The Germans, however, were by that time . . . penetrating
deeply into eastern Poland . . .

The Polish defence was already reduced to random efforts by
isolated bodies of troops when another blow fell: on September
17 1939, Soviet forces entered Poland from the east. The next
day, the Polish government and high command crossed the
Romanian frontier on their way to exile. The Warsaw garrison
held out against the Germans until September 28 . . .

When the Nazis laid siege to Warsaw . . . over 10,000
citizens perished and more than 50,000 were wounded, before
the lack of supplies forced a surrender.
        The New Encyclopaedia Britannica, Volumes 14 and 19

The last days of August. Hazy late summer sunshine, trees heavy with
ripening fruit, drowsy butterflies stirring over the bright multicoloured
asters and dahlias. Blissful silence. Sweet peacefulness.

I am back at Konstancin, reunited with Sophie, ailing Grannie, dear
Auntie Maria. Father in the army, somewhere in a Warsaw military
hospital. Mother away in our Warsaw flat, to be as near him as possible.
He was called up as a reserve officer six days ago and Grandpa Maks
phoned to the Spa Hotel with the message. Lots of men spending their
holidays in the Spa got the same message on the same day and a true
exodus began at once. With little chance to get on the overcrowded
train, Father managed to hire a taxi to get to Warsaw as quickly as
possible. We all travelled one whole day and night, stopping only to
have a hasty meal wherever we could get it. There were queues of cars,
wagons and bicycles on the roads; people hurried in all directions driven
by the same fears. We drove by quiet fields and woods, passed small
villages already stirred by anxiety. Once we stopped in Rawa Ruska, a
sordid little town near the Russian border. It was dark, but the narrow
streets of the town were swarming with panic-stricken Jews packing their
shabby bundles into their shabby carts, wailing in Yiddish. I picked up
one word I could understand: '*Krieg*' – war. They were obviously trying
to run away – but from whom and where to?

When, in the small hours of that same night, we approached Warsaw,
we were stopped for a while by passing troops. Young, perhaps just called
up, the soldiers looked sleepy and frightened. They were singing an
enthusiastic military song with so little enthusiasm that it sounded sad.

Back in my peaceful Konstancin garden, among loving people and
reassuringly familiar objects, I can't help thinking about all this, I can't
stop going through the horrors of our journey again and again. I don't
know what to do with myself, the time drags by. When I switch on the
radio, all I can hear are jolly military marches interrupted now and again
by strange, enigmatic announcements like, 'Attention . . . attention
. . . approaching . . . Chocolate . . . chocolate . . . Co-ma   six
. . . co-ma six . . . ' It is frightening. A nauseating anxiety fills my soul.
Where is Father, what will happen to him, what will happen to all those
other people, those poor panicking Jews, those dismayed young soldiers?

In the garden, in the villa, life seems to go on as usual. Grannie in her armchair suffering from a new wave of pains, Auntie Maria busy with her daily tasks, the gardener, a weatherbeaten old man with a big moustache, telling me off for picking an unripe peach from the tree. But apart from that, no one says much, not even Sophie. We are all waiting. But what for?

About nine o'clock on Friday morning we heard from a radio announcement that war had begun. High in the clear sky we could see planes flying from the west and back. Polish planes, we presumed, but we could not be sure. The tense atmosphere brought about by waiting for the unknown was now suddenly broken. The villa was full of people again, as some relatives came and stayed with us. Stefan and Jadwiga had to cut short their holiday and returned from the mountains, sunburnt, more beautiful than ever. With their arrival, even war ceased to be frightening for me and became a kind of adventure. I decided to keep a diary and got on with it for the first six days of war.

By Saturday, we had learnt these were German, not Polish planes, speeding above us towards Warsaw. The radio now announced, now called off an air raid. Warsaw was being bombarded. We could hear the hollow sounds of distant explosions as well as the spanking noise of the anti-aircraft defence. We could see heavy clouds of smoke darkening the bright September sky.

Towards evening, Mother arrived from Warsaw, pale and distressed. She had been in a raid with Father, whom she had managed to meet for a while. A bomb had gone off quite near. They saw people wounded by the blast. An elderly man was killed. Father insisted she travel back to the villa and stay with us. He looked so handsome in his uniform, she mentioned, and burst into tears.

I knew my father's uniform by sight; it could be admired in his wardrobe among his civilian clothes. There were also two medals, a slightly faded photograph showing Father as a slim, handsome officer in his early twenties, and a bullet shell – all cherished by the family as keepsakes of his military past. Father did not fight in the First World War, he was a medical student then. He joined up as a qualified doctor in 1920 when the Polish Army fought against the Bolsheviks approaching Warsaw. Working for the field hospital, he moved up and down the front line on an armoured train, picking up the wounded. He was wounded himself and almost died of typhus on the same train. That was a long time before he met Mother. Now he was in danger again and had Mother, Sophie and me worrying desperately about him.

Stefan was expecting to be called up any time. He was not an officer, just an ordinary private. In the meantime, glued to the radio, tuning and retuning it from the BBC to Paris, from Paris to Berlin, he was trying hard to make out what was going on. With no career so far but with a sound British education he was the most brilliant and competent member of the family. If only Great Britain and France would declare war against Germany, he kept repeating – we would be saved. This partly came true. On Sunday afternoon we heard Chamberlain's speech on the BBC, which Stefan interpreted for us, delirious with joy: Great Britain was at war with Germany. And so was France.

On Monday a glamorous car with the initials CD and a tiny British flag pulled up in front of the villa. Three gentlemen and a lady smartly dressed in dark clothes presented Stefan with some documents stating their right to move in with us. They were from the British Embassy which had just been evacuated from the city to Konstancin. The rest of the Embassy staff was allocated to other villas in the vicinity. Far more pleased than put out, we quickly moved downstairs, leaving the upper floor for the strangers. Their presence was reassuring. The powerful British considered our place safe. Cramped in the downstairs rooms, sleeping close to one another, so unusual for us, we felt much safer.

The first thing the strangers did after they had settled down in their rooms, was to ask the gardener to lend them some tools. They went to the garden and dug a deep ditch at the foot of the hillock on which Sophie and I used to play with sand when we were younger. After that, whenever the radio announced an air raid, which happened with increasing frequency on that and the following days, our lodgers rushed downstairs and hid in their ditch. It seemed funny to us. We ourselves stayed put wherever the raid happened to find us. The bombs were not dropping on our suburb, after all.

On Wednesday, 6 September something unexpected happened. Following a telephone call, the embassy people hurriedly packed their belongings and left in their gleaming car. Just before their departure, Stefan, who had already made friends with one of them, asked the reason for this sudden decision. But the British didn't want to say, or perhaps they did not know themselves. They had just received an order to evacuate again.

There was not much time left to think about it all, because half an hour later Father arrived in his Chevrolet. He looked strikingly handsome and strange in his uniform. He was tense and very hurried. There was no time to enjoy our sudden reunion or ask questions. He had come to take us to Warsaw. While we collected a few basic belongings, he explained briefly what had happened. Konstancin was no longer safe. The German Army was approaching Warsaw. As the capital was ready' to fight hard in self-defence, the suburb might be occupied by the enemy and very soon cut off from the city. We did not discuss the matter. We packed in no time at all and left the villa. For ever.

So there we were trying to make our way to Warsaw again. This time Father was at the wheel himself, and Grannie and Sophie were with us. Stefan, driving his own car, accompanied by Jadwiga, Auntie Maria, the cook and the maid, was just behind. The road was crowded with panic-stricken people again, and convoys of vehicles with soldiers and officers were creeping along. They saluted Father and he saluted them, and I watched this with mixed feelings of pride and agony. Grannie and Mother, still mourning grandfather's death, wore black dresses and black veils. We drove very slowly and when I recall this journey now it seems like a funeral.

We arrived in Warsaw just after an air raid and managed to reach Border Street by the time the next one began. Mother decided we would not go to our flat in Sienna Street, but stay with Grannie. Jadwiga did not want to part from Stefan, so she stayed at Border Street too. Father had to rush back to his hospital, despite the raid. Just after he had left and the air raid was over, we heard on the radio the dramatic voice of President Starzyński, the heroic Mayor of Warsaw. He announced that the German Army was approaching the capital, that we were preparing to fight back in defence. Soon after that, another voice ordered all men of military age who had not been called up to leave Warsaw immediately. I do not think he said the government was planning to leave Warsaw the following night; I believe we learned about it much later.

In profound gloom, in the midst of scattered bundles and pieces of furniture which were being moved to accommodate more people in the flat, Stefan was preparing to leave. Jadwiga, pale and grave, no tears in her eyes, busied herself packing his bag with warm socks and sandwiches. Just then Uncle Jerzy phoned to say he was leaving Warsaw in his car, taking his wife, little daughter and parents-in-law. Soon after that Father turned up again. His hospital was to be evacuated by that night. Doctors were ordered to follow the ambulances in their own cars if they had them. They were allowed to take their families. Father came to collect us – Mother, Sophie and me. There was no time for discussion. Without the slightest hesitation Mother said, 'No'. She could not possibly leave her dying mother in a besieged town. Father insisted, but with no success. So he decided to take Stefan instead. Then suddenly, Uncle Józef appeared. He also had been ordered to leave Warsaw and contact his unit outside, though he was already called up and in his officer's uniform. Father took him in his car as well. They said goodbye and left. I had an overpowering feeling that I would never see my father again and cried all night.

The siege of Warsaw began the following day. The city was under constant artillery fire and was bombarded from the air in the daytime. At the beginning, we all stayed in the flat during the raids. We were now joined by some other people. Mother's deaf-mute uncle came and stayed, so did Jadwiga's father, a middle-aged divorcé, who wanted to be with his daughter now she had decided to stay with us. Then Sister Franciszka arrived. She was a qualified nurse who for years had assisted my grandfather in his operating theatre. Deeply devoted to him and his family, she came to see how we were and quickly made up her mind to stay and take care of Grannie. She was a short, taciturn, matter-of-fact person with a plain face, cropped hair and a foreign-sounding voice – she was of German origin. Soon she had assumed command in the household. She managed to acquire a quantity of medical and nursing supplies and organised a first-aid station, employing most of us, Sophie included, in preparing dressings, rolling up bandages and generally assisting her as she attended to all the injured people waiting in the front gateway of our big apartment house.

The streets of Warsaw were full of refugees from small towns and villages who thought they would be safer in the city. Many of them had nowhere to stay and nothing to eat as most of the shops were already empty and closed, if not wrecked by bombs. A lot of people had been injured by falling debris. While Sister Franciszka was busy helping them, Auntie Maria and other women from next-door apartments organised some simple meals for the starving. Most of our neighbours, including those who owned the ground-floor shops, contributed to this enterprise. Everybody had large supplies of food at home: the outbreak of war had not come as a surprise, after all. Auntie Maria, the cook and the maid kept to the kitchen, cooking soups and potatoes in the huge pans lent by Mr Kleinbaum, the owner of a household goods shop downstairs. He also lent them numerous tin bowls and spoons out of his stock. All these were taken down to the gateway and the meals distributed to the queuing strangers by volunteers. I tried to be useful where I could.

On the third day of the siege, Grannie's bed had to be moved into the corridor – it had no windows and seemed safer. Mother was with her all the time. In fact, Grannie was no longer with us: for most of the day she lay sunk in the blessed oblivion of morphia, mercifully administered by Sister Franciszka.

Once, during a morning raid, the explosions came so close that Sister Franciszka ordered us to leave our second-floor flat and run to the cellar, while she stayed alone at Grannie's bedside. We obeyed and left hurriedly, but did not manage to make it to the bottom of the stairs, so crowded was the staircase with homeless people trying to find shelter there. We could not go back either, the stairs being blocked by neighbours from upper floors trying to make their way down. So we all stood there stuck on the stairs. The building was shaking and swaying with explosions, the wailing of diving aircraft pierced our brains. The staircase windowpanes shattered into smithereens and it was dark with smoke and dust. Children were screaming, women moaned. Next to me, a woman clutched her three-year-old boy in her arms, trying to calm him by constantly, almost mechanically repeating, 'Don't cry, my darling, you're safe, your mother is with you.' That woman and her child were both killed by a blast three days later.

While we were all busy giving first aid and meals to strangers, or attending to Grannie's needs, Jadwiga was not with us. She had found something else to do. Dressed in an overall, her thick auburn hair hidden under a scarf, but still looking beautiful, she started a meticulous search through the bookshelves. There were thousands of books in my grandparents' apartment, for they were keen readers and collectors. Stefan, too, had his own collection in his room, which Jadwiga was now occupying. Enthralled by her work, surrounded by piles and piles of books from shelves and bookcases, Jadwiga seemed to pay no attention to the war roaring around her. She looked uncannily self-controlled and for a while I thought that her anguish over Stefan had made her lose her mind. But she was not mad at all. After three or four days of hard work, she asked me to lend her a hand. All the shelves and bookcases were tidy again, only a few books and pamphlets were left piled up next to the dining-room tile stove. I was given the task of tearing them into shreds, while Jadwiga lit a fire and fed the remains to the stove. Puzzled, reluctant, I had a good look through the books before I started destroying them. Some were about Communism, but most dealt with Fascism,

Nazi Germany or Hitler himself. One was particularly voluminous. Bound in hard, dark cardboard, its title was *The Brown Book*. It was about the persecution of German Jews and Nazi concentration camps in Germany. It was lavishly illustrated with photographs showing all kinds of atrocities committed by the Nazis. I let myself sink into those documents with horror. Suddenly I realised that everything that Great-Aunt Eugenia had told us two years before was true, even worse. We had not believed her then, but meanwhile *The Brown Book* had been published, my family knew the truth – and had only been keeping me in the dark. I stared at Jadwiga in silence. Calm and competent as usual, she answered my unasked question. I was old enough to know how things were, she said. We could expect the Germans to enter Warsaw any time now. There was little hope that the besieged town would resist the powerful German Army. And when they came we should expect them to interfere in our private lives, search our homes, severely punish us for anything they considered to be against the Nazi regime. That was why we had to get rid of any documents that were critical of their regime. To reassure me, as well as herself, Jadwiga added that she did not believe the Nazis would deal as severely with us as they had with their own Jews: Poland was a foreign country to them, after all. Moreover, we had powerful allies, England and France. I remember how I hurt my fingers tearing up that hard brown book. It took us a long while to burn it.

On the tenth day of the siege we had to give in and move down to the cellar for good. It was no longer possible to stay in the flat. The raids and the artillery fire had come too close for safety. All windowpanes were already broken, water, electricity and gas cut off.

The vast basement of the house had already been adapted to accommodate a large number of people. The partitions between individual quarters had been demolished, all sorts of lumber thrown away. The only supplies left were coal and potatoes. The space was already tightly packed with sheltering families – people from the flats as well as homeless strangers. They were all squeezed in next to each other on mattresses or bedding laid out on the filthy, cold cellar floor. Yet, somehow, we managed to find a place for our own mattresses. Some of the strangers protested loudly, but eventually they helped us and even tried to make Grannie as comfortable as possible in the circumstances.

So we began our mole's life in the stuffy air, dirt and semi-darkness, relieved only by the light of a few candles; with no water and no hot meals; in full awareness that we might die in a fire or be buried alive under rubble at any moment.

There were all kinds of people camping with us. Jews and non-Jews, people who were well off and people who were poor. Some of them were panic-stricken, some women moaned and screamed. Others were numb with fear or calm and self-controlled. I remember a Mr Bachner, a shopkeeper, who pretended to be quite calm and whenever a particularly heavy explosion seemed to shatter the walls, he just repeated, 'Nothing happened, nothing happened, just one more plant pot dropped down from the window-sill up there.' Nobody laughed at his joke. One old Jew prayed constantly. A young Christian woman whispered her prayers next to him. From time to time people squabbled noisily over two inches of space or access to a candle. But on the whole, we were all understanding and helpful with one another.

Mr Kleinbaum with his wife and two daughters were squeezed in next to the family of a middle-aged businessman. There was something going on in the darkness between the businessman and Kleinbaum's younger daughter, Lucy, a fleshy twenty-year-old blonde. I could sense rather than see it. I could bet that in the most dangerous moments she drew close to him and he stroked her fair silky hair. Lucy's parents certainly knew it but did not interfere, while the businessman's wife crouched sobbing next to him.

Two boys kept showing off how brave they were. They obviously wanted to impress me, or Jadwiga, or both of us. I found them ridiculous. There was a third boy, though, whom I liked. He sat quietly with his mother on our left, trying to read in the faint candlelight. As I was trying to read by the same candle, we soon became acquainted. His name was Artek and he was just three months my senior. He lived on the second floor, opposite my grandparents' flat. His father had left with the army on the same day as my father. Artek turned out to be a serious, sensitive boy. Not really handsome, but gentle-looking. We talked a lot and made friends at once.

On 25 September – it was Monday, the day of Rosh Hashana, the Jewish New Year – all hell on earth broke loose. We learnt later that it was the final German storming of Warsaw, but squatting in horror amidst the quaking and rocking walls of the basement we thought the Nazis meant to raze the nearby Jewish quarter to the ground, choosing a Jewish holiday to do so. This was true enough. Time stopped, life seemed to be coming to an end, we could only pray to be swallowed up by the inferno quickly and painlessly.

Once in the space of that dark, stagnant time, I was taken by the hand and led through the underground labyrinth up to a deserted ground-floor shop. I was suddenly dazzled by tremendous light, deafened by a mixture of weird sounds – roars, jingles, wheezing. An immense wall of flame stood in front of the shop's broken window: the other side of Border Street was on fire. There was nothing but brightness and sound. We stood in perfect emptiness, Artek and I, out of the human world, on the brink of life. Spellbound we held on to one another tightly. We did not utter a word. Just stayed there enthralled by the flames, for hours and hours, or maybe for a few seconds only, I do not know. Then we kissed, the first kiss of my life and his. And the last – we believed.

The storm went on all that day and the following night. Soon we learnt that the whole of our district was in flames and there was nowhere to escape to. We just waited to die. But suddenly, in the early hours of the night, a complete stranger camping with us in the cellar took command and ordered all the men and younger women to follow him up to the roof. He would not take me, but Artek went, Mother, Jadwiga, Sister Franciszka. They fought the fire from dawn throughout the whole day. There was no water – they just used sand and axes to keep the flames off our house. They succeeded.

So we were all alive when the storm came to an end and ominous silence took the place of a pandemonium of sounds. In this sudden silence we tried to guess at the future. There were the optimists, like Mr Bachner, who believed, or just pretended to believe that the German Army had been defeated by the Allies and that General Sikorski* with his troops had come to the rescue of Warsaw. But most of us were defiant. When, after a time, we ventured out of our shelter to explore the upper floors, a voice reached us from a radio set left surprisingly intact. It was the voice of Mayor Starzyński, hoarse and breaking as he announced the surrender of Warsaw.

We returned to our flat covered now with thick layers of broken glass, white dust and black soot. Cold draughts roamed freely around the rooms bringing a sharp smell of smouldering ruins. At first, there was no sign of the conquerors in the street, and we did not even think about them. We set to to make our place fit to live in. Our food supplies were already exhausted and somebody had to go out and look for something to eat. Jadwiga found two large baskets – one for herself, the other one for me – and off we went. What we saw I can only describe as a dead town, ruined and burnt to the ground – or so it seemed at first. Many buildings

*General Władysław Sikorski was well known for his bravery in the First World War and for his political activity between the two wars. From September 1939 to July 1943 he was Prime Minister and Commander-in-Chief of the Polish Army in exile.

were still smouldering, pavements destroyed, deep bomb craters all around. A few emaciated people could be seen wandering to and fro like us, looking for food. On one occasion, we saw a crowd swarming around a bomb crater, doing something we could not understand until we came close. Deep down in the crater lay the corpse of a horse killed by the bomb. Excited people dived down into the hole with knives or penknives to hack off bits of the horse's flesh. Soon the corpse was opened wide and the plunderers fought over the steaming liver. We retreated, sick with disgust. The incident brought home to us, however, that our search for food was hopeless. On our way back we ventured a walk through Ogród Saski (Saxon Garden), the beautiful eighteenth-century public park where I had played as a young child. It was deserted and peaceful with no signs of devastation. The ancient trees, all gold and scarlet, stood still under the blue sky. Thick layers of dry leaves rustled under our feet as we walked in silence. Then, in the grass, under a horse chestnut tree, we saw lovely glossy, ruddy chestnuts. The lawn was littered with them. I had never seen such a lot of chestnuts before, there had always been a host of children preying on them at other times. Now they were all mine. And Jadwiga's. With mindless joy we began to pick them up and fill our empty baskets up to the top. We felt almost happy carrying our useless load back home.

The following day we saw the Germans for the first time. They were marching along Border Street, just beneath our front windows, tall, well fed, neat in their field-grey uniforms. They sang out loud their *Heili Heilo*, the odious song of evil's victory I had already heard in Gdańsk. This sight and sound marked for me the real beginning of the German occupation.

As the days and weeks went by we little by little adjusted to our new life. The huge apartment house in Sienna Street had been burnt to the ground. Nothing was left of our apartment and all its contents. Mother would not have gone back there anyway, as long as Grannie was still alive. Henryk, Jadwiga's father, and Ludwik, the deaf-mute uncle, were busy repairing damage done to our present home and had little thought of leaving Border Street. Uncle Ludwik's own place was ruined, anyway. Jadwiga stayed, of course, and so did Sister Franciszka. In order to keep warm we settled ourselves in just three rooms of the large apartment. I remember those days and weeks as a bleak time of autumnal chills, Grannie's suffering, bitter daily hardships and vain hopes of hearing from Father and Stefan. But there were joys as well. Great joys when my father's parents and other people we loved turned up alive and well; small joys when plywood boards were found to replace broken windowpanes, when water began to trickle again from dry taps and electricity was restored. The odd loaf of bread or handful of rice found somewhere in the reviving shops and brought home by somebody, caused genuine euphoria.

It was Sister Franciszka who mainly provided us with food. She still attended to Grannie but would disappear for long hours, day after day, and return with priceless articles such as flour, potatoes or soap. She did not talk much and we did not ask questions. Once she asked me to go with her and help her fetch a large load of tins. We entered a big grocer's shop in the main street, which I remembered very well from shopping with Mother before the war. Surprisingly enough, the shop was stocked with as many goods as it had been then, though now there were only a few customers. To my puzzlement Sister Franciszka presented a mysterious ticket to the shop assistant and in return received two big boxes with tins of meat and vegetables. Only when we were leaving did I notice a small label stuck to the shop door: 'Nur für Deutsche' ('Germans only').

We were dragging along the main street with our heavy treasure when all at once we heard *Heili Heilo*. Here they were, marching and singing again, the brave, strong conquerors. Sister Franciszka stopped. Automatically, I stopped too, without any intention of looking at them. I looked down at the pavement. But when I glanced at Sister Franciszka I could not believe my eyes. She stood engrossed, her mouth half opened in a vague half-smile, her eyes gleaming with a sort of worship or pride, her short, square body stiffened to attention.

Shattered, perplexed, I told the others at home what I had seen. We knew now that Sister Franciszka had reclaimed her German origins and become a *Volksdeutsch* – an almost-German citizen favoured by the Nazis. We believed she also worked for them as a nurse. Yet we could not make ourselves hate her. She had not changed in the least, after all. She was still the same generous, caring person, our most devoted friend. There had never been much talk between her and us, and so it remained after my discovery. She left us only after Grannie Eva died, two months later, in January. We have never heard from her since.

One dark November morning I heard a gentle knocking through my sleep. Half awake, I climbed out of the bed I shared with Sophie and ran to the kitchen. Someone was at the back door. In the darkness of the staircase I recognised Stefan. Trembling with cold and emotion, I flew straight into his arms and clung to him sobbing. Then, pulling myself together I whispered what seemed to be the most urgent news: 'We're all alive. Jadwiga too. And you can be proud of her.'

The story we heard from Stefan when all sobs, laughter and embraces were over, was as follows. Father, Józef and Stefan had followed the hospital vehicles in the car along the overcrowded roads, on and on, towards the east. They were constantly bombarded from the air and every so often had to leave the car and hide in the roadside ditches. Józef tried his best to find his own military unit, but it was utterly impossible: chaos had overcome not only the civilian population but also the army, it seemed. There was no end to this horrifying journey which was more like a flight from the enemy than any attempt to face him. Soon they learnt that they had been following the government speeding along to safety. There was no safety in the east, though. On 17 September, the Soviet Army, hand in glove with the Germans, entered the eastern territories of Poland and annexed them without resistance. Stefan, Father and Józef, together with thousands of other officers and soldiers, were stopped by the Russians, deprived of the car and interned. This was in Ukraine. As they marched in convoy through Ukrainian villages, hostile peasants went for them with dung forks and scythes. They survived only thanks to the Soviet guards. Soon they were transferred further east and confined in an internment camp in Kozielsk. Stefan was separated there from my father and Józef, since they were officers while he was just an ordinary soldier, still in his civilian clothes. Like other soldiers he was amicably treated by the Russians, fed with simple but nourishing food, and eventually discharged. He was offered free transport back to the Soviet-German 'green border' which he managed to cross under cover of night. Then he walked to Warsaw: it had taken him over a fortnight.

So he was back with us for better or worse and we all felt happier. Stefan did not know exactly how Father and Józef were doing in their officers' camp. He supposed they were being treated in a less friendly way than soldiers. Yet, he said, at least they were not starving and stood a better chance of surviving the war far from the bombs and Nazis. The only letter we received from Father from Kozielsk two months later seemed to confirm Stefan's belief.

In the midst of wintry gloom, Jadwiga and Stefan rejoiced in a state of blissful reunion. Once, on a freezing December afternoon, they came back from town covered with snowflakes, beaming with silent happiness. We were all gathered round Grannie's bed in her warm, well-lit room, when they came in. Grannie lay calm, her vacant eyes wide open. Stefan and Jadwiga knelt at the bedside and stretched their right hands. A flash of two golden wedding rings caught Grannie's lifeless eye. And something unexpected happened: she smiled, happily, approvingly. Nobody uttered a sound.

Grannie died soon after that, at the very beginning of 1940. On the day of her funeral the cold reached minus 25 degrees. The gravediggers could hardly dig a proper grave. No one came to the funeral but the closest members of the family. Even Sophie and I were left behind, though we loved Grannie dearly and cried for her at home.

While our daily hardships had been going on the Nazi occupying forces had settled down in the country and established their cruel order. Homes were searched, people – both Jewish and non-Jewish – arrested and deported to concentration camps or kept in prison without reason. News of executions was heard day after day. In the streets of Warsaw Jews wearing traditional dress were stopped by the Nazis and forced to perform humiliating and exhausting physical exercises in front of watching passers-by. Their beards were cruelly cut off together with the flesh. White armbands with blue stars of David became compulsory for all Jews over thirteen.

We tried not to go out unless it was necessary. The only person who did not seem frightened was Uncle Ludwik. As a deaf-mute, he sported a special armband together with his Jewish one, and ridiculously enough, felt secure because of that. He would disappear for days and nights, causing us great anxiety. Stefan was furious with him. 'What kind of urgent business has the old fool to attend to?' he groaned. 'Why can't he just stay quietly at home.' But Uncle Ludwik would not stay quietly at home, though he was not a fool. Despite his handicap, he was a lively cheerful fellow in his fifties, and a very bright one too. He was pretty aware of everything that was going on, could understand people's conversation by lip-reading, and could easily communicate with them in his own language of funny sounds and telling gestures. But he would not divulge his secret reason for staying away from home.

As a curfew had been imposed on Warsaw ever since the arrival of the Nazis, we had to stay at home from early evening till morning. As a result, unusually close relationships began to flourish between neighbours. People who had had very little in common before were now becoming good friends. No evening would pass without a visit from a few neighbours who would call in and stay late to exchange news, discuss the situation and wonder about the future. The two main subjects discussed during those nocturnal gatherings were: should we expect to be confined in a Jewish ghetto? and what is the Soviet Union up to? Everyone thought the Russians might decide to move west again and take Warsaw from the Germans. This was the current gossip and even people who hated and mistrusted the Bolsheviks no less than the Nazis had to admit that their arrival would be the best solution. For Jews at least. Other gossip whispered by the most notorious optimists claimed that General Sikorski and his army were getting ready to strike from their exile in the early spring. Mr Bachner kept chanting the absurd popular couplet: 'The higher the sun in the skies, the closer comes Sikorski on his white charger.' I doubt whether he believed it, but certainly it cheered him up a little.

For lack of any better source of information or entertainment, we took to séances. We settled round the table with our neighbours, our fingertips gently touching a small plate placed upside down on a sheet of paper marked with letters. Somebody would solemnly call up the ghost of a dead person – usually Marshal Piłsudski's* – asking him to answer a question. After a while, slowly, reluctantly, the plate would move round and round, the arrow drawn on its edge pointing at different letters to form the words of the answer. Often the words were rude, so rude that I could hardly understand them and kept pestering everyone to tell me what they meant. But sometimes they were amazingly relevant. I clearly remember the very important question we asked our rude ghost: 'What is the Soviet Union going to do?' – 'With the USA against Japan' came the answer. It is easy to dismiss this as obvious now. But who could have possibly anticipated this strange zigzag of world history then, at the beginning of 1940? I know now who it was: it was Stefan, with his profound knowledge of international relations and his unbelievable political instinct, who, apart from the omniscient ghost, was the only person able to give such an answer. Yet he was not responsible for the rude words, I am sure. He was far too well brought up for that.

I do not remember exactly how and when I learnt about the courses organised at my school. From the very beginning of their rule over Poland, the Nazi authorities had set about destroying Polish culture. The universities were closed, academic staff deported to concentration camps, secondary schools banned. In the primary schools which were open, Polish history and geography classes were prohibited. All this had

*Józef Piłsudski was the founder and leader of independent, post-World War One Poland. He died in 1935.

triggered off an instant response in the nation. Teachers, parents, pupils themselves started up a whole system of underground education. The illegal courses began to function soon after the defeat.

Ignoring all the dangers of going out, I rushed off to school as soon as I heard it was open. Under the guise of sewing and cooking lessons the most important subjects only – Polish, maths, science and history – were taught by just a few teachers to a handful of girls. In my class were no more than ten girls from the previous year, all of them serious, really keen to learn – 'the elite'. Needless to say, I was the only one wearing the band marked with a blue star.

After class on my first day we were all about to leave together. In the hall one of the girls to whom I had never been close whispered in my ear, 'Slip it off.' Taken aback, I obeyed and hid the armband in my pocket. To my great surprise none of the girls said goodbye to me in the street. They all seemed to be heading in the same direction. We talked and laughed as we walked together. It was strange. The year before I had never had any company on my way home, I had always been alone. The following morning two of my new friends were waiting for me at the gate. I slipped off my band again and we went to school together. And so it was ever after: two girls with me in the morning, six or more in the afternoon. I had a warm, reassuring feeling of being among friends.

As far as my old friends were concerned – Renata, Zula, Hanka – they had all survived the siege, but we could not see each other often, as it was foolhardy to go out unless really necessary. Now Artek was becoming my only substitute for all of them. We would meet every day in his place or mine, talk a lot or play cards. Sometimes we kissed, but not very often, since we both believed routine could easily lead to boredom.

In the early spring the house at 13 Border Street was raided and searched for the first time. A vehicle full of armed Nazis pulled up at the gate. Soon two of them were banging at the front door of our apartment. We let them in and watched their determined efforts to find something in our wardrobes, drawers and bookshelves. What exactly they were looking for we never learnt. They were cool and polite. They found nothing and left.

The second visit was different. The authorities had just announced that Polish citizens were forbidden to own wireless sets and must hand them over by a certain deadline at local police stations. Some people obeyed at once and were seen dragging their sets along the pavements as though they were dogs on the leash. Others tried to hide them. Our radio, which Stefan had brought from England and greatly cherished, was a particularly big and heavy Philips. It was hard to hide and even harder to part from; it was, after all, our only link with the outside world. While we were wondering what to do, three men banged at our door. Two were uniformed Germans, the third, a civilian, was Mr Richter, my grandfather Aleksander's chauffeur, who had driven him for years until Grandfather died. Apart from his German name, Mr Richter had never had anything to do with Germany, nor could he even speak German. Now, seeing him with the two Germans, we thought at first that he had been arrested by them, but soon his behaviour made it clear that he came as an enemy. Always before full of respect and servility, he now took hardly any notice of us as he entered with his superiors. He led them straight to Stefan's room and pointed to the radio. We heard him saying in ridiculous, broken German, 'Schöne Radio Apparat' ('Fine set'). The two Germans laughed briefly, gibbered something amongst themselves, then helped Mr Richter to disconnect the radio. Carrying the huge object in his arms along the corridor, his square face scarlet from effort and excitement, he kept mumbling, 'Present schön, danke schön' ('Fine present, thank you, fine').

Soon after, or perhaps even before this, Grandfather Maks' and Grandma Viera's flat was raided and searched. It happened late at night. They were woken from their sleep and together with Uncle Julian, the doctor who lived with them, were forced to stand still facing the wall while the invaders turned the flat upside down. It was not clear whether they found anything suspicious or not, but they arrested Grandpa Maks and Julian that night. They kept them in prison for several days, beat them, then let them go. Grandfather and Julian returned home frightened. The injuries from the beatings were not serious and healed quickly, but for Grandpa Maks, who was in his late sixties, the shock was too great. A week or so later, he died suddenly from a stroke.

So I lost my beloved grandfather, too, and had just one grandma left, the one I had never particularly liked. But as she was the only one, my feelings for her grew stronger and our relationship became closer than before.

The school year was limping to an end earlier than usual. Some teachers had been arrested, some pupils had had to give up school and start working to help their fatherless families. On the last day, Mrs Kwaskowska, who now was my form tutor, made a little speech. We were just seven, sitting with her intimately in a tiny little classroom. For security's sake she could not give out any written certificates, she said, but our results had been recorded. They would be kept well concealed in her private residence and wait for better times. We were all brave girls and excellent pupils, she continued, but since the school year was incomplete, she believed it would be fair to give all of us just a 'sufficient' mark for each subject we had studied. Her eyes moistened when we said goodbye.

The spring came and went with no sign of a white charger speeding to the rescue of my oppressed country. From the high skies the sun warmed the ruins around us and they blossomed with weeds.

By mid-summer we knew that there would be a Jewish ghetto in Warsaw. Ghettos had already been established in some provincial towns. There was now little hope of any change for the better. France, our powerful ally, was defeated and occupied. So were Belgium and Holland. Great Britain was having to struggle for her own survival. The United States were obviously trying to keep out of the European war, and the Soviet Union did not seem willing to move further west. Helpless and hopeless, we were left at the mercy of Hitler.

No one at our nocturnal gatherings sounded optimistic now, not even Mr Bachner. The new question was: Would it be better to stay in the ghetto, or hide on the 'Aryan' side? For my family it seemed out of the question to hide among non-Jewish people. None of us could pretend to be 'Aryan'. Our dark hair, bridged noses, sad eyes would give us away. We were resigned to living behind the walls. For a long time, though, we did not know whether Border Street would be part of the ghetto or on the 'Aryan' side. We were right on the border between the two worlds.

By the end of September we learnt that we would have to move to the northern part of town, which was traditionally inhabited by the Jewish population. Border Street was to remain on the 'Aryan' side. Moving now became our practical problem, since the deadline for all Jews to settle within the walls that were now going up was the middle of November. Many Jewish families were in the same position and were trying to exchange their flats with Christian families forced to leave their homes in the Jewish quarter. We meant to do the same, but soon after the decree about 'The Jewish Dwelling Quarter' was announced, we received a letter from the authorities saying that our flat had been requested by a German official. The 'German official' so keen to inherit my grandparents' beautiful apartment was nobody else but Mr Richter, the chauffeur.

A solution came unexpectedly from Henryk, Jadwiga's father. He had left us soon after Stefan had returned to Warsaw and now lived alone in his own little flat, often coming to see us. Shortly before the war his wife håd divorced him and left for Argentina, taking their younger child with her, while Jadwiga stayed with her father. Henryk owned a draper's shop. He never really bothered about his business and never made a fortune out of it. He was a friendly, light-hearted fellow. In his late forties, he still looked young and very handsome. Jadwiga took her beauty from him.

Henryk had a Christian friend who lived at Leszno Street. This street had now been denoted Jewish, whilst Henryk's home was to remain outside the walls. The two friends had instantly decided to swap their homes: they were the same size, both had two rooms and a kitchen. Jadwiga and Stefan were to move in together with Henryk. While Mother was making desperate efforts to find somewhere for the three of us to live, Henryk suddenly turned up with a generous offer: we, too, were welcome to move in with him, he said. And he meant it. For lack of any alternative, Mother accepted his offer.

We were now getting ready to move, packing only the most necessary things to take with us. The cook and the maid had to say goodbye and return to their families somewhere in the country. Auntie Maria decided to stay with one of her numerous sisters and keep in close touch with us. She had been delaying her departure as we could hardly face life without each other. Meanwhile, she did all she could to remove the most valuable objects from the apartment and hide them in her sisters' flats in order to save them for us.

The only member of the household whose housing problem had not been solved so far was Uncle Ludwik. Stefan was trying his best to find a Jewish family willing to take him as a lodger. But Ludwik, it appeared, had his own plans. He turned up at home with a short, plump, lovely lady in her fifties. She had rosy cheeks, smiling blue eyes, and she was deaf-mute. In his funny way, Ludwik presented her to us. 'Ludwika,' he scribbled on a piece of paper. With gestures, he showed us a big nose, long beard and side curls, which he vigorously crossed out with the next gesture. It meant: 'She is not Jewish.' The following message conveyed with the fingers of his right and left hands 'walking' together side by side, was: 'I am leaving with her.' Then Ludwika had her say. She pressed her arms to her abundant bosom and rolled her blue eyes: 'I love him so much.' 'And so do I,' announced Ludwik in his own way, which also meant: 'Now you see why I couldn't stay quietly at home,' and 'Don't you worry, I'll manage.'

They said goodbye and left soon after. We never saw them again. Two or three years later, Auntie Maria learnt that Ludwika had hidden her lover for quite a long time before they were discovered and shot dead together.

Friends and acquaintances who happened not to be Jewish kept calling unexpectedly to see us before our disappearance behind the walls. Some of them cried, some cursed Hitler with the strongest words; 'You're the first, we'll be next,' they said.

Shortly before moving to the flat at 15 Leszno Street, a couple of particularly dear visitors turned up at the door. My Aunt Halina, Vładek's Christian wife, suddenly called with Jurek, her lovely three-year-old son. I had hardly known her, we had not seen her since our first and last visit three years before. We had not expected her to come at all. Yet she did come, showing she bore us no grudge. She brought her little boy to see and remember his close relatives. She told us that Vładek was to stay on the 'Aryan' side and hide away from home. She also said we could count on her if and whenever we needed help. She kept her promise later.

The last friend to whom I said goodbye was Artek. He came over as we were just about to leave, upset and shy, not knowing what to say. I felt something sweet and serene was coming to an end.

Then we packed some of our belongings on to a hired cart pulled by a horse, and followed the cart to the ghetto on foot. It was only a ten-minute walk, after all.

3 Behind the Walls

———◦———◦———◦———◦———

Originally some 400,000 Jews – Warsaw residents and refugees from the provinces – were crowded into the area of the Warsaw ghetto, that in November 1940 covered 340 hectares, including a Jewish cemetery . . . Later reductions in its size necessitated internal shiftings and further overcrowding, so that thousands of families were often left without shelter . . . The situation had been further aggravated when 72,000 Jews from Warsaw district were transferred to the ghetto, bringing the total of refugees to 150,000 and the total of the ghetto population up to 500,000 . . .

Average number of persons per room was 13 while thousands remained homeless . . .

The gates of the ghetto were guarded by German and Polish police from outside, by Jewish militia (*Ordnungsdienst*) from inside. Only those with special permits could enter or leave . . . In October 1941, the authorities declared that leaving the ghetto without permits was punishable by death . . .

The ghetto population received a food allocation amounting to 184 calories per capita a day, while Poles received 634, Germans 2,310 . . . The average allocation per person was ½lb of sugar and 4lb of bread a month. The dough was mixed with sawdust and potato peel . . .

The ghetto suffered from mass unemployment . . .

There was an acute shortage of fuel to heat the houses. In the winter of 1941–1942, 718 out of 780 apartments investigated had no heat . . .

These conditions led to epidemics, especially typhoid. The streets were strewn with corpses due to starvation and disease. Bands of children roamed the streets in search of food . . .

It is estimated that by the summer of 1942, over 100,000 Jews died in the ghetto proper.

Encyclopaedia Judaica, Volume 16, Warsaw: holocaust period

The flat was small but nice. I felt excited when I entered it for the first time. A new kind of life was ahead, something I had never experienced before. Bad – but perhaps not too bad, different, thus exciting. Never before had I lived in a multistorey annexe meant for the less prosperous inhabitants of a smart apartment building; never had I had to climb five steep flights of stairs to find myself at home. During the day the flat was full of light. From its windows I could see endless rows of roofs and chimneys, and imagine vast fields somewhere far beyond.

Henryk did everything he could to make us comfortable. Mother, Sophie and I were to live in the bigger of the two rooms; Stefan and Jadwiga in the smaller one. Henryk himself did not need a room at all, so he said, and he put his narrow couch in the corridor between the kitchen and the loo. Mother felt very uneasy indeed about this but could think of no better arrangement. Feeling guilty, she agreed. There was no bathroom in the flat. We put a washbasin, a jug and a bucket in our room and concealed them behind a screen. Jadwiga and Stefan did the same, while Henryk had to wash in the kitchen. Strangely enough, central heating had been installed in the house just before the war. But no central heating worked during the war in Warsaw. So we had to put an iron stove with a long black pipe in our room, and keep searching for fuel. This stove, which for some curious reason everybody called 'the goat', smoked like a factory, covered everything with soot and was the ugliest thing I had ever had to share a room with, but it did make our place as hot as hell, provided we were lucky enough to find something to put in it. Three beds, a ramshackle wardrobe and a large round table at which we all sat and ate together, completed the furnishings. The walls were painted yellow and this sometimes made the room look bright and gay. The corridor walls were a pea-green colour, while Jadwiga and Stefan lived in sky blue. All this was so unusual, so different from all the other homes I had ever known that I could only wonder what other surprises life could bring.

We settled down somehow and began a more or less normal

existence, living from one day to the next. At first nobody from the household went to work. For the second year running we were living on what was left from before the war. Getting food, though it was not the kind we were used to, was not a problem for those who had money. One could not possibly survive on the ration allowed. It was the black market, thriving in the ghetto despite its borders and heavily guarded gates, that kept us alive. Stefan and Henryk were in charge of finding food and fuel for the 'goat', while the women ran the house. Keeping it tidy, free of bugs and lice, was Jadwiga's job. Mother was the cook. Totally inexperienced in matters of cookery, embarrassed by the necessity of economising, she was at first miserable. Then Henryk came to the rescue again. Far more competent in the kitchen than any of us, he eagerly took it upon himself to initiate Mother into the mysteries of 'the art of cooking from-what-is-available'.

The children of the house – Sophie and I – were exempted from major daily tasks. We were expected to continue our studies instead. This we did. There were many good teachers trapped in the ghetto, and plenty of children wanting to learn. I found a few of my old friends now living close to me, we got in touch with some teachers from a good prewar grammar school for boys called '*Spójnia*' ('Bond'), and within a couple of days we had begun our third year of secondary education. I had only to cross the street or walk for no longer than fifteen minutes to find myself in one of my friends' shabby flats where we gathered daily to study; or they would all come over to my place and, sitting with the teacher around our table, we would translate Horace from Latin or toil over the theorem of Pythagoras. Sophie, now nearly eleven, also joined a study group of children of her own age. Unfortunately, all her friends lived in 'the little ghetto', a district fairly remote from the central part we lived in. Day in and day out she had to walk far through the crowded streets, and cross a busy traffic lane used mainly by German vehicles.

When I recall this first winter in the ghetto, I can still smell the sharp mixture of odours produced by the 'goat' and the kerosene lamp in the evenings. For most of the time there was no electric power, and all windows were thoroughly blacked out, so that after the early sunset of winter the streets were pitch dark – everywhere in the occupied Polish towns, not only in the ghetto. But in the ghetto one could hardly move after dark. So many people were trying to make their way through the darkened street that they were constantly bumping into and tripping over one another. Fluorescent lapel-pins, invented and sold by some resourceful craftsmen to those who could afford them, helped just a little.

Physical contact with strangers was what we tried most to avoid. A lot of people were already destitute, living side by side with those more fortunate. The 'professional' Jewish beggars from before the war were now just a drop in the ocean of new poverty. Refugees from small provincial towns, robbed by the Nazis of their homes and belongings and thus reduced to rags, were crammed into the Warsaw ghetto by force. The homeless, tattered, undernourished people we brushed against in the streets were covered with lice and often suffered from infectious diseases.

Nazi propaganda played on this, claiming that Jews were the carriers of lice and germs. The Germans really feared us because of this and seldom entered the ghetto, except in heavy vehicles. This made us feel much safer in the ghetto than before. Besides, no matter how miserable we were, living in a sealed community among people equally vulnerable to outside violence, not being singled out in a crowd, produced a vague, deceptive feeling of relative security.

The first enemy to violate our home and ruin the illusory peace of our daily life did not wear a Nazi uniform. At the end of winter, when the snow had already melted and a fluid blend of mud and garbage flooded the narrow, never-cleaned pavements, Stefan, who now worked in the hospital as a voluntary auxiliary nurse, came home from work with a severe headache, chills and a high temperature. We thought it was flu, but when on the fourth day his temperature reached the dangerous point of 41 degrees and Stefan's body turned red with a rash, we realised it might be typhus. The doctor we called for at once confirmed our suspicion, ordered some drugs against pains and fever and summoned a sanitary unit. The few ghetto hospitals were bursting with sick people, supplies of medicines were scarce; the only thing a Jewish doctor could do for a Jewish patient was to order him to stay in bed, if there was one. The flat was sprayed throughout with carbolic acid by the sanitary unit, then sealed off with the six of us inside. A huge yellow poster saying 'Typhus epidemic – keep out!' was stuck on the front door. Every day a kind neighbour would leave some food in front of our closed door, knock twice and run away. Confined to home, we waited to see who would be the next to show symptoms of the deadly disease.

Stefan was young and strong. He did not die. After a critical period of suffering and despair, he eventually recovered. None of us caught typhus from him. The quarantine was over.

When, after long weeks of house arrest, I dived out again into the open air, the town was at the height of spring. In the bright sunshine the streets seemed to fester. The living corpses of the beggars who had survived the winter had emerged from holes and dens, trying to warm their bones, calling piteously for food. But the sky was blue and I was not yet fifteen. On that day, I wrote in my diary:

16 April 1941, evening
Freedom, freedom at last! Everything was fun today, even sitting on this awful settee in Ala's room, squeezed between Zula and Hanka. Even the maths. I've missed quite a lot, by the way, but Hanka says she'll help me make it up in no time. They all seemed extremely pleased when I appeared out of the blue. Renata was so surprised that she kissed me, forgetting all sanitary precautions. Nina said she had rather expected me to die from typhus, the silly cow.

Lots of news. Lena's five-times-removed relatives – six people including kids – have arrived from Grójec and are staying with her, so we can't meet at her place any more, no room. They were robbed, forced to leave and were brought to Warsaw in a cattle truck. Scared to death.

Irena wanted to join our group, but eight is enough, said the girls, and flatly turned her down. So she asked the teachers to let her join the boys. They didn't mind and the boys were delighted, at least she says so. They are nine all together now. Could be nice to meet them – same teachers, same problems.

Tomorrow Polish and I'll see L. again. I'm looking forward to it.

It took me a couple of days to cool down and look soberly around.

18 April 1941
Two little boys are begging in the street next to our gate. I see them there every time I go out. Or they might be girls, I don't know. Their heads are shaven, clothes in rags, their frightfully emaciated tiny faces bring to mind birds rather than human beings. Their huge black eyes, though, are human; so full of sadness . . . The younger one may be five or six, the older ten perhaps. They don't move, they don't speak. The little one sits on the pavement, the bigger one just stands there with his claw of a hand stretched out. I must remember now to bring them some food whenever I go out. This morning, on my way to lessons, I gave them my bread and butter meant for lunch.

They didn't show any excitement or gratitude, just took it from me and began to eat at once. I saw other people giving them bread or some money, too. This keeps them alive. But, my God, what kind of life is it?

On my way to Pawia Street, strewn all along with starving people leaning against the walls or sitting on the pavements, not strong enough to walk, I kept accusing myself of being well fed and for that reason entirely indifferent to their plight. I talked to Hanka and Zula about it after class. 'Don't you think the way we live is highly immoral?' I asked. 'We eat our breakfast, lunch and supper, we occupy our minds with the French Revolution or Polish poetry, or just which one of us L. fancies the most; then we go to bed with a good novel and peacefully fall asleep. At the same time they are starving and dying.' 'There's nothing we can do for them,' said Zula sadly, 'for the hundreds and thousands of them.' 'Of course not. But for some of them perhaps? Each of us for somebody?' 'Would you and your family be willing to take home these two begging boys?' asked Hanka very seriously. 'To share not only food but also beds with them, live with them for better or worse?'

I had no ready answer to her question, and the more I think about it now, the clearer I see the answer is 'No'. No point in asking my family, I don't want them myself. The idea of stopping our lessons and giving the money we pay for them each month to the poor won't work either: the teachers who live on it would soon be reduced to poverty. So what can we do? The only conclusion we have managed to come to so far is: we must find a way of being helpful, giving our time, skills(?), physical strength . . . Yes, but how?

The problem was neither forgotten nor solved. Not for the time being, anyway. Days passed by, new problems arose to wonder about or struggle with.

29 April 1941
Went to see Teresa this afternoon. Zula and Hanka with me. We seldom part these days. We haven't seen Teresa for ages and all we knew was her address where she lived with her mum only, her father apparently dead, as they haven't heard from him since the siege, when he left, exactly like my dad and Hanka's.

We walked all the way, though we could have taken the tram which has been introduced recently in the ghetto. Funny tram, pulled by two horses like an eighteenth-century stagecoach. It's called 'Kon-Heller tram' after the names of the two owners who are Jews, of course, but Gestapo agents at the same time. So people say. Nobody decent would use this service. So we walked.

We sat in Teresa's tiny little room sipping ersatz tea and talking about all manner of things: what we're going to do after the war, which of us will marry, which won't, and so on. Teresa who, to be frank, isn't the brightest person in the world, said she was going to be a famous writer, and Hanka, she said, a great scientist. Here I must agree. Zula, said Teresa, will become a courtesan of the high-class sort; and I, a devoted wife and mother, apart from anything else I do. Zula seemed quite pleased with the prophecy. With her fiery red hair, milky complexion faintly dotted with freckles and lively eyes that remind me of shiny little cherries, she will certainly attract dozens of men in the future. Which doesn't mean at all she couldn't do better than to become a courtesan, I told her. I was furious with Teresa's view of myself. 'Devoted wife and mother' – is that really all she thinks of me?

We talked and talked for hours, while Teresa's mum was busy dusting books in the corridor. (They keep their books in the corridor because there's no space in the room.) In fact she probably didn't want to bother us with her presence. All of a sudden we heard her cry out and we all four rushed into the corridor. What we saw was Teresa's mum hanging on the neck of Teresa's dad, who stood in the middle, all rags and filth, with a rucksack on his shoulders. 'Dad's alive! Dad's back!' yelled Teresa and ran into her father's arms too. Slowly, softly the three of us retreated from the flat and ran down to the street like mad things. None of us said a word. Zula, whose father died during the siege, sobbed openly. I tried hard not to break down. In fact, I cried silently all the way back, and I can bet Hanka did the same in the dark.

I decided not to tell Mother about the incident.

I was worried about my mother. She was missing Father terribly and could hardly sleep at night. She had certainly been thinking about all possible horrors that could have happened to him. Sometimes in the silence of the night I could hear her gently knock on the wooden bedpost: she 'touched wood' to avert the evil of the images she had been conjuring up in her mind. It was not like my mum, she had never been superstitious before.

There was something else I did not like at all. The way Henryk had been staring at her. I noticed he always tried to be with her – in the kitchen whenever she was there, always in our room when I came back from class. With growing anxiety I kept an eye on them. For the first time I realised that Mother was not yet old: she was just over forty. She had never been a beauty, but she had lovely warm, brown eyes, a shapely figure and gorgeous legs any younger woman would envy. She had always been neatly dressed in clothes of exquisite quality and taste. Even now, when they were considerably worn, she still looked fresh and tidy.

My imagination, stirred up by having recently read *Climates* by Maurois and Flaubert's *Madame Bovary*, made me think there was something secret going on between my mother and her brother's father-in-law. I started behaving like a jealous lover, watching closely all their gestures and glances.

One day, on a mild evening, there were just the three of us in the flat – Sophie was playing in the courtyard, Stefan and Jadwiga were out. As usual, Mother and Henryk were both in the kitchen, making supper for all the family. The kitchen door was wide open. In a sudden fit of jealousy, I shut myself in our room which faced the kitchen and, abandoning all dignity, peeped through the keyhole. They were still busy cooking, but after a while I saw Henryk's arm come round mother's shoulders, his cheek touch hers. A red mist dimmed my eyes. In an outburst of fury I flung the door open, flew into the kitchen, and slapped Henryk's face with all my strength. 'Why? Why?' he whispered, taken aback.

I shut myself back in the room, sobbing my heart out. Some time passed before Mother came in, very pale and trembling. She did not seem to be angry with me, which made it all the worse. For a long time she just kept stroking my hair. Then she started talking to me softly and frankly, as if I were not her daughter but her closest friend. Henryk was in love with her, she told me. He had fallen in love with her a long time ago, during the siege. But she had not had the slightest notion about it until recently. If she had known she would have never accepted his offer to share the flat. Now there was nothing she could do about living under the same roof. We had nowhere else to go, nowhere else to live. We had to wait till the war came to an end. Nevertheless, Mother continued, I could trust her. All her thoughts and feelings were with Father, somewhere far away in the remote Russian camp. Never in her life would she betray her one great love. I knew it was true and loved her more than ever that night.

Next morning, dying with shame, I apologised to Henryk. He forced a smile, trying to turn the incident into ridicule, but I knew that deep in his heart he felt uneasy. After that day I never saw Henryk make any advance to Mother. Perhaps she became more strict with him. Or maybe I lost all interest in spying on him. Anyway, a far more dramatic incident soon made all this wretched matter sink into oblivion.

15 May 1941, 2 a.m.
It was – and still is – the worst day of my life. Worse than the raids, worse than typhus. I can't sleep, I can't even lie still. I have to wait till the morning when we'll run back to hospital and learn . . . Mother paces the room, four steps up and four steps down, her face blank, her eyes dry, as if she had already run out of tears. I don't know how to comfort her, so I don't even try.

For me this all started at noon. I was walking back from Zula's place deep in thought about maths, the Polish essay L. wants us to write, and other things like that. When I entered our gate, that Goldberg woman from the third floor was there, very nervous. 'What news? What news?' she shouted when she saw me. 'News about what?' I asked. 'About your sister of course!' Then she realised I knew nothing and told me the story. This morning Sophie was on her way to her classes, as usual. As she was crossing the traffic lane a heavy German lorry, one of the eight-wheel type, knocked her down and drove away at top speed. It happened just in front of Dr Korczak's* Children's Home and some kids saw it from the window. They called the doctor and some other staff. They all ran down and picked up Sophie who lay in the middle of the road, unconscious and spattered with blood.

They somehow managed to get her to hospital (I wonder how, it's a long way, the hospital is at the end of our street). By

*Janusz Korczak was a doctor, writer, educator and social worker, and the founder and head of an orphanage in the ghetto.

coincidence a nurse called Sabina, who used to work with Dad, recognised Sophie and sent somebody to fetch Mother. The person said Sophie was still alive. 'Your poor, poor mother,' sobbed Mrs Goldberg, but I didn't stop to listen. I rushed to the hospital. First thing I saw in the hall was Sophie on the stretcher on the floor next to the entrance. She was unconscious and not herself. Her head was tightly bandaged, her face white, her left eyelid enormously swollen. Mother crouched next to the stretcher wiping Sophie's face with a damp sponge. Sister Sabina came and said the doctor who had already seen Sophie suspected her left foot and left eye were seriously damaged. He also said she had concussion. It was too soon to say whether she would survive and if so whether her leg and eye would be saved.

We stayed there in the hall for the rest of the afternoon. There was no spare bed for Sophie. All wards, halls and corridors of the hospital were tightly packed with seriously ill people. But towards the evening Sister Sabina came down, a spark of triumph in her eyes. A patient had just died, she said, and she had used all her influence to keep his bed for Sophie. Stefan, who was on duty, helped Sister Sabina carry the stretcher upstairs. Mother and I followed them to the ward. As we lifted Sophie from the stretcher, she suddenly opened her right eye and stared at us. Then, in bed, she touched her bandaged head, neck and shoulders as if she were searching for something. She didn't find what she was looking for. Her beautiful black silky plaits, her pride, had been cut off first thing in the hospital. To our great amazement, we saw tears streaming – drop, drop – from her healthy eye. It meant she was conscious again. Soon we had to leave since the curfew was approaching. Now we wait.

Same day, 8 p.m.
Sophie is going to live, the doctors say. The concussion is slight, it will heal if she lies still for a week or two. The eye doesn't seem to be damaged inside, either. The worst thing is her foot, both flesh and bones mangled. They might decide to amputate the leg if it shows any signs of gangrene. Poor, poor little Sophie. I've never realised how I loved her. Or what an unusual child she was. My God, she was only nine and a half when the war began. Yet she lived through all the horrors of

raids, fire, starvation without a word of complaint, never cried, never panicked, always so calm and silent. I think she understands everything as well as me and better perhaps than some grown-up people who give way to their fears and other instincts we share with animals. Now she lies there, in this awful hospital, crying about her beautiful hair, not in the least aware that she may be crippled for the rest of her life. Why did it have to happen to her, why not to me?

A young man from Dr Korczak's came over to ask after Sophie. He says the children who saw the accident are positive the German driver did it on purpose, knocked Sophie down because he wanted to. He could easily have avoided it, they say.

Whatever the crisis, however close and inescapable disaster came, we had always had a bit of luck, Mother, myself and Sophie. We did not burn alive, we did not die from typhus, we made our narrow escapes time and again throughout the war. After a couple of weeks Sophie was back with us. Her life was no longer in danger, her sight unimpaired, her foot saved. She was an invalid for no more than six months, during which time she had to have daily massages and exercises for her foot. She learned to walk again. The only souvenir of the accident she kept for ever was a large, thick, ugly scar on her foot.

During Sophie's slow recovery, two major events occurred, one of paramount importance for the world, the other one just for me.

The first event was entered in my diary only briefly.

22 June 1941
I saw people staring at the sky this morning. All that could be seen up there were tiny glittering dots of planes flying very high. But people whispered about the outbreak of war between Germany and the Soviet Union. I wondered how they could possibly know this and dismissed the whole thing as one more piece of gossip.

But it is true, the Bolsheviks really are at war! Now (late afternoon) Stefan, 'wrapped up' in his *Völkischer Beobachter* (Nazi official newspaper) that he managed to get just recently, is reading between the lines, as usual. From time to time he bursts out with his own views – very different from those in the paper. He says the balance between the warring powers has shifted in favour of the Allies, and Hitler's defeat is now inevitable. He sounds enthusiastic.

The other event stemmed from my earlier worries and the talks I had with my friends in April. The matter of how to become useful was soon picked up by the rest of the girls in our study group. The most enterprising couple, Ala and Lena, went to the Jewish Council to make some enquiries. They were sent from one official to another, turned down many a time due to somebody's incompetence, often dismissed with a joke. Yet they persisted and after two weeks or so turned up beaming with victory: there was something great for us to do.

The organisation that Ala and Lena had finally come across was called 'Toporol' which stood for Agriculture Promoting Society. Financed by the Jewish Council but based on voluntary work, the society aimed to use every bit of free ground in the ghetto for growing vegetables. Any crops grown would be given to starving people. 'Toporol' needed us, our free, dedicated work. They could not offer us any recompense – no money, no vegetables, not even an *Aussweis* – a written certificate stating we were employed. The only benefit they could promise us was a good training in agriculture.

The 'school year' was just coming to an end, so we started working almost at once. Our group was allocated the patch of ground where the prewar hospital of the Holy Ghost had stood – it was destroyed during the siege. It was at the back of Leszno Street, very near where I lived. The hospital's ample grounds were covered with thick layers of rubble from the ruined buildings. Clearing it away was our first job.

23 June 1941

What a day! Eight long hours of hard physical work under the blue sky. Can't imagine anything better. There are fifteen of us including the ones we don't know, ten girls and five boys altogether. The instructor from the Jewish Council called Tadek is a strict, matter-of-fact fellow in his early twenties. Handsome, too, though not very tall; blond and sunburnt. A perfect organiser: we didn't waste a single moment. The girls, standing in two rows, picked up and passed the bricks to the barrows, the boys wheeled the barrows to the far end of the grounds and emptied them. We were too busy to talk to each other except in the short break, when we sat on the rubble and ate our sandwiches. Back home I was so tired I could hardly speak. My legs and hands are scratched and swollen, my face sore with sunburn. When I close my eyes I can see nothing but bricks, bricks, bricks . . . I'm happy.

It took us over a week of daily work to clear the ground of rubble. The following fortnight we were busy digging. The job of turning over the hard, dry soil still full of debris was far more exhausting than coping with the bricks. It was too much for some: Nina and Zula dropped out. Nina because she was too lazy, Zula, though keen and passionate, could not take the work, fainted twice, then gave up.

For those who stayed, however, a great day came when the ordeal was over and the joy of proper gardening began. Following Tadek's expert instructions we now sowed and planted vegetables: carrots, onions, cucumbers and tomatoes, everything our plot could hold. Every morning I ran eagerly to work to see how it was all growing, to tend the fragile little shoots, to weed the soil. Thanks to Tadek's efforts, our unit received an incubator to start a chicken farm. Tadek went crazy about it and wanted to run it himself. He needed just one assistant. All my friends volunteered. I did not, being too fond of my plants. Tadek chose Renata and within a day managed to infect her with his own passion for the job.

Once the hard work was over, we could take more breaks to rest and talk. This long warm summer spent on a green island in the midst of hell I still recall – truth to tell – as a happy time of my youth.

3 August 1941

After three days of heavy rain, warm sunny weather again. Oh, how it is all growing! The frail pale-green plumes of carrot leaves sway in the breeze, the tiny baby cucumbers are creeping along the narrow trenches we have dug for them. Zula is back with us, which makes me happy. I have missed her badly. True enough, I had Hanka. But Hanka can't replace Zula for me, or vice versa. They are so different. Sometimes I think they're only friends because they have me in the middle. With Hanka I can talk about all kinds of serious matters, discuss the books we both read, not only novels and poetry but also things like Descartes, for example, or the *Communist Manifesto*, or *The Life of Termites* by Maeterlinck. Zula would yawn and interrupt if she were there. But when it comes to boys and love, I've only got Zula to talk to. Hanka would dismiss the subject, blushing terribly as she did so. So I've had to wait for Zula to talk about Renata. How much she's changed since Tadek made her his assistant! She hardly ever notices her friends these days, she's miles away, her eyes hazy, all her behaviour vague. She seems to be in a dream even when she is dealing with the hatching eggs. Is it just love for the chickens or is it Love? Zula's been watching them since I told her. She says yes, it must be Love, true and mutual. Strange, Renata is only fifteen like us, and a very quiet, unpretentious girl, too. She isn't even attractive, both her face and body are a bit flat. But Tadek who is an adult, handsome man looks at her warmly. Tenderly, that's the right word. No need to hide it from Zula: I envy Renata. I envy her not because I fancy Tadek, which I don't, but because she's in love and somebody is in love with her. Zula says she feels exactly the same. Neither of us has ever been in love. I can't say I loved Artek. We kissed, all right, but it wasn't the same. As for L., we are, all eight of us, enchanted by him – by his slim figure, inspired eyes, the way he recites poems. But that's a collective feeling, nothing personal. L. is more a Hamlet than a Romeo for me. And it's Romeo I'm longing for.

Back from the romantic mood to the squalor of the surrounding world, I was growing more and more used to the daily horrors. Corpses lying in the streets of people starved to death or shot by the Nazis had ceased to shock me. I passed them on my way to and from work without taking much notice. The work, conceived out of my deep concern and pity, turned into sheer joy. Little by little my conscience was lulled to sleep by the soothing awareness of *doing something for them*. Only from time to time would a sudden flash of sharp recognition make me reproach myself.

20 August 1941
I'm a beast. A callous hypocrite. Yesterday I had an argument with Mother. The matter was trivial: I've grown out of all my summer dresses, they're all too short and tight for me. No wonder: they were made for a thirteen-year-old child with no breasts. Mother insisted I wore the only one I still can squeeze into because it's loose, the silky red one. I've always hated it, ever since I got it two years ago. But I couldn't make Mother change her mind by just saying I didn't like the dress. So I told her that if I walked the streets all bright red, I might easily be spotted by that crazy German who comes to the ghetto every day on his bike just to shoot dead a few Jews in the crowd. This argument did the job instantly – Mother stopped nagging and gave me one of her own dresses, the lovely grey one made of

linen. Now I look gorgeous and hate myself.

Something else happened this morning. Regina, the girl who works with me in the field, was singing all the time we were weeding. She has a nice voice and knows many of the prewar hits. I was really quite enjoying it until she started on 'Bel Ami'. Suddenly I became hysterical and yelled at her to shut up. The reason is that I've been forced to listen to this stupid song day in day out in the early evenings. A beggar woman sings it endlessly down in the street, just under my open window where I sit, trying in vain to concentrate on my reading. And how she sings it, my goodness! With a harsh, broken voice, Polish, Yiddish, French words all mixed up together. Her face is swollen so I can't tell her age. She has two children with her, one in her arms, the other clinging to her filthy clothes. Their feet are bare. When I drop down a coin or a bit of bread for them, or if someone else does so, she stops for a second, then carries on with her 'Bel Ami' even louder and harsher. I really hate her, I hate all of them. That's why I say I'm a callous hypocrite. I really am.

Summer went by and we returned to our studies, the main work in Toporol having been finished, crops harvested and delivered to the Jewish Council. Only Renata kept working at her thriving chicken farm and often missed a lesson or two.

I remember my second winter in the ghetto as a time of weird 'stability'. I somehow learned to live with evil claiming its victims all around, with the tide of misery lapping my doorstep. I took it for granted like summer heat or winter frost. I was not the only one to live like that – but if I blame others, I should first of all blame myself.

My family were still able to survive on what was left from better times. Auntie Maria had taken all the most valuable objects from our flat in Border Street. She kept the old silver and precious paintings from my grandfather's collection. These valuables kept us alive in the ghetto and after. Auntie Maria sold them one by one on the 'Aryan' side and found any way she could to get the money to us.

Since October 1941, entering or leaving the ghetto without a special permit meant death for those who dared and were caught. Yet, despite the terrible danger, links with the outside world were not cut. There were holes in the walls, secret passages through houses neighbouring with the 'Aryan' side; there were guards to be bribed – German as well as

Polish and Jewish – at the ghetto entrances. Many Poles working for the water authorities or electricity board were authorised to enter the ghetto to carry out their duties. All these ways were used daily by both Jews and non-Jews to provide the ghetto with food and other goods. Some of these daring people, including children, were just struggling to keep their families alive; some made fortunes; some died, shot or beaten to death.

A large building at Leszno Street housed the municipal Court of Justice that acted for both Jews and non-Jews. There were two entrances to the building, one from the ghetto, the other from the 'Aryan' side. The court's halls and corridors were heavily guarded, of course, but with money and luck people from the two worlds could meet there and talk. Mother and Auntie Maria met in the Court of Justice several times. Auntie Maria's brother-in-law, who was an electrician and had a special permit to enter the ghetto, would also call on us from time to time with letters, money and all kinds of useful things from her.

By that winter shops with luxury goods, cafés and restaurants had opened in the ghetto. Once, having met Auntie Maria in the court and feeling rich for a while, Mother took Sophie and me out to lunch in a restaurant at Leszno Street. I had never been to a restaurant before and found this new experience exciting. Despite the bright day outside, the windows of the large room were all completely blacked out. The place was discreetly lit with a few kerosene lamps, the tables covered with white tablecloths, the waiters wore black suits. A pianist and violinist softly played sentimental Jewish tunes and Gypsy romances. Most of the tables were occupied. People were eating and talking loudly – they did not look smart to us, and yet one could tell they felt at home. We felt very out of place. Mother examined the menu on the table and became even more uneasy. There were all sorts of luxurious dishes, as well as French wines and exquisite brandies. The prices were horrifying. If it hadn't been for Sophie and me, Mother would have got up and left, but she didn't want to disappoint us, so we stayed and ordered the least expensive items from the menu: chicken broth with noodles, cholent – a traditional Jewish stew made of cheap meat, potatoes, beans and pearl barley – followed by milky pudding with cherry syrup. It was a true feast, the best meal we had had for ages. Though so far we had never starved in the ghetto, our daily meals at home were far less substantial and tasty. Sighing, Mother paid the bill, and filled with goodness we left the restaurant.

In the bright sunshine of the frosty afternoon there he was, the wild, hairy man, stark naked under a filthy, torn, feather quilt flung over his shoulders and only partly covering his skinny nakedness. Leaning against the wall next to the restaurant entrance, his feet bare, he waited for alms from the well-fed customers. I had seen this man before, he had been a regular feature of the ghetto scenery for some time. Before Mother could get her purse out, a Jewish policeman turned up from nowhere. Yelling at the beggar, threatening him with his truncheon, he tried to force him to leave. It was some time before the man moved from his spot and began to shuffle along Leszno Street, a little cloud of feathers flying out from his torn quilt.

The restaurant venture was the first and the last for me, I never felt like going there again. As for the naked beggar, I saw him dead some time later. He lay on the pavement covered with newspapers held down with a brick. I could tell it was him only because a ragged edge of the dirty quilt stuck out from under the papers.

At Leszno Street, not far from my house, prewar 'Femina' cinema was turned into a concert hall that winter. There were enough prominent musicians who happened to be Jews to set up a first-rate symphony orchestra in the ghetto; it was conducted by Szymon Pulman. I knew nothing about classical music. I had never in my life been to a concert before. It was Hanka who first persuaded me to go to 'Femina' with her. The orchestra played Tchaikovsky's 'Pathetique' symphony. Everyone in the dark auditorium sat still, profoundly moved. Then an eighteen-year-old girl sang 'Ave Maria' by Schubert. She had a strong, clear voice that seemed to burst through the walls of the hall and rise high above our world with all its daily troubles. The audience cried and I cried myself. The name of the young singer was Maria Eisenstadt. She did not survive the war. Neither did the conductor. As far as I know, they both died in Treblinka in the summer of 1942.

After that first concert I could hardly wait for the next, and never missed any until they came to an end. The orchestra was eventually banned by the Nazis for performing works by German composers, something that was strictly forbidden to Jews.

I passed a message to Auntie Maria begging her to send me my gramophone. I believe she had a hard time convincing her brother-in-law that such a thing was of vital importance to someone living behind the walls, but she managed and he brought me the gramophone. There were some records of tangos and foxtrots inside, but this was not what I was now interested in. As soon as I got hold of it and told my friends, we made a date with a boy we knew from Toporol. This boy used to complain of not having a gramophone to play his classical records. One cold evening we went over to his place with the gramophone. Some other young people were already waiting for us and we all went to a strange place next door; it was an empty room half demolished by fire and terribly cold. We sat down on the floor. Our host brought out two records – the only two he had not yet sold. One was Beethoven's Fifth Symphony, first and second movements; the other, Beethoven's Fifth Symphony third and fourth movements. Freezing in our coats and gloves, we spent all evening listening to these two records. When the fourth movement was over we started with the first again, until it was nearly curfew time. After that we met at the same place and listened to the same records once a week till the end of the winter. We had no other records of classical music. We had just the Fifth Symphony.

At that same time, I heard that medical lectures were being given in the big building next to one of the ghetto gates. The building belonged to the 'Aryan' side, but the lectures were sponsored by the Jewish Council and were meant for Jews. In fact, it was an almost standard unofficial university course in medicine. We rushed there at once, Hanka and I, and managed to cross the sinister gate alongside bona fide students who were showing their permits to the German guard. Once inside the building, we easily slipped into the lecture hall and immersed ourselves in the world of genetics. The lecture was being given by a prominent scientist of Jewish origin, Professor Ludwik Hirszfeld. It was clear and fascinating. We could follow it without effort, though we were only secondary school pupils without sufficient learning to attend the university. The following week we crossed the gate again and listened to the next lecture on genetics. Later on the checkups at the gate were reinforced and on the third attempt we luckily escaped a beating, just by the skin of our teeth. So we had to give up our medical studies. Yet, after forty years, I can still clearly remember the main principles of heredity.

Most of my innumerable relatives lived, like us, in the Warsaw ghetto. I kept in touch only with those I particularly liked.

There was my Grannie's sister, Great-Aunt Bella, who lived alone not far away, at Nowolipie Street. I would call on her sometimes, attracted by the stories of her youth that she enjoyed telling me. Before the war she had lived in luxury, indulging in sensual and intellectual pleasures. Her husband had deserted her soon after their wedding, leaving her with a son and all his debts. Coming from a rich family, however, Bella had her own resources and had enjoyed herself despite all adversities. I remembered her prewar flat furnished in Art Nouveau style, full of precious things of that period. She had taken some of them to her tiny, gloomy room in the ghetto. A plump but shapely blonde woman with the remains of great past beauty despite being in her mid-sixties, Aunt Bella had, in the past, kept her front door wide open. Painters, poets, philosophers would gather in her parlour to discuss art and literature, and also to eat, drink and dance. Now she was lonely, her only son gone with the army, her old friends left outside the walls, if not dead. Yet her sense of humour, her innate optimism protected Bella from gloom. She had set a definite aim for herself: to outlive Hitler.

The other relative I liked very much was my mother's cousin, Maryla. She was still in her prewar flat at Żelazna Street, as it was in the ghetto area, and lived there with her old mother and their prewar Christian maid, who did not want to part from them and had stayed in the ghetto. Maryla's only brother, Karol, had gone away with the army too, and much later was reported killed in Africa at the battle of Tobruk. Maryla was a tall, smart woman, by then in her early forties. Though not beautiful, she had the special charm of a witty, independent professional woman. She had been educated in Switzerland, was fluent in four foreign languages and before the war had worked as an English and French interpreter as well as a shorthand secretary. In the ghetto she earned her living by teaching foreign languages. To Maryla I owe my first steps in English: she taught me twice a week, in the winter of 1941 to 1942.

Then there was my Grandma Viera and Uncle Julian, now in the 'little ghetto'. Uncle Julian had joined the Jewish police and wore a policeman's uniform: a special cap and a truncheon. We at Leszno Street did not like it at all. Mother, Jadwiga and especially Stefan had nothing but contempt for the Jewish police. Once, at the beginning of the ghetto, Stefan had been offered a job with them too, but he flatly refused and went to work as a volunteer in the hospital, slaving away at the most appalling jobs there, just to be useful. For him the Jewish police meant Nazi lackeys and collaborators. True enough, joining the police was for some young men their only way of earning money and supporting their families. But Julian was a doctor, he could easily have managed otherwise. On the other hand, he did work as a police doctor. 'Don't you think that working as a doctor is all right whatever the circumstances?' I said to Stefan, trying to defend my paternal uncle against my maternal uncle's scorn. But Stefan said that in the war and ghetto we were all so much exposed to evil, so vulnerable to being infected by it, that we should take the utmost care not to become involved in any morally ambiguous situations; just keep away from such things as long as we could. Which did not mean, of course, that I should keep away from Julian, he added. So, from time to time, I would go to see Julian and Grandma Viera, crossing the bridge which had by then been built over the dangerous traffic lane.

Despite her age, widowhood and endless anxiety about the three of her four sons who were away, my grandma held herself well. She was always very pleased when I called and fed me with good food. Unlike my mother she was a perfect cook; besides, she could now afford to buy more than we did at Leszno Street. Once when I came, Grandma asked me to go with her to the café that had recently been opened in the little ghetto. A programme of entertainment had been advertised there and she wanted to see it with me. We sat at a little table drinking a filthy black liquid over-sweetened with saccharine, and watched a smutty show, stupid and rude. Grandma was very embarrassed at having brought me to see it. Nevertheless, we stayed till the end in the vain hope that there might still be something good. When the programme was over the band began to play a tango and several couples went out onto the dance floor. All of a sudden, somebody came to our table and asked Grandma politely for her permission to invite me to dance. It was a young, innocent-looking boy. Grandma gave him a scrutinising glance and said she did not mind. I did not mind, either.

So I danced the tango with a stranger, feeling thrilled and guilty at the same time, since I did not approve of having too much fun when people were dying in the street. I even told my partner this, but he said smiling, 'We, too, can die very soon, you and I.' It was true. I smiled back, quite relieved. I liked that boy. His eyes were pale blue and sparkling, his hair fair and soft. I could feel its softness as it gently skimmed my temple while we danced – he was just a little taller than myself. And just a little older. He told me it was his sixteenth birthday that day; his parents had taken him to the café to celebrate. He too was disgusted with the programme. We could not talk any more because the band had changed to 'Rosamunda', that loud, fast piece of music which inundated the whole of Europe during the war. 'Rosamunda, you came with the northern wind,' sang the young pianist. One cannot talk with 'Rosamunda' in the air, one can only dance. So we danced till the band stopped. As we walked back to my table, I hoped Grandma would invite my dancer to sit with us for a while. But she said it was time to go home. The boy bowed politely to her, waved his hand to me, and disappeared. He did not tell me his name. Nor did I tell him mine.

Spring came again, the third spring of the war, my second in the ghetto. I was almost sixteen. Vague intimations of life awakening from its wintry slumber somewhere far beyond the walls, a fresh breeze coming through the window from over the endless roofs, all this made me yearn for the freedom of open space. I was suffocating in the tightness of my cluttered room, in the stench of the sickly streets. Images of green woods bright with sunbeams, of boundless fields panting with fecundity haunted my dreams. So when in May I went to the Jewish Council to ask for a new job in Toporol, it was not this time just because I wanted to help the starving.

Only Hanka went with me. We still had lessons, but the fourth year of our secondary schooling was nearly finished and there was ample time left for revising, so we could easily spare two days a week for work. We were allocated straight away to a team working in the cemetery. The Jewish cemetery was now cut off from the ghetto and even people going to funerals had to have special permits to cross the ghetto gate. We received our permits from the Jewish Council and went to work the same morning.

The way to the cemetery was long and led through the worst, most appalling part of the ghetto, a part I hardly knew. Almost immediately my bag of sandwiches was snatched from my hand by a starving child who did not even run away but stopped and devoured the bread on the spot. The cemetery plot, still free of graves and allotted to Toporol for cultivation, was twice as large as the hospital's grounds. We were expected to work hard since the team was small. Instead of onions or cucumbers, we were now going to grow potatoes, cabbages and beet-roots. A rough, middle-aged man with none of Tadek's wit and charm was in charge of the team. On that first morning he showed us how to plant cabbages and we started work at once. After an hour or two I heard to my astonishment some words of appreciation from this rude, quarrelsome instructor. 'Look at her,' he told my fellow workers, pointing at my back doubled up in effort, 'she does it right, and fast. Try to do it like her.' Never before had I been praised for my physical endeavours and this comment made me proud and happy. I got on with my work with the utmost zeal. Eight hours passed in no time at all.

That spring I was too busy to read, think or keep my diary properly. After a day of hard physical or mental work I would go to bed dead tired and fall straight into peaceful sleep. I would reach for my diary and scribble in it only if some strong emotions of that day kept me awake till late at night.

20 May 1942

Tomorrow back to work. Just an hour ago Jadwiga took me to her room to talk to me privately. And seriously. A woman-to-woman talk. I must say she's been getting on my nerves lately. Either she's changed or I have, I don't know which. Once she used to be my idol. Everything she did or said, the way she behaved, dressed, thought about things was right with me. I wanted to be like her. Now I can see she's got her faults like anybody else. She tries to impose her own rules in the house, she's vain and conceited. I doubt if her knowledge is really as sound as I used to believe. There are some subjects she only pretends to know about, yet would never admit I know more than she. Strange though it may sound – she's jealous of me, my own aunt, ten years my senior! I could see her furious glances when Mr N., Stefan's friend, talked to me last week. Silly, what does he care for me, an old man over thirty.

Anyway, we sat together on her bed this afternoon and she was preaching to me about the dangers I'm exposed to working in the cemetery. Danger one: 'Frankenstein' at the gate – he loves to have a few Jews dead, apart from the one they're seeing off to the grave. Which means I could be shot just by chance. Danger two: there's this black market business going on in the cemetery, Jews meeting non-Jews, Polish and Jewish policemen chasing the vendors to squeeze out some bribes, Germans hunting with guns for all of them. I could get involved in this, again by chance. Danger three, Jadwiga assumed a solemn expression: a girl like me, young and pretty, could easily be raped somewhere in a deserted part of the cemetery. When she said that, out of sheer cussedness I said something stupid that I am now ashamed of. 'Good,' I said, 'I wouldn't mind being raped, provided the rapist were young and handsome.' Jadwiga is not a prude, she didn't tell me off for being indecent. On the contrary, she took it seriously and went on explaining to me what a difference it made to a woman to lose her virginity in a rape rather than losing it out of love. I must admit she was great talking about it and I felt I was still very fond of her, in spite of all her faults. I kissed her and promised to be careful. Tomorrow, next week and all my life.

21 May 1942

We were sent to the other part of the cemetery first thing this morning, and worked at singling beets for the rest of the day. Just Hanka and I, since we are 'reliable workers who don't need to be watched' – so the old man said. We worked honestly, indeed, till noon. Then we took a break. We had nothing to eat because we had given our sandwiches to some children on our way, not waiting till they were snatched from us. So, terribly hungry and tired, we stretched ourselves flat on the ground and gazed at the sky. It was a lovely feeling, as though I were an integral particle of the world, rooted deep in the crust of the earth under a huge, blue dome. There wasn't a soul around, no Germans, no vendors, not even rapists – and not a single sound, apart from birds' twitter. Breathing the scent of the moist soil, little by little we were falling asleep, when all of a sudden we heard wailing coming closer from the cemetery entrance. We got up at once and saw a horrifying funeral procession moving fast along the nearest cemetery pathway. Two Pinkert men*
were pulling a cart loaded up to its edges with corpses, covered carelessly with a single sheet on top. An old Jew, perhaps a Rabbi, followed the cart, humming and lamenting perfunctorily while he tottered far too fast for his age. They passed quickly and soon disappeared from sight.

The world was bright and peaceful again. But we couldn't stop thinking about it or start work as if nothing had happened. We felt impelled to go and see the spot where the corpses were buried. We soon found it. It was just a huge, deep, rectangular hole in the ground, half filled with the naked bodies of men, women and children, thrown down in layers, one on top of another, facing up, facing down, arms and legs mixed together, not human bodies, in fact, but bones coated with rotting skin. A hideous stench of decay we hadn't smelt before almost knocked us down. We ran away and didn't speak to each other till the end of working hours. I shall not forget this as long as I live.

Indeed, I have never forgotten that grave waiting open for more corpses to arrive.

---

*Pinkert was the only undertaker in the ghetto.

By the beginning of the summer very worrying rumours about the future of the Warsaw ghetto began to be heard more and more often. People talked about Nazi plans to clear the capital of Jews by mass deportations to labour camps in eastern parts of the country. These rumours came from the Jewish Council and were anxiously whispered time and again. People dismissed them as *Greuel propaganda* (terror propaganda) or tried to convince themselves that living away from Warsaw in some well-organised camp might be better than rotting in the ghetto. My family did not share these views. Stefan firmly believed that the Nazis had decided to exterminate the Jews and one could expect no change for the better from them. There was nothing, however, we could do to prevent what was coming, so we just got on with our daily concerns as before.

Despite the constant feeling of danger, or perhaps just because of it, some people in the ghetto indulged in pleasure with particular zeal. I knew a few who were living like that, and mused upon this kind of living with mixed feelings.

30 May 1942

I'm furious with Zula. Something has been going on recently in Renata's and Joanna's home night after night and we were both dying to know what it was. Renata wouldn't say. Apparently she's nothing to do with it, much too absorbed in her own romance. But we've heard gossip from people who have been to Joanna's night-time parties. Very vague, though. It would never occur to me to go and ask Joanna, or try to get invited by her – she's older, after all, and has never been my friend. Yesterday, without even consulting me, Zula went uninvited to the party and stayed there over night. This morning she's told me all about it. In the tiniest detail. Thirteen people were there, including Zula, boys and girls, all but her about eighteen. Renata wasn't in. It appears she hasn't been sleeping at home lately. Where does she sleep then, I wonder? The parents don't object. They don't object to Joanna's parties, either. They slept peacefully in their room all night, Zula says.

Joanna and her friends didn't mind Zula being there, they were rather pleased to have her with them. They were playing games when she went in. It involved sitting on each other's knees and kissing. From time to time, they would drink vodka straight from the bottle. Somebody passed Zula the bottle and she drank, too. When the bottle was empty one of the boys got another and they sent it round again. After a while Zula felt tipsy, but she can remember they danced, then switched the light off and lay down on the floor, all next to each other. She fell asleep straightaway, but woke up after a time and heard a couple making love next to her. She thought the other couples were doing the same in the dark, and felt so terribly uneasy that she began to sob. A boy came over to comfort her and wanted to make love to her. She was very frightened and refused. The boy didn't sound offended though. In a fatherly way he told Zula that with life as it is we shouldn't wait for our one true love before making love, because we might never live that long.

We've been thinking and talking about what he said all day. Perhaps he was right, perhaps we've been wasting the last bits of our lives not even trying to find out what love is? Yet, the very idea of doing it drunk and in the presence of other people makes me sick. I would rather die not knowing . . . Zula says I'm right. She seems deeply distressed after what she saw last night. Serves her right. She shouldn't have gone there in the first place.

Our school year was drawing to a close. In the middle of June we sat the unofficial exams, supervised by our own teachers only. Irena, my friend from before the war who had joined the boys' courses a year earlier, came to me with a message from her group. The boys wanted to meet the girls from my group and suggested a party to celebrate the end of our exams. I said I had to ask my friends first, so Irena went off without any definite answer, leaving me torn by ambivalent feelings. I had no doubt that throwing a party at a time like that was shameful. On the other hand, I longed to meet the boys, to dance, to laugh.

Next morning I told the girls about the invitation. Hanka and Renata said at once that they were not interested. The remaining five were only too pleased to accept. I had to give Irena the answer but still couldn't make up my own mind. I was just thinking about it and had almost decided not to go, when two boys turned up grinning on my doorstep. To my great surprise one of them was the stranger I had danced with in the café, three months earlier. No less surprised than myself, this time he introduced himself to me. His name was Roman. He and his friend Marian belonged to Irena's study group. They came as deputies of the group to hear my answer, and, if it was 'yes', to ask me to lend my gramophone for the party. It was going to be given in Roman's house. I was so excited and confused that I said, 'Yes, of course,' forgetting all my doubts. For a while we stood awkwardly in the corridor discussing the details of the coming event, then talking about everything and nothing. I noticed Roman was a bright, witty fellow, not nearly as shy as I had thought when I had first met him. Slightly suntanned, his open-necked blue shirt matching his sparkling eyes, he seemed far more attractive now than he had in the winter. I was pleasantly aware of being suntanned too, and knew that my summery green blouse matched my eyes as well. I could see that Roman and Marian had both noticed this.

The following days and nights were all dreams and sweet expectations. I was longing to see Roman again. On the appointed day, however, Marian turned up alone to fetch me and the gramophone to the party. Roman was too busy sorting things out, he said. I tried hard not to show my disappointment. In the street Marian stopped a rickshaw, being too lazy to carry the gramophone to the 'little ghetto'. I had never travelled in a rickshaw before, I found it disgusting to be pulled by a poor cycling man. I sat stiffly in the cart next to Marian, looking away from people in the street and dying with shame.

The party itself was not a success, either. The room Roman shared with his parents was large enough, but it was the only one they had in the big apartment, so the parents stayed there all the time. My friends behaved like silly geese, the boys talked mainly to each other, and Roman was busy with the records most of the afternoon. I danced with him only once and enjoyed it less than I had expected. We ate some tiny little sandwiches washed down with erzatz lemonade and the party was over. When all the people had left, I stayed behind to help Roman and his parents with the tidying up. Then Roman came to help me carry the gramophone home.

He did not even think of calling a rickshaw. For the first time the two of us were alone, except for the noisy, swarming crowd. We walked, talked and laughed all the way, finding there were lots of things to tell each other. We stopped at the entrance to my house. Roman pressed my hand and asked whether I would like to meet him again. His bright eyes were serious this time.

On the following evening I heard him whistling 'Rosamunda' in the street below my open window. I ran down and we went for a walk again. For the next three weeks we spent all our spare time together, day after day. I was working in the cemetery full-time by then; Roman, too, had his own commitments, earning money by giving maths lessons. So there were only the evenings left. Usually we walked in the streets, since there were no nice places to go to. Sometimes Roman would come upstairs and stay in my room till almost curfew time. Mother and Sophie were always with us and they both enjoyed Roman's visits as much as myself. His special gift for telling stories, his vivacity and his wonderful sense of humour made us think he would later become a writer or actor or both.

Once Roman invited me to the cabaret. It was called 'Sztuka' ('Art') and had been opened at Leszno Street the previous winter. I had been longing to go there all those months, and sitting there with Roman made me feel infinitely happy. The programme was good. Apart from old hits sung by prewar stars, it dealt with the daily life of the ghetto. Bitter and sharp, the sketches and couplets mercilessly lashed corruption and indifference, hinted at the hollowness of our 'cosy stability', brought laughter to the audience as well as tears. We left profoundly moved.

It was easy to talk to Roman, it was easy to be with him. We liked the same things, read the same books. It was also good being quiet together. I wanted to be alone with him and longed for him at night when I imagined something awful might happen to him. I was in love.

21 July 1942

There is nowhere to go, there is no way to be alone. The streets moan and yell with a thousand voices, they reek of rotten fish and dying bodies. Wherever we turn, whatever we look at, all is ugliness. So we run away and hide from it all in the flat. Here at least we are safe from sounds and smells. Not from other people, though.

We've spent this afternoon sitting on Henryk's couch in the corridor. For a while there was no one around and Roman stroked my cheek, and I stroked his, and we moved close to each other. But then Jadwiga suddenly opened her door and went to the loo, then back; then Sophie went up and down; then Henryk came home from his afternoon walk and, winking at us, shut himself in the kitchen to let us feel undisturbed. I could hardly bear it, so I asked Roman to go. My eyes filled with tears as I said it.

As we were saying goodbye Roman whispered something strange in my ear. He said the only way we could be left alone is to go to a hotel. There is a secret hotel in the ghetto, he said, and he's got enough money to book a room for a single night. We could go there tomorrow if I wanted to. He didn't look at me as he said it and he ran away in a hurry.

Now I'm sitting at the window thinking about it all.
Everybody else is sound asleep. I wouldn't talk to anyone about
it, anyway. Not even to Mother. What shall I do? How shall I
answer him tomorrow? A hotel room . . . Something seedy,
degrading . . . judging from the French novels, at least. A
picture of a fallen woman in rags comes to mind. On the other
hand, this is the only way we can be on our own. For a
while . . . for an hour . . . for a whole night . . . God! I want
it, I long for it . . . Yes, I'll go with him tomorrow!

> 'Come gentle night, come loving black-brow'd night,
> Give me my Romeo . . . '

The next day, 22 July 1942, the mass deportation of people from the
Warsaw ghetto began.

4 The Walls Tighten Around Us

The number of deportees averaged 5,000–7,000 daily, sometimes reaching 13,000 . . .

Some of the victims, resigned to their fate as a result of starvation, reported voluntarily to the *Umschlagplatz*,* lured by the sight of food which the Germans offered to the volunteers, and by the promise that their transfer to 'the East' meant they would be able to live and work in freedom . . .

In the beginning, the Germans exempted from deportation employees of the ghetto factories, members of the *Judenrat*† and Jewish police, and hospital personnel, as well as their families. Thousands of Jews made feverish attempts to obtain such employment certificates. In the course of time even these 'safe' categories were subjected to deportation . . .

The number of victims, including those murdered in the ghetto and those deported to Treblinka, totalled approximately

*The Nazis turned the station depot at Stawki Street in Warsaw into an assembly point during the mass deportations. The victims were dragged there and kept in a yard surrounded by a high fence or crammed into an abandoned building until the freight cars arrived to carry them away. The depot was guarded by contingents of SS troops, support troops, and the Jewish Police.

†The Jewish Council was established during the German occupation on Nazi orders as an extension of the prewar Jewish council. It was supposed to care for the ghetto community and execute the orders of the German authorities.

> 300,000 out of 370,000 inhabitants of the ghetto prior to July
> 1942 . . .
>
> This major *Aktion* lasted from 22 July until 13 September
> 1942 . . .
>
> *Encyclopaedia Judaica, Vol. 16*

The first three days of the *Aktion* I spent in the flat, following Julian's firm instructions not to set foot in the street. He appeared at our doorstep on the morning of 22 July armed with his truncheon, wearing his navy-blue cap, very nervous. He said the deportation would begin in an hour or two. We were safe as long as there were volunteers and beggars to make up the first daily contingents of deportees. Provided we stayed at home. Otherwise, we might be caught and put on a train with the beggars. He said we must do everything we could to avoid being put on a train to the east, because conditions in the labour camps would certainly be dreadful. We didn't need to be told this: we at Leszno Street had never trusted the Germans anyway. Julian promised he would take care of Mother, Sophie and myself and try to find a way out for us as soon as possible. First, however, he had to think of his own mother. He suggested that Stefan, Jadwiga and Henryk do everything they could and use all possible connections to get a job at one of the German factories in or outside the ghetto. They should go out to do this, despite the danger.

I stayed at home wondering in agony what would become of my love. I wanted to be with Roman whatever happened. I was more desperate for news from him than for the safe place that Julian had promised to find for us. But there was no news.

On the fourth day I could wait no longer and, ignoring Mother's pleas, set out to the 'little ghetto'. At first the streets seemed uncannily quiet, almost deserted. I walked fast, not looking around, quick, quick along Leszno Street, until I plunged into the tangle of narrow lanes leading to Roman's flat. There, all of a sudden, I found myself in the middle of a panic-stricken crowd. In a little square a score of men – both Jewish policemen and civilian helpers – tried to hold a swarm of screaming people inside a ring of tightly locked hands. Other policemen ran up and down the back alleys searching for more victims, pulling them violently along, pushing them by force into the ring. Just concealed behind a large building, two lorries waited for their human load. A couple of Nazi soldiers leant leisurely against them. Their guns ready to fire, they watched the round-up lazily, talking and laughing in the bright sunshine of the mid-summer day.

I hardly had time to be frightened when one of the men forming the deadly enclosure broke away from the ring, rushed at me, seized my arm, and began to pull me, as if intending to force me into the ring. He was just pretending. I recognised him at once: he was Mr. N., Stefan's friend. As an employee of the Jewish Council he had evidently been ordered to take an active part in the round-up. His face was white, twisted with fear and agony, his hands trembling. With feigned brutality he pushed me into a dark gate and whispered imploringly, 'Run away, child, run back home as fast as you can!' He showed me a narrow passage between two buildings. Terrified, I darted away without another word. I do not remember my journey back.

On the following day, a little boy whom I did not know brought me a letter from Roman. 'My sweet Princess,' it said, 'I'm trying my best to find employment in the Schultz factory *for both me and you*. We *must* be together whatever happens, we *must* survive. Don't despair, my sweet little girl, I'll be with you as soon as I can.' There was no way to reply: the little boy vanished and the postal service had stopped working in the ghetto since the beginning of the *Aktion*.

We waited. There was no news from Julian, nor from the people who had promised to 'find something' for Stefan, his wife and father-in-law. The *Aktion* was already well under way. Day after day, including Saturday and Sunday, it started at 8 a.m. and ended at 4 p.m. We soon learned to live according to this timetable, going out early in the morning to be back home before eight, then in the evening again, until curfew time. The streets, deserted during the long hours of daily horror, came to life again during those short spells. People hurried to see whether their relatives and friends had survived the day's *Aktion*, to make another attempt to get into the factories, to telephone friends on the 'Aryan' side, to find some food. All shops, cafés and restaurants had been closed since the beginning of deportation, all entrances to the ghetto thoroughly blocked by the Nazis. Food was getting scarce. Yet, in the evenings the streets swarmed with resourceful vendors selling bread, potatoes or sweets at sky-high prices.

There were no more beggars lying on the pavements and no calls for help were heard. The 'human refuse' had been swept away and put on the trains during the very first days of the *Aktion*. The ghetto orphanages, old people's homes and refugee shelters had been gradually cleared away as well. Now the Nazis, keenly helped by the Ukrainian and Latvian troops as well as by the Jewish police, launched a systematic house-to-house hunt. Houses were surrounded by the troops, all gates and exits blocked, residents summoned to the back yards. Their documents were checked. Only those with an *Ausweis* that proved their usefulness to the Germans were exempted from deportation. All the others were forced to form ranks and march to the *Umschlagplatz*. Meanwhile, the flats were searched; anybody found hiding was, as a rule, killed on the spot.

At the beginning of August we learned that the 'little ghetto' had ceased to exist, the inhabitants deported or forced to move farther north. We knew that Julian and Grandma Viera were all right, they had moved elsewhere. There was no news from Roman, however. All hope of seeing him again dwindled little by little. We expected our turn to come any time now, without much hope of getting an *Ausweis* before then. And when it really came, on 13 August, we were still without the coveted documents, all six of us.

The house at 15 Leszno Street was surrounded and closed off first thing in the morning. From our fifth-floor flat we heard the uproar of troops bursting into the courtyard, the ear-splitting whistle, then the loud cry: '*Alle Juden raus, schnell, schnell, alle Juden herunter*' ('All Jews out, quick, quick, all Jews down here') repeated in Polish. Then the sound of dozens of feet running down, down to disaster. Then shouts, screaming, whistles, lamenting in the courtyard . . . Two single shots . . . A turmoil of violence and misery.

We stayed in our flat, waiting, listening. We had decided long before not to obey, not to go down. To be shot dead instantly seemed far better than to endure the long, slow process of dying in pain and humiliation. Besides, there was no chance of survival if we obeyed the order; there might be some if we disobeyed. So we sat still, listening.

Soon we heard a rumble of heavy boots climbing up the stairs, of smashed locks and doors flung open by force: the hunters were searching through the flats. We could hear them coming up and up, approaching the third floor, then the fourth. We could already hear their voices, make out Polish and Latvian words. The fourth floor was taking them a long time: they were obviously busy plundering. Now we had only minutes left. We waited.

Then suddenly a long, sharp whistle and a German command from the courtyard announced the end of the round-up, summoning back the hunters.

We had survived.

We stayed in the flat till the end of the day, unable to move, to think, or to decide what to do next. We kept straining our ears, but there was dead silence all round. The house seemed empty. Towards evening, Stefan ventured out to see what was happening. He soon returned with news. Two neighbours who were employed in German factories had come back from work to find their homes plundered, their families taken away. A poster stuck on the gate announced that the inhabitants of our house, and most of the other houses in Leszno Street, were to leave the following day. We should move farther north if exempted from deportation, or report to the *Umschlagplatz* if not. Those who disobey – the poster said – will be shot dead. The numbers of the houses that were to be cleared were meticulously listed at the end.

After a sleepless night, my family decided to move, at least for the time being, to a cousin who lived very near in Leszno Street in a house which was not mentioned in the poster. We packed all we could carry with us and were just about to leave when Julian came to see whether we had survived the round-up. He almost cried with relief to find us alive and promised again to take care of Mother, Sophie and myself very soon. We left home reassured.

Uncle Leo, whose home we invaded that morning, was neither pleased nor indignant to see the six of us with our bundles and chattels on his doorstep. He just took our coming for granted. He was an unusual man. Like most of my uncles, he was a doctor. But unlike anybody else among our relatives, he had a political past. Before the war he had been involved in some leftist activities and was said to be a member of an international organisation that helped persecuted communists. Now he was over fifty, stout and balding but still full of charm. He lived in the ghetto in his own prewar flat, with his wife, her sister and two adult nieces. Since the *Aktion* had begun the household had tripled in size, including now two young male pianists, students of Leo's wife, the two nieces' boyfriends, my Aunt Maryla with her mother, and a young couple with a baby son. Now we had arrived too. We put our bundles on the floor in one of the four rooms and thus began a new kind of life.

Uncle Leo, the embodiment of energy, was frantically busy getting in touch with anybody who might be able to provide safekeeping for his family and friends. He feared his house would be surrounded and cleared very soon.

As a doctor working in the hospital he had a 'good' *Ausweis* himself. His wife was 'safe' for the same reason. But nobody else in the household had any such security. So Uncle Leo, glued to the receiver of his telephone, tried desperately to make arrangements with friends, acquaintances, influential patients, both in the ghetto and outside. In growing suspense his little crowd of dependants waited for news. As the day wore on, the luckiest of them gradually left, one by one.

We spent a second sleepless night lying on the floor. At sunrise the walls of the room came to life with the moving black dots of bedbugs thirsty for our blood. In the morning, in anticipation of a round-up, Leo ordered everybody to spend the day in the hiding place which had been carefully made ready long before. It was a tiny little room next to the kitchen. Before the war it had been the servant's bedroom. It had no window. The door leading from the kitchen was covered with tiles exactly like the kitchen walls and had no handle, so when locked from inside it was perfectly concealed, invisible from the kitchen side. It was equipped with two narrow benches to accommodate about ten people, jugs of water, piles of dry biscuits and two buckets. Little holes pierced in the outside wall gave us just enough light and air to see each other and not suffocate. We were thirteen in there, including the three-month-old baby, who was given a little alcohol and slept quietly for most of the time. We spent eight hours pressed tightly to each other, hardly breathing, hardly talking, in frowzy anguish and boredom. We strained our ears to make out what was going on outside. From time to time, we heard some sinister sounds from the street. In the late afternoon, Leo, who had not been hiding with us, came to our rescue. We learned from him that several houses in the vicinity had been surrounded and cleared during the day. Not ours, though. It was still to come. Meantime, he had succeeded in sorting out something for the next six people. An hour later, our hearts bleeding, we said goodbye to Stefan, Jadwiga and Henryk who had finally got jobs in the Schultz factory. They went in a hurry. Then a mysterious man in long boots and a leather jacket turned up to guide Maryla, her mother and Leo's sister-in-law to the 'Aryan' side. He did not look Jewish. They left quickly too. Leo and his wife were going to stay in the hospital, which seemed safer for them. So Mother, Sophie and myself were left in Leo's flat with just the young couple and the baby. The young father was making desperate telephone calls to his friends on the 'Aryan' side trying to find a hiding place for the three of them. Our future was still in Julian's hands.

We heard from him the following morning. He rang to say that he had finally found something for us and would take us to a safe place the next day. Meantime, we should leave Leszno Street at once and go to the northern part of the ghetto. He suggested Great-Aunt Bella's place in Nowolipie Street. He would collect us from there the following evening, and from then on we would not need to worry.

We now had a clear-cut objective: to survive a couple of days. It was too late, however, to leave Leo's flat that morning. We heard the German vehicles pulling up along Leszno Street earlier than usual. Together with the young family, we rushed to our hiding place and stayed there again till the late afternoon. We only dared come out when all sounds from the street had finally died away.

It was a torrid, drowsy afternoon, the world outside the windows seemed uncannily still. Hastily, we picked up some of our belongings and small supplies of tinned food, wished our hiding companions good luck, and left the flat. Just as we were about to go out through the front gate, we suddenly heard the familiar rumble of harsh voices and heavy vehicles braking nearby. There was no time to run back upstairs, there was no time to think. On an impulse, we turned round and rushed into the courtyard. The voices, the heavy footsteps were already approaching the gate . . . In seconds the hunters would spot us in the middle of the sunlit yard. Then at the end of the court I saw a ramshackle fence. Without thinking, I rushed to it, pulling Mother and Sophie with me. With all my strength I pushed at the loose planks and they gave way. In the nick of time we found ourselves on the other side of the fence, in a quiet green place strikingly familiar to me: we had landed in the grounds of the ruined hospital where I had worked a year earlier. In a flash of inspiration I ran towards the remaining foundations of the building. I remembered it well. Concealed in the rubble, there was a narrow entrance leading down to an undamaged underground passage. Plunging into its darkness we could distinctly hear the sounds of the round-up from the place we had just fled. Slowly, noiselessly, we moved along the pitch-dark passage until we reached its end; the other way out was cut off by rubble. We stopped and waited in the darkness, our hearts throbbing, our ears alert. Whistles, shouts and cries came to us muffled by layers of brick and debris. Time had slowed down, the whole world ceased to exist; there were just the raging hunters under the blazing sun and the three of us sunk in the darkness. Time drifted away.

All of a sudden we heard the sound of footsteps above our heads. Two men were there, talking loudly. We understood at once: they were searching the grounds. Petrified we clung to the rubble. I felt my heart flutter deep in my throat. The steps were coming closer, then down. The hunters had entered the underground passage, then stopped as though they were reluctant to go any further. 'Anybody there?' – the loud, harsh shout multiplied by echo was like a deadly shot. A sharp shaft of light edged watchfully along the damp corridor walls . . . coming nearer and nearer, but not reaching us . . . not yet . . . My heart stuck in my throat . . . death, death coming close . . . Then a harsh, dismissing '*Niemand!*' ('No one!') The light disappearing, the sound of footsteps dying away. Silence. Darkness. Fear.

Numb, glued to the corridor wall, we dared not leave the den for the long hours that followed. When finally we did, late night and curfew had already wrapped the world in shadows. There was nothing we could do at that hour but go back to Leo's flat. We found its front door ajar, the furniture turned upside down, the floor covered with broken glass from smashed dishes and feathers from ripped pillows. We rushed to the kitchen. There was nobody there. The door of yesterday's hiding place was wide open; there was nobody there, either. The baby's empty pram stuck under the kitchen sink . . . The baby's wet nappy on the table . . . The baby's dummy on the floor . . .

We made our way to Nowolipie Street early next morning. As we entered the house it struck me suddenly that Great-Aunt Bella might have been deported or shot dead long before. Surprisingly enough she was still there. She was pale and unusually slim, but lively and self-possessed. She welcomed us warmly with her usual cheerfulness. 'I'm still fighting Hitler, as you can see,' she said, kissing us in turn. 'It's not much fun these days, having to live on barley instead of caviar.'

The day dragged on endlessly. It was terribly hot and stuffy in her little room, deadly quiet all around. We kept straining our ears, reliving the events of the past day and night. I was trying to make out what day it was, what date. Great-Aunt Bella, who had been keeping a diary, helped me: it was Tuesday 18 August, which meant it was my birthday, probably the last. I was sixteen.

Julian came, as he had promised, to take us away just before curfew. He was sorry he could do nothing for Bella, but she cheered him up by saying she had been thriving on her own all that time and did not need anybody's help. We offered her our last three tins, and, filled with remorse, left the old woman to her fate.

Our new 'home' turned out to be just five minutes from Bella's place, farther north, at 18 Nowolipki Street. Julian told us that the ghetto had now been reduced to single blocks of houses, lodging only those Jews who were officially exempted from deportation: German factory work-ers, some of the Jewish Council employees, some hospital staff and the Jewish police. The exempted people received special registration cards stating that they were allowed to live in the ghetto. Wives of the exempted men were exempt too, but neither their children nor parents.

Sounding a little boastful, Julian said that he had used a high-placed acquaintance of his, as well as a large sum of money, to secure two registration cards for his two 'wives': one was Grannie Viera, the other my mother. Grandma was the 'wife' who would live with him on the hospital premises, Mother would have to be a policeman's wife and live without her 'husband' in the police block. There were, of course, no registration cards for Sophie and me. Nevertheless, we would stay with Mother: there was nothing else we could do.

This new place of ours and the days that followed I can just vaguely remember. There were four or five families of doctors serving in the Jewish police crammed into the same seedy flat, with their children, bedding, pans and suitcases; rude, quarrelsome and restless. Alas, without a man to take care of us, we were immediately put in the worst room which everyone else had to go through on their way to and from the loo. Not that it really mattered. After the horror of the past days and nights, we felt somewhat relieved. Some strange mechanism made us believe that we were safe there. For the time being at least. The same mechanism made us indifferent towards what was still going on outside the police block, towards the plight of the tens of thousands of human beings driven daily to the *Umschlagplatz*, then to the trains. Every day we heard hair-raising stories about the *Umschlagplatz* from eyewitnesses: from policemen who were doing the job, or from people who had been helped to escape in return for money or out of pity.

By then, I believe, news of the gas chambers awaiting the deportees in Treblinka, instead of labour camps, had already been brought back to the ghetto by the few who had managed to escape. But it was quite a time before we heard about it. We did not give much thought to what might have happened to our innumerable friends and relations. We had lost all contact with them since leaving Leszno Street. Even my love was gradually fading away, sinking into the past, becoming more of a dream than a real happening. Yet I kept straining my eyes to see Roman among the strangers huddling in the courtyards and passages between the houses of the police block.

Since the day we had said goodbye to Stefan, Jadwiga and Henryk, I had become the real head of the family. Without her brother, Mother felt insecure and helpless. Now it was I who had to take care of our day-to-day life, of settling down, finding food, even cooking. I also had to tell Mother and Sophie what to do and make all kinds of decisions for them. They gratefully accepted my leadership. Sophie, my brave little aide-de-camp, was always ready to help and cooperate. Silent and composed, she rarely asked questions, she understood.

All blocks still left in the shrunken ghetto were now surrounded with fences or barbed wire to prevent communication between them. The block occupied by the Schultz factory workers was very close to where we lived, but separated from the police flats by a high wooden fence. I do not remember how it happened, but we got in touch with Stefan and managed to make an appointment at an exact time and place on the two opposite sides of the fence. There was a gap between two planks in the fence, wide enough for us to see each other and talk. The early evening was mild and quiet. For once there was nobody around. They came all three of them and we kept changing places on our respective sides of the fence to let each of us see the others and exchange a few words. Stefan said he believed neither in their nor our safety: we should get in touch with Auntie Maria and beg her to find us a hiding place on the 'Aryan' side as soon as possible. Jadwiga told us they were working extremely hard, sewing underwear for German soldiers ten hours a day. From her I learnt that Hanka and her mother were alive and well, they were employed in the same factory. With sudden hope I asked about Roman. No, Jadwiga had not seen him. However, she said, there were thousands of people working in the factory and living in the block, it was impossible to see all of them.

Henryk was the last to talk to us. He begged us to kiss him through the fence. He pressed his cheek into the gap between the planks and we kissed it, one after another. Then we did the same and he kissed our cheeks by turns. I felt terribly upset, though I did not then know that we were parting from Henryk for ever.

In the early hours of Sunday 6 September we were suddenly awakened by our flatmates running madly up and down, collecting their belongings. A new announcement had been posted to the walls of the block at 4 a.m. that morning. The residents of the police block were ordered to clear out before 10 a.m. and move, for the time being, farther north, to Wołyńska Street. The flats were to be left open. Anybody found in the block after 10 a.m. would be shot dead.

We had less than four hours to get ready. There were rumours that we were moving to Wołyńska Street just for a new registration, but the sinister word 'selection' could also be heard. Whichever rumour was true, for me and Sophie they both meant the final threat. We were 'wild'* residents in the police block, with no registration cards, no right

*In ghetto slang, a 'wild' person was anyone living without German permission in the reduced ghetto area after the first deportation, a person without 'the number of life'.

to live. Should we go with Mother, or stay in the block? Or should we stay behind together and find a place to hide? But this would mean Mother would miss the chance of getting the new registration card so vital for us. She lost her head entirely and I had to decide what to do. All our neighbours were taking their 'wild' children with them. Nobody wanted to part with their family, and we least of all. I quickly made up my mind: Sophie and I would go with Mother. Whatever happened, we should be together.

Then there was the question of what to take with us. Poor as we now were, we still had some clothes, bedding and keepsakes that Julian had managed to fetch from Leo's the other day. We decided to take only a few of them. We already knew what an impediment the things would be if we had to hide or run away. Since it was obvious that the flat would be searched when we went, Mother insisted on burning her dearest keepsakes that she had always kept with her in a little suitcase. She could not make herself do it, though. I went to the kitchen, lit the fire in the oven and burnt the contents of the suitcase one by one. There were old photographs, some poems Mother had written when young, Father's love letters, a bunch of dried mimosa. I knew Father had given it to Mother when he had first declared his love. It caught fire instantly and vanished in a blaze of flame. I could not help crying.

It seemed sensible to take some food with us. But we had nothing but some raw potatoes which I had bought a day before from a Jewish worker employed outside the ghetto. I decided not to take them with us. It could not be long before we came back or died.

In the streets thousands of people with their babies, bundles and heavy bags were huddling along towards the north. Apparently all the blocks of the ghetto had to be cleared, and all the residents were ordered to gather in a narrow space that morning. People from factories and council blocks were now mixing with us. I heard somebody saying, 'The Jewish police, serves them right!' I caught some scathing glances and felt deeply upset. Yet my eyes were busy searching for Roman in the crowd.

Wołyńska Street, which I had never seen before, was one of the poorest, shabbiest, filthiest streets in the Warsaw ghetto. The former inhabitants of the dreadful houses must have been deported long before. All the doors of the flats stood ajar showing sickening pictures of devastation and filth. The newcomers were driven in by the Jewish policemen on duty, and settled down on the floor next to each other. We entered one of the sordid flats and sat on the floor, our backs propped, luckily, against the wall. People kept flooding in. Women moaned loudly, children cried. In a matter of seconds the room was tightly packed. From a policeman attending to his own family crammed next to us, we heard that our stay in Wołyńska Street might last several hours or several days. Nobody knew exactly what it was all about. Suddenly we realised that we were without food. It was nine o'clock, one hour to the deadline. Despite Mother's pleas, I decided to go back to Nowolipki and fetch the potatoes. One of the families with whom we had shared the flat at Nowolipki, Dr Koenig with his wife and two sons, were now sitting next to us. The elder son, Adam, a shrewd thirteen-year-old lad, volunteered to go with me, bringing his mother close to hysteria. We slipped out and began to make our way against the crowds still surging northward. As we got near the corner we saw Latvian and Ukrainian soldiers trooping along Nowolipki Street. We stepped back and instinctively hid in the gate of the nearest house. It was dead quiet there, all inhabitants gone. I wanted to run back to Wołyńska, but Adam seized my arm and pulled me up the stairs. The front doors of the flats were, as ordered, left unlocked. We burst into the first of them. Before I realised what we were doing in someone else's home, Adam was already poking about, searching for food. Soon he came across six tins of sardines in oil hidden on the top of a wardrobe. He slipped a couple of them into my pocket, kept the remaining four for himself, and off we went. We returned safely to Wołyńska just before 10 a.m. I had a mixed feeling of shame and pride.

We spent the day sitting on the floor, squeezed between other families hardly able to go out to the courtyard where the only wooden privy was besieged all the time by an impatient crowd. Nothing happened. We went on waiting. Julian was now with us. He told us that Grandmother had been moved to the 'Aryan' side a day earlier. She was now relatively safe in the care of her younger daughter-in-law Halina. Julian had kept her registration card for somebody else. His new 'wife', a good-looking young woman, was sitting next to him, nestling to him lovingly. But Julian did not seem to care, he looked distressed, remote. I realised he was a little drunk.

When night came we dared open one of the tins I had brought and ate the sardines with our fingers. Our neighbours were cooking barley on a primus stove they had providently brought with them. We had nothing to cook. Slowly, very slowly, the stuffy night echoing with human anguish gradually passed by.

In the morning we heard that the registration was to take place in the nearby square, at noon. There was word from those who had survived their registration the day before that thousands of people were being sent to the *Umschlagplatz* straight from the square. Not only those without the old registration cards, children and the elderly first of all, but also hundreds of workers employed in German factories. Seized with terror, hoping against all reason, people tried to use the few remaining hours to save their children. Julian, once awakened from his stupor, feverishly searched for a friend, a young policeman whose wife had been shot dead in the street a week before. He hoped the widower had kept his wife's registration card. He found him at last and asked whether he could take me as his wife to the registration. But the policeman had already promised to do that for another 'wild' woman. For me all this was pointless anyway: even if I could have, I wouldn't have gone with that man and left Sophie behind.

The *Aktion* began at just about eleven. The ear-splitting whistle and a loud German command summoned the crowds out to the streets. Terrified but resigned, people emerged from the houses, their old registration cards ready to be shown, their bundles forsaken. In a burst of desperation, Julian told Sophie and me to stay where we were, pushed Mother and the young woman to the door, and all three of them disappeared in the stampede.

Now we were left on our own, just Sophie and I, in the deserted flat, in the empty house, among the scattered chattels. Deadly silence had suddenly replaced the hue and cry of the last hours. We wandered drowsily from flat to flat in hope of finding some other human beings, some children perhaps, or old people left behind. But they had all gone. Or were hiding perhaps: I wondered where. Strangely enough, the simple truth that we could be found and shot dead on the spot any moment now did not occur to me. All my thoughts, feelings, imaginings were now in the square, with Mother.

'If Mama doesn't come back, I don't want to go on living any more,' Sophie said suddenly. This was exactly what I had been thinking. We were now back in the flat where we had spent the previous day and night. I went to the kitchen and examined the cooker. But it was just a simple oven heated with coal: gas was obviously too much of a luxury in this squalid part of town. My eyes caught a glimpse of a long rusty knife and I shivered in horror: no, never, not this way. On the kitchen table I saw a primus with an empty pan on top. Next to it was a huge bottle half filled with purple methylated spirit. The label 'Poison!' with a black skull drawn below seemed to be winking at me, 'That's what you need!' Sophie was next to me, staring at the bottle, her eyes wide open. She knew what I was thinking, she agreed without saying. I found two filthy mugs, washed them thoroughly under the tap, and put them on the table next to the bottle. Then we brought two ramshackle stools, sat at the table and waited in silence. It did not occur to me that if we drank the purple liquid, we might not only survive but also go blind. Some time passed and I was about to fall asleep, when I heard Sophie saying, 'I'm awfully hungry.' I suddenly realised that I was starving too. Our second and last tin contained four plump sardines. We each took one and sipped a little oil from the tin, leaving the rest for Mother in case she came back. There was still hope . . . Waiting, we fell asleep.

The uproar of the returning huddle made us spring to our feet. Mother was the first to burst into the flat. Crying and laughing at the same time, she went on repeating that never in her life would she part with us again. On her breast, hanging down on a piece of string, a large orange card displayed a black, four-digit number and a seal. The people still pouring back from the registration were all wearing the same cards. This meant they were permitted to return from Wołyńska Street to their former dwellings. Most of them were in a state of shock and distress, though. During the registration hundreds of people, even those with old registration cards, had been picked up and driven to the *Umschlagplatz*, children and the elderly as a rule. Jewish policemen and their families were no longer an exception. Many of our companions had lost their children or parents. We had survived again.

We now had to face a new danger: the return to the block. We soon received an order to leave Wołyńska and gather in the spacious yard in front of the Jewish Council. Julian was not with us now, Mother had lost sight of him just after registration. We set out with the others, Sophie and I glued to Mother's arms, the only ones without the life-saving numbers. Our breasts not covered with the orange rectangles, we felt almost naked. Being a child, not even tall enough to pretend otherwise, Sophie seemed in particular danger.

In the fiery light of the sunset, the Nazi officers and soldiers, armed with rifles and whips, rushed up and down the yard, shaping the unruly mob into an orderly column. Shouting, whistling, using their whips, they forced people to line up in close array, five persons to a line. Together with a couple of strangers, we were instantly pushed to form a line of five and join the column. The other fives followed quickly: the Nazi performance was efficient and fast. People looked scared, they only breathed loudly, not daring to utter a word.

'Look, there are two wild girls among us!' – a sharp, hysterical voice rang out suddenly behind me. I turned round, frightened. A well-dressed, intelligent-looking woman in her forties was staring at me with indignation from the line behind. 'They have no right!' she said to Mother. 'Innocent people may die instead of them!' 'But they are innocent, too . . . ' whispered Mother in agony. A loud German command ordered us to march, thus interrupting the argument. The column quivered and began to move on, watched intently from a distance by a Nazi team. We were just approaching them when the woman behind screamed: '*Herr Offizier! Herr Offizier!*' Stop . . . The man in the uniform barred our line with his rifle: I felt its butt pressed hard against my numberless breast. '*Wer schreit?*' ('Who shouted?') '*Herr Offizier!*' screamed the woman again. '*Ruhe!*' ('Quiet!') In a fit of rage the Nazi slashed her face with his whip. She howled with pain and lapsed into silence. '*Nachzuschicken!*' ('Forward!') the Nazi roared, taking his rifle back. '*Schnell, schnell!*' ('Quickly, quickly!') He did not even look round. We resumed our march, now almost running to join the ranks ahead.

When we finally reached Nowolipki, the Nazis vanished, the lines dispersed into small clusters of dismayed people huddling towards their dens. There was nobody in when we entered the flat. We were the first if not the only survivors. The signs of search and robbery we took for granted. All our clothes had disappeared, but the potatoes were left. Numb, unable to think or feel, I began to peel them automatically. Then a single question sprang up in my mind, throbbing, nagging, tormenting. Was the woman right? Might someone die instead of me?

A stranger turned up at the door, a strong, tall man with a bulging sack on his shoulders. He asked whether the Riders, a couple we had shared the flat with, had come back. They had not. Hearing that, the stranger pondered a while then took off his burden and put it on the floor. 'Open it at once, miss,' he said and left without a word of explanation. My hands shaking, I undid the sack. Curled up in peaceful sleep a little girl was hidden there, the two-year-old daughter of our flatmates. The parents had apparently believed that the man stood a better chance of saving her life than they did themselves. Perhaps they had paid him for it, or he had done it out of sheer compassion. Anyway he had succeeded, he had risked his life and brought the child back from the deadly courtyard.

The little girl had obviously been drugged. Mother took her on her lap, trying to wake her up. She kissed her pale little face, gently stroked her fair curly hair. I felt a wave of warmth surge into my frozen heart:

love for this helpless human crumb, love for Mother.

The child eventually woke from a drugged sleep and began to cry. With returning energy, I took her from Mother and started feeding her with warm water sweetened with the only bit of sugar I had managed to find. It helped. She stopped crying and began to sip greedily. She was nestling to me, soft and warm. I wanted her to be mine for ever. I wanted to care for her, to protect her from cold, from pain, from death.

Dr Rider and his wife returned safely later that night. They had just been kept longer in the courtyard. They claimed their little treasure back, shedding tears of relief. From Adam and his family we did not hear until the following day, when they all turned up alive but scared. During the registration Adam and his younger brother had been taken away from their parents and driven to the *Umschlagplatz*. In despair the parents decided to follow them to the deadly place, and when they got there used all their brains and money to rescue the boys and escape with them. The other families we had shared the flat with never returned.

Julian survived, and when he came to see whether we were alive he was obviously drunk. It was a rainy morning and we were shivering from the cold, all our warm clothing having been stolen. Saying little, Julian went out for a while, then came back loaded with coats, warm dresses and cardigans. He did not say where they had come from, and we did not ask. A yellow woollen dress which I put on immediately seemed vaguely familiar to me, as if I had already seen somebody wearing it before.

So our clothing problem was easily solved, but not that of food. Since the registration was still going on and all traffic between the ghetto and the 'Aryan' side had stopped, it was impossible to find anything to buy. For a couple of days we lived on potatoes but they were already running low. Then Adam, who had quickly recovered from the shock of his recent experiences and was the same brazen, shrewd lad again, talked me into a daring expedition. He said he knew where we could find food, and I went with him without hesitation. Making our way up and down through a tangle of lofts and staircases, we found ourselves in a ghost house once more. The unlocked flats were all deserted but they had evidently not been robbed yet. It looked as though the tenants had left in a hurry several days before. In the first flat we entered, bowls of half-drunk soup and broken slices of bread were still lying on the kitchen table. Both soup and bread were covered with greenish mould. Next door a bridge party must have been abruptly interrupted: four hands of playing cards and the unfinished score scribbled on a pad were left on the table. An open bottle of wine and four empty glasses completed the story. Trembling with excitement and hunger, I reached for the bottle and drank straight from it. There were some strange soft bits in the wine. I poured the rest into a glass to see what it was. They were dead flies.

We went on prying and in one of the flats came across a pile of books. They were good books: Freud, Mann, Zweig. I picked some up and took them with me. Next day I went there again and took some more. I quickly got used to poking about in dead people's homes and even learned to find pleasure in it. I knew that corruption had found its way into my soul and did not care a damn.

'Registration' lasted from 6–12 September. 54,000 people were deported and more than 2,600 died, shot dead or by committing suicide.[*]

The Encyclopaedia Judaica, Vol. 16 writes:

Following the deportations, the ghetto area was drastically constricted again and some factories and several blocks of buildings were left outside the new walls and cordoned off with barbed wire to prevent anyone finding shelter there. The Germans also fixed the number of inhabitants allowed to remain in the ghetto at a maximum of 35,000 persons . . . The leaders of the underground movement appraised the new situation. At their first meeting they decided to create the Jewish Fighting Organisation and take active steps to oppose further deportations. A few members of the underground managed to escape from Treblinka, and brought to the ghetto information about the real fate that awaited the deportees, namely physical annihilation . . .

Some 30,000–35,000 Jews, most of them factory workers and their families, remained legally in the ghetto and were employed within or outside . . . In addition there were between 20,000 and 30,000 Jews living on in the ghetto 'illegally' . . .

In this period, intensive preparations were made for armed resistance . . .

At the end of September the police block was moved from Nowolipki to Zamenhoff Street. From the window of my new dwelling I could see the memorable courtyard of the Jewish Council, with the heavily

[*]Archiwum Ringelbluma: Ghetto Warszawskie, lipiec 1942 – styczeń 1943, P. W. N. Warszawa 1980, pp. 294–5.

guarded gate of the shrunken ghetto to its left. The Riders and Koenigs moved in with us, and another family consisting of a middle-aged couple, their adult son and their young servant girl, also joined us in the four-room flat. This time Mother herself decided that we should take the smallest room – part of the passage – in order to avoid any argument with our flatmates. I found an old blanket and hung it up in the passage to cut us off from domestic traffic and provide some privacy.

The *Aktion* stopped for a time and life gradually took over again from death. From my window I watched the processions of Jews employed outside the ghetto crossing the gate on their way to work in the early morning and back again at dusk. However strict the checkup, they usually managed to smuggle some food through the gates. Later at night they sold it in the back yards. Life was in full swing only in those inner yards and passages now: walking in the few streets that still remained within the walls was far too dangerous.

Little by little, we recovered from the stupor that had come in the wake of the terror of the 'registration' days, and as our feelings returned we counted our losses. The first one was Henryk. He was driven away from the factory ranks on the day of registration. He never came back. Stefan and Jadwiga were with him when it happened. Helpless, they watched people being 'selected' for deportation and dragged away to the *Umschlagplatz*. There was nothing they could do. They survived the registration but left the factory soon after and settled in a deserted attic in the police block, staying there as 'wilds'. They thought it was better to go into hiding than stay exposed and defenceless in the factory.

There was no way of finding out whether Great-Aunt Bella was still alive. Nowolipie Street had been off limits for a long time now. The area cleared in August was cordoned off and stood uninhabited. A special Nazi unit called *SS Werterfassungstelle* (SS Centre for Collecting Valuables) was put in charge of collecting the possessions abandoned by the deported and sending them to the Reich. Jews were employed to do the hardest and filthiest of jobs. One day in October a stranger came to see Mother. While helping the Nazis to clear a house in Nowolipie Street, he had found an old woman lying on the floor. She was dying from starvation, yet conscious. There was just one SS man around. The stranger asked him to save the old woman's life. As it happened, the German was in a good mood and allowed his helper to take care of the 'old hag'. The man brought Bella to the ghetto and put her in the hospital. She asked him to find Mother and tell her to come to her deathbed. She did not know where Mother was, but the stranger went to all the trouble of finding our new address through the Jewish Council. And here he was.

Mother rushed to the hospital immediately. She refused to take me with her. She returned deeply shaken. What she had seen in the hospital was a human shred, bones coated with yellow skin, the face that once was beautiful now sunk and covered with some kind of growth, the eyes already dulled by a deadly mist, but still conscious. Her voice fading away, Bella strained desperately to tell Mother her story. She had stayed in her flat all that time. By a strange coincidence nobody had come to kill her. She had gradually eaten up her meagre supply of rice and barley, and then had gone out to look for food. But the streets were already deserted. Later she became too weak to walk. She tried to cook her own clothes cut into pieces but could not make herself eat them. So she lived on water from the tap. For how long? Four, five weeks perhaps, she could not tell. 'That's how charming Bella loses her fight with Mr Hitler,' were the last words Mother heard from her. She died three days later. Mother did all she could to secure a proper burial for her: she was buried in an individual grave, and a wooden board with her name scribbled on it was set into the earth.

Winter was quickly approaching. Short days and long nights dragged on, bringing cold, misery and anguish. Nobody believed the danger was really over. We expected the *Aktion* to start again any time, and were now fully aware that deportation meant death in the gas chambers. Somewhere in the vast world the war was reaching its peak. The battle of Stalingrad, that had been going on since the summer, made a Nazi victory ever more unlikely. Yet for us, in our town, in our street, the Germans were still the same unassailable masters.

In the evenings neighbours gathered again to talk over recent events. Stefan and Jadwiga came down from their attic. Together we racked our brains over possible ways of escape.

My days were now filled with reading and searching for food. Thanks to the Jewish Council, the legitimate residents of the block, those with life-saving numbers, were now entitled to daily rations of free soup. With Mother's number and a bowl, I queued for this soup in the back yard day after day. Enriched with barley, potatoes or whatever else we could find or buy, this was our main if not sole daily meal. Late at night I often set out for bread. There was a secret bakery in a back alley. The ingenious baker, supplied with flour by smugglers, worked only at night, baking bread and selling it still hot before dawn.

My way to the baker's led through a labyrinth of cellars and underground corridors. Adam always went with me. I would not have dared go alone. Even with him at my side, I felt my flesh creep as we descended into the dense shadows of this underground world. Moving very slowly, often on our hands and knees, we often came across strange objects blocking our way. Once I bumped into something soft and wet that might have been just a pile of rotten straw. Once I stepped on a dead cat. Sometimes we had to climb over a barricade of old cases or furniture barring the way. A weird rustle nearby would make me shiver. There were rats scurrying in the darkness, or someone else was making the search for bread. The return was usually less frightening. The warm fragrance of the bread made me feel safer. I could hardly help nipping its lovely crust.

Our bread expeditions improved slightly when Adam managed to steal a torch from a neighbour. Once in its faint light I saw a leaflet posted on the cellar wall: 'Brothers,' it said, 'don't die in silence. Resist the Nazi terror. Let's fight.' It was signed, 'ŻZW'.* The appeal sank deep into my mind.

On 29 October we heard shots from around the corner and soon learned that the head of the Jewish police, Jakob Lejkin, had been shot dead in Gęsia Street. People whispered that it was an act of retaliation by an underground Jewish organisation. Someone said that a teenage girl was among those who had planned it. All this made me restless.

In those dark days of temporary stability I had no close friend, nobody of my age to talk to. After a long break I started keeping my diary again.

2 November 1942

They say 'Fight'. Yes, of course, it's the only way, though there won't be much chance of survival if we do. But what else can we do? There is something called 'dignity', much forgotten these days. Yes, I'm ready to join at once, but who? Who are they, where can I find them? I've been trying to find out the people behind those three letters. The people I see are Dr K. and Dr R., decent chaps worried to death about how to save their wives and kids. Then young F., in the room opposite, fooling around half naked all day long. All he's interested in is their servant's skinny bum which he keeps pinching to make her squeal. He must be mad.

Then my two uncles, Stefan first of all. I talked to him, of

*ŻZW: Żydowski Związek Wojskowy (Jewish Military Union) was a little later incorporated into ŻOB (Jewish Fighting Organisation), responsible for the uprising in the Warsaw ghetto.

course. About the leaflet and so on. He said that in our circumstances the very idea of taking on the German army who had conquered the whole of Europe could only have been conceived in a sick mind. The only way to resist the Nazis, he says, is to prevent them from killing us. That's why he's trying hard to get us all out of here to a good hiding place on the 'Aryan' side.

Last but not least – Julian. I wanted to talk to him as well, but I've given up. He was drunk again when he came yesterday. He's in charge of an ambulance now and very busy, he said. I hated the way he looked at me when he said I'd grown up lately. He asked me to take care of a bottle of pure spirits for him, because, he said, one can hardly trust one's neighbour these days. I locked the bottle in that huge empty cupboard which stupidly blocks half our room, thinking vaguely about Adam and his skills.

It's hard to admit this even to myself, but I have come to loathe Julian. It's really awful, I know: he's my beloved father's brother, looking so much like him; he has saved our lives; he's still helping us now. Perhaps I hate him just for that reason, just because we depend on him so much.

If only Father were here . . . We would be so much safer with him and so much better off. He would certainly know exactly what to do and how to cope with the worst. I know Mother thinks the same. I know she's longing terribly for him and often cries. Last night I heard her whisper to herself, 'Why have you forsaken me?' She must have done it in her sleep.

In fact, I'm happy Father isn't here. He certainly wouldn't put up with the part of a Jewish policeman. And if he did, I couldn't possibly bear it. Besides, I'm sure he's much safer wherever he is. In our circumstances the fewer loved ones we have around us the better. Love is a terrible thing these days. I think I'm really lucky not to have a husband or a child. Not to have a child most of all . . .

Lack of friends, the impossibility of carrying on my studies, the bitter awareness of being idle when there was an underground fight going on, all this began to upset me.

12 November 1942

Sophie has just come in from the back yard, singing. She has made friends lately and spends most of the day with them. Good for her. They have taught her a Hebrew song which she now sings constantly in her clear voice. I've just been reading *The Magic Mountain* by Thomas Mann, it needs a lot of concentration. I snarled at her to shut up and ridiculed her for singing something she can't possibly understand. Sophie felt insulted and said she knew quite well what the song was about because her friends had translated it to her word for word. It was all about young Jewish boys and girls who don't want to live in humiliation and leave their native countries to build a new homeland in the deserts of Palestine.

Now I can't read any more. I keep thinking about people who know what they're doing with their lives: people who decide to fight an overwhelming military power; people who set their hearts on building a better life somewhere far away; or those who do the same in their own countries by fighting social inequality. I'm none of these. I belong nowhere. Have I lived for anything? Is there any reason why I should keep running for my life?

One day, on my own in a sombre mood, I remembered the bottle of spirits which Julian had entrusted to me. I had never tried strong alcohol before, but had often heard it helped overcome gloom. I crept into the cupboard and closed its door behind me, so as not to be caught red-handed by anybody coming in. Once inside, I uncorked the bottle and took a sip of the pure spirits. It was like swallowing fire, it burned through every fibre of my body. I began to toss wildly in my confinement, gasping for breath and thrashing about against the plywood wall at the back. Suddenly it gave way and I found myself in a dark closet. It didn't take me long to realise what it was: a hiding place for ten, perhaps fifteen people if they clung tight to each other, was perfectly concealed behind that huge oak cupboard which robbed us of space in our little room but was too heavy to be moved. Unlike Uncle Leo's hiding place, this one was empty, yet I had little doubt that somebody had thought hard about making it safe. Where were these people now? What had happened to them? Had they been caught before they had managed to reach it, or were they discovered in it and dragged out? Anyway, we had inherited this place now and could feel a little safer if something happened again. Dizzy from the spirits, I crept out of the cupboard and hurried to tell the good news to the others.

The *Werterfassung* now needed more people to help in the deserted houses, and the unemployed wives of the factory workers, policemen or council clerks were summoned to compulsory work from time to time. In the middle of November Mother received a written order to go to the Jewish Council courtyard at 7 a.m. the following day. She was in bed with flu. Not reporting at the due time and place could have been disastrous – she could have lost her life-saving number. I realised I could easily go in her place: they checked numbers not faces, human beings weren't important, it was the orange rectangle that counted. So, on the following morning, with Mother's number hanging round my neck, I reported at the square. It was bitterly cold and the women gathered there crouched frozen and restless. There were young girls as well as women over fifty, not all of them 'wives', I was sure. I spotted one of them who seemed vaguely familiar to me. It took me a while to realise that I used to see her in the street before the *Aktion*. She used to walk up and down Leszno Street at dusk wearing gaudy make-up. She was a prostitute. I had always wondered who could be attracted to that woman, plain, vulgar and not even young. Now without her make-up she did not look vulgar at all, but haggard and squalid. My heart contracted with compassion.

We were ordered to form ranks and march. Escorted by two Jewish policemen and a single German guard, we crossed the ghetto gate and walked into the deserted area outside. Soon we stopped in front of a row of big, wealthy houses. Now, in couples, we were sent to the flats to scrub floors and clean windows. I found myself in a huge, six-room flat together with the prostitute. She was kind and friendly. We split the job fairly between the two of us, she took three rooms at the back, I three in the front.

The flat had already been cleared of its contents and stood empty, ready for new lodgers to move in. In one of the front rooms, however, I came across a vast quantity of china and cut glass, apparently brought in from other flats and ready to be taken away to Germany.

Scrubbing floors and cleaning windows was not my favourite task. I was slow and awkward at the job and didn't like it at all. Besides, I thought with disgust about those for whom I was slaving: Germans perhaps or that mean sort of Pole who would have liked to take over the flats of murdered Jews. So I didn't even try to work properly or fast. Left on my own I sank deep into my thoughts, a rare chance I really appreciated. From time to time one of the policemen would look in to glance casually around, not even pretending he cared a damn about what I was doing.

In the room where the china was kept I decided to have a break. I sat down on the floor to take a close look at the collection. There were exquisite dinner and coffee sets made of the finest china and lavishly hand-decorated; sets of fragile crystal glasses; priceless vases and figurines, some very old, some of rare beauty. I had always been fond of beautiful things and found pleasure in handling them. Now I could indulge myself in picking up these precious objects and stroking them gently. At the same time I thought of those who had once owned and enjoyed these cups and vases and who were now dead. Soon new owners, Nazi officers and their families most likely, would spread their own tables with these valuable objects, devour food stolen from all Europe from these fragile plates, quaff superb French wine from these shapely glasses . . . Feeling almost physical pain, I began to destroy, as quietly as I could, the most precious cups, plates and figurines by knocking them hard one against another. It was my first act of resistance. And my last.

Mother soon recovered from her flu, but when the next order came from the Jewish Council, I again went to work instead of her. And so it went on. I didn't want her to do these filthy jobs, to be humiliated by the stupid remarks of rude policemen, to be searched and jabbed by German guards on returning to the ghetto. I hated it myself, but being so much younger, could more easily put up with the ordeal. So I reported to work each time a new summons for Mother arrived.

I was usually sent to clean empty flats. Most of them were filthy, bearing signs of miserable lives and a sudden end to their former inhabitants. I plunged into the unspeakable dirt of beggars' rags and bedding, deep into their wretched existence so abruptly stopped on a bright day that last summer.

My fellow workers were not only women. Once I was assigned to a block of apartments together with a young man. We soon recognised each other: Natan had been a friend of Roman's, they had studied together and he remembered me well from the party which had taken place just before the *Aktion*. Excited by the lucky coincidence, we forgot all about our drudgery, settled down on a pile of mouldy feathers which we were supposed to take out of the flat and burn in the backyard, and began to talk in earnest. Trying not to show how much I cared about his answer, I asked Natan about Roman. No, Natan had not seen or heard from him since July. We quickly changed the subject. There was such a lot we had in common. Natan, like myself, lived 'wild' in the police block. He had lost his parents and two little sisters during the *Aktion*. Like myself, he reported for compulsory work in someone else's place, but he did it in return for food. He longed to join the underground movement too, but belonging nowhere he had no idea how to do so, just like myself. And, of course, he longed to start studying again. Sitting on that pile of dirt we struck up a true friendship. The dull December day became a little less bleak; the appalling place, the sickening task we were doing ceased to upset us for a while. It was great to have a friend, to share thoughts and feelings. When the working day came to a close, we parted, determined to join forces and try to do something useful with our lives.

A few days later another friend turned up. I was just queuing for the soup ration when someone gently touched my shoulder. A young, unusually handsome policeman was grinning at me from under his navy-blue cap. I could hardly believe my eyes: I had known this boy in the distant past, he had belonged to the same little group of children learning at home long before the war. Yes, I remembered little Danny, the laughing stock of other children. Bright, but terribly spoiled by his wealthy parents, always dressed in little dark-velvet suits that set off his fair girlish curls, he would burst into tears for the slightest reason. Once he peed in his trousers during the lesson and choked with sobs while the others split their sides with laughter. How on earth had he come to wear this cap and truncheon?

I heard his story the same evening when he called in for a long talk. Like Natan, he had lost both his parents in the early days of the *Aktion*. They had been taken away from their home during a round-up. Daniel was not at home at the time, he had been to see a friend that day and so had survived. To start with he had felt entirely lost, but his friend's father, who was an influential member of the Jewish Council, had taken care of him and helped to get him into the Jewish police. Slightly younger than myself, but tall and strong, Daniel was not even sixteen when he had received the emblems of authority and was ordered to take part in the *Aktion* alongside the German and Latvian troops. 'It was a lousy job,' he said staring blankly away. 'But after a time I learned how to cope. You can cope with the worst things if you've got brains and guts,' he added vaguely with the shade of a boastful grin.

I listened incredulously, perplexed. This last remark, obscure as it was, brought a little hope to my frozen heart. There *were* some noble policemen, after all, who had risked their own lives helping victims to escape. I knew Julian did all he could, even for strangers. Daniel, too, might have been one of the few. I smiled back, asking no questions, and when Daniel suggested we should meet again soon, I had no objections.

He showed up a few days later to take me out. It sounded preposterous: those days 'out' meant back yards and cellars for me. Mysterious and solemn, Daniel declared that he wanted me to have great fun that evening, to enjoy something I had been deprived of. Before we left he handed me a little gift, with the same solemn expression. It was a locket of rare beauty. Made of silver, engraved at the back, set with turquoises and rubies in the front, it was an old, very precious piece of craftsmanship. Enchanted and puzzled, I was uncertain as to whether to accept it or not. I presumed it had once belonged to Daniel's mother and did not feel I was the right person to inherit it from her. Daniel laughed and said that the locket had certainly belonged to a mother, somebody's mother, but not his mother. He explained that he had simply found it in a deserted house during the *Aktion* and had taken it away to give as a gift to the first pretty girl he came across. I was the right person to own it, he said. I felt an irresistible desire to accept the gift. I realised that the precious locket would soon have embellished a Nazi wife's neck, had not Daniel found it and dared to put it in his pocket. So, my remorse fading away, I hung the locket round my own neck. However, I felt uneasy as we made our way through the back alleys to the mysterious place of fun.

It proved to be a small basement, its entrance concealed behind a large heap of lumber. No sound could be heard from outside, but as soon as we entered a loud hubbub of people enjoying themselves struck our ears. Lit with a few candles, the basement was full of men, most of them wearing navy-blue caps. There were just a few women. They were all busy eating and drinking at a long rough table. Another table serving as a bar displayed drinks and food on sale at fantastic prices, bottles of vodka, joints of meat, hard-boiled eggs, loaves of fresh bread. Half the table was covered with large baking trays containing lovely-looking cake.

The strong aroma of food struck my nose and I felt dizzy. Stunned, I almost fainted. Since the summer I had been starving. Not badly enough to die, but enough to feel ravenous and weak at any time of day or night. Daniel gripped my shoulder, preventing me from collapsing. I quickly came round. He was now talking to a stout, scruffy woman in charge of the bar. He handed her a little pile of banknotes. In return we received two gorgeous plump wedges of warm apple cake wrapped in newspaper. Daniel gaped at me as I greedily bit off the first piece. He seemed to be pleased with himself. He offered to buy me a glass of vodka but I flatly refused it. Slightly disappointed, he ordered one for himself. Filled with warm bliss, I watched him fiddling with his glass. He took off his cap and now, with his blond curly hair shining in the candlelight, he looked like a child, like the spoiled little boy I still remembered. His innocent face twisted slightly with disgust. I was sure he hated the very smell of vodka. He drank it down in a single mighty gulp just to show off, to impress me with his manliness.

I finished my cake and looked around bewildered. The raucous joking of coarse men indulging in food and drink, the shrill laughter of their drunken women made me feel sick. No, we did not belong here, neither I nor Daniel. I longed for fresh air, I wanted to leave this repulsive place of self-indulgence immediately. On our way back I was silent. I wondered whether I wanted to meet Daniel again. Still a child, but with power already in his hands and without much strength to resist temptation, he was obviously sliding into evil. He had no parents, no brother or sister to help him. It suddenly came to me that it was my duty to hold out a helping hand. How, I did not yet know, I had to think it over. When we parted, I asked Daniel not to call on me until I got in touch with him myself. He agreed and said that he would be on duty at the ghetto gate every evening the following week. I would certainly see him from my window, he said, and he would be delighted if I would come down and talk to him for a while.

A couple of days later I heard good news from Natan. He had met a teacher who offered to coach us – just in maths and physics to start with, but he promised to do humanities as well if some more students would join us. I thought of Daniel at once. He was the right one, bright and gifted. It would be great to study with him. Besides, it would take his mind off his wretched job.

I could hardly wait to see him at the gate that evening. I kept peeping out of my window. At last I spotted his slim outline next to the stout figure of a German guard. They were busy checking a long line of labourers returning to the ghetto from work on the 'Aryan' side. I hurried down from my third floor and was walking fast towards the gate when a terrifying spectacle made me stop dead in my tracks. I saw Daniel struggling with a thin, elderly worker. He pulled off the man's shabby coat, found a bulky bag fastened to its lining, tore it out briskly, and tipped its contents onto the cobblestones. Frightened out of his wits, the man tottered about trying to explain something, or begging for mercy. The German guard, busy with other workers, his back turned, took no notice. Leaning over the scattered goods, Daniel rummaged in the bags and parcels of groceries. He did not see me. Almost crying, the poor man pulled a bank note out of his pocket.

Shocked, seized with abomination, I jerked back to run away and disappear unnoticed. I would feel even more ashamed if Daniel knew that I had witnessed this act of disgrace. But it was too late. He straightened his back to take the bank note and suddenly our eyes met. He shuddered and for a split second there was terror and shame in his eyes. Then, abruptly, his face contracted with a ghastly smile. He gripped his truncheon, and with all his strength began beating the frail old man about the head, about the face. Next he knocked him down to the cobblestones and kicked his helpless body with his heavy boots. I ran away and have never seen nor heard from Daniel since. I kept the locket, though, and have it still.

December slipped by. I went to evening classes with another girl and Natan, my friend. The teacher was a middle-aged man, worn and scared. He lived 'wild' in a dark little room nearby which he shared with strangers – a family of three. We sat in this room trying to concentrate on logarithms, while the family of three gaped at us vacantly. Despite our initial zeal, it was no good. We were all starving, we expected the *Aktion* to start again any time. Hair-raising rumours of the imminent end of the Warsaw ghetto grew louder from day to day.

My family was determined to leave the ghetto and go into hiding on the 'Aryan' side. Since October Auntie Maria, with the help of some friends, had been making desperate efforts to find shelter for us. She would have done anything to save our lives, have gladly died if this would have helped, yet she was unable to take us in under her roof: she did not have a roof of her own. Living in my grandparents' home till the war broke out, she now lived with her sister and brother-in-law in a single room.

After a long break we were in touch with Auntie Maria again. On appointed dates she would visit her other sister, who was a midwife and had her own telephone. There Auntie Maria waited until she heard from us. It was not easy to find a telephone in the ghetto. Usually Mother made her calls from the ambulance duty room when Julian was in charge.

In the second week of January we heard good news. There was a family ready to take Mother, Sophie and me. Someone else, a single woman, agreed to take Stefan and Jadwiga under her roof. Our future hosts also undertook to provide us with forged identity cards stating our 'Aryan' origins. For this they needed a large sum of money and special photographs disguising our Jewish features.

So we could not leave the ghetto yet. Auntie Maria first had to sell some more paintings and silver to raise the necessary money, while we had to get the photographs. This wasn't a problem: there was a clever photographer in our block who made his living by faking people's likenesses. A few days later I was musing over a picture showing a girl with a short nose and straight hair.

17 January 1943
Here I am, a Christian virgin looking hopefully forwards to the future. To a safer future perhaps. No point in kidding myself: I don't look like that. This photo could safely be shown to even my worst enemies – but not my real face. I'm going to be shut in behind someone's closed door, not able to go out, not able to see anyone but the strangers who are risking their lives by having us with them. And while I'm living there, safe and bored, my friends and neighbours behind these walls will gradually die. And perhaps fight before they die. I know I should stay and share their plight. It's strange but Julian seems to feel the same. He came this morning to talk over the details of our escape. He's got it all planned. We shall leave the ghetto with the night-shift factory men. We'll never come back. Julian said he'll never escape to the 'Aryan' side himself, his place is here with the other Jews. He sounded sad and bitter, he wasn't drunk. I think he may be involved in the underground fight, after all. Somehow I was too shy to ask.

After he left I went to the dentist. It was my last appointment. Let's hope I won't need a dentist before the end of the war, otherwise I may lose all my teeth and die from pain, being unable to go out. My present dentist has got on my nerves ever since I first went to see him. I can't bear his wife and mother-in-law staring into my open mouth all the time, though I can forgive them this, they've got no other entertainment these days. I don't blame him either for the terrible pain he has always caused me – not having proper tools and anaesthetics is not his fault, after all. What I really mind and can't put up with is his talking to me while he fumbles with my aching tooth. He keeps snivelling about malnutrition, insecurity and so on, asking stupid, rhetorical questions, such as, 'Can we survive? Will we survive?' And each time he's finished with me and I'm able to speak again, he shoots his last and most important question, 'What does your uncle say?' Then he waits in suspense for my answer. He's done it every time I've been there. What on earth can I tell him? Does he think Julian is all-mighty God? A Jewish policeman is only a Jewish policeman, he doesn't know more than any other Jew these days, I reckon. So, when this morning the bloody dentist asked me his stupid question again, and stared at me with hope and anxiety, I felt an irresistible urge to say something nasty. 'Uncle Julian says,' I announced gravely, 'that the new *Aktion* is going to begin tomorrow.' It was a cruel, shameful joke. Now I'm terribly sorry I said that.

The second wave of deportations began on 18 January 1943 when the Nazis broke into the ghetto, surrounded many buildings, and deported the inhabitants to Treblinka. They liquidated the hospital, shot the patients, and deported the personnel. Many factory workers who had been employed outside the ghetto were included among the deportees. The underground organisations, insufficiently equipped and ill-prepared, nevertheless offered armed resistance, which turned into four days of street fighting . . .

   As a result, the second wave of deportations was suspended after four days, during which the Germans managed to send only 6,000 persons to Treblinka. About 1,000 others were murdered in the ghetto itself.

Encyclopaedia Judaica, Vol. 16

We spent four days hidden behind the oak cupboard, fifteen people altogether, crammed tight in the bare, pitch-dark closet. There were three young children with us who could have cried out and betrayed our hiding place at any time; as it happened they did not. On the first morning our flat was invaded and searched. We could hear heavy steps and harsh voices coming from our own room. Somebody peeped into the cupboard and said in German it was empty. Then the hunters left. We had survived again.

Some time later we heard gun shots and hand grenades. At dusk, when the first day of the resumed *Aktion* came to an end and we emerged from the hiding place, we learned that a handful of armed Jews had attacked the German troops that morning. One Nazi and a couple of Jewish fighters had been killed in our street. The German was already taken away, but when I ventured out the dead bodies of a girl and a boy were still lying on the pavement just outside our gate. I felt a strange urge to see their faces. I could see in the faint light of the early sunset how young they both were. The girl's dark hair was spread over the snow which was stained with her blood. I knew her. I knew a lot about her. Her name was Halinka; like myself she was a doctor's daughter, a year my junior. In the ghetto, she had attended a younger group of the 'Bond' students. My friends, even myself, used to gossip a lot about her with confused feelings of outrage and envy: at less than fifteen she had already had a lover. This lover, a dark handsome boy of eighteen, now lay dead in the snow next to her. My heart contracted with pain. In helpless agony I cried for them and hated myself, a righteous virgin hiding like a coward while others fought and died.

Late at night a neighbour who during the day had been caught and dragged to the *Umschlagplatz*, returned safely home. He told us he owed his escape to Julian. Driving the ambulance up and down the deadly place, my uncle had picked up odd men and women from the crowd whenever he had a chance, had packed them into the vehicle and driven them back to the blocks. He was a true hero, the man said. Hearing that, I made a quick decision. I was sure I had been misjudging Julian; obviously he was the right person to turn to for guidance. I wanted to see him and talk to him immediately. But first I had to find Natan: we had promised each other long before to be together if ever there was a chance to join the fight.

In the middle of the night I left home and ran hurriedly to Natan's place. The flat he shared with strangers stood open, deserted. The usual signs of violence and plundering told me my friend's tragic story. I knew I would never see Natan again, never hear he loved me, never grow to return his feelings. In blind despair, oblivious of the danger lurking in the dark, I plunged into the underground labyrinth, making my way to the hospital.

The building stood unusually still and dark, but in the ground-floor extension, which housed the ambulance office, I saw a faint light coming through the cracks of the blackened window. I prayed Julian would be there. Noiselessly I entered the tiny hall. There was nobody around but I could hear Julian's voice from behind the plywood partition. I stopped dead, not wanting to talk to Julian with someone else there. I waited. Without meaning to eavesdrop, I listened to my uncle's conversation with another man, who, I knew, was his assistant nurse and driver. My mind totally set on what I was about to say to Julian, I took no notice of what they were talking about. Suddenly I realised they were counting money. Taken aback, I could hardly believe my ears, yet it was true: they were counting money, lots and lots of it. Bewildered, then terrified, I understood. Or perhaps I only thought I did. Holding my breath, softly, noiselessly, I retreated and ran back to my block.

The three days of hiding that followed I remember only vaguely as a nightmare of agony and despair. The muffled sounds of odd shots and explosions coming from the streets meant fighting was still going on. At the same time the *Aktion* was well under way. In the evenings, out from our hole, we would hear horrifying stories of the days that had just passed. The ghetto hospital had ceased to exist, its patients murdered on the spot, doctors and nurses taken away straight from work or from home.

By chance, I heard my dentist's story from someone who, hidden in the same flat, had watched the incident. He was dragged away from his little room together with his wife and mother-in-law. He did not even look surprised when the Nazi troop, assisted by a Jewish policeman, entered his room. Ordered to get out, he calmly helped the two women to put their coats on, took his own coat from the rack and reached for his galoshes as it was snowing heavily outdoors. While he fumbled to put on these galoshes, the Nazi kicked him painfully and burst out laughing. 'Leave it, you fool,' he roared, 'you won't need your galoshes any more.'

Driving round the *Umschlagplatz* with his ambulance, Julian survived the *Aktion*. When on the fifth day the Nazis withdrew from the ghetto, the street fighting came to a standstill and the survivors emerged from their holes, he did all he could to arrange an escape for us. I could not look at him when he came to tell us what to do. It was the last time I ever saw Julian. He stayed in the ghetto till its end, and died in its ruins the following spring. I shall never know whether he fought in the ranks of the Jewish Fighting Organisation. Nor shall I know why he needed the money which some of the victims evidently paid him for his help. Was it just greed, or did he take it on the orders of his organisation who desperately needed money for buying arms and ammunition? I do not know, so I do not judge Julian. May he rest in peace.

Mother, Sophie and I left the Warsaw ghetto on 25 January 1943. At dusk we put on all the clothes we had and filled the pockets with our small belongings, in my case my diary and Roman's photograph.

Carrying bundles was out of the question, since we had to pretend we were going to work. We joined the crowd of workers gathered in the Jewish Council yard and reported to the man in charge, who had promised Julian to get us out of the ghetto. He told us to line up at the front of the column, and soon we were heading the shabby procession towards the gate in the wall. We crossed it quickly, followed by the workers. We were now outside the walls. In dead silence the column proceeded through the deserted area which separated the ghetto from the 'Aryan' side.

All of a sudden I realised we were already there, on the other side. The streets of the old town, clothed in the shades of a wintry wartime evening, yet touchingly familiar to me, looked unnaturally quiet. The few passers-by trotted hastily, close to the buildings, not looking around, just giving quick, furtive glances at the ranks of the blue-starred destitutes that marched drearily along the cobblestones, off the outlawed pavement.

To this very day there is a stout, round billboard post jutting out from the corner of Koźla and Senatorska Streets in Warsaw. We were just approaching it when our guide, who led the column, turned round and whispered an order to slip down our armbands and clasp the billboard post. Then, sheltered by the passing column, one by one we circled the post and hurried down Senatorska Street, quick, quick into the open gate of number 10. In its welcoming shade, a little crouching figure clasped me lovingly in her arms: 'Praised be Jesus our Lord!' whispered Auntie Maria through sobs. 'Holy Virgin help us!'

5 Beyond the Walls

Re: Death Penalty for assistance to Jews who have left Jewish residential areas without permission.

Numerous Jews have recently left the Jewish residential areas to which they were assigned without permission. They are still for the time being in the Warsaw district.

I hereby declare that by the third decree of the Governor-General concerning residential restrictions in the Government-General of Oct. 15, 1941 (UBL GS p. 595) not only will Jews who in this way have left the residential areas assigned to them be punished with death but that the same punishment will also be imposed on any person who knowingly harbours such Jews. This does not only include shelter and food but also any other sort of assistance, e.g. by conveying Jews in any sort of vehicles, by purchase of Jewish goods, etc.

I hereby instruct the population of the Warsaw District to inform the nearest police station or police command post immediately of any Jew who stays without authorisation outside a Jewish residential area . . .

Warsaw,
6 September 1942

THE SS AND POLICE CHIEF,
Warsaw District

*Proclamation of the SS and Police Chief quoted by Josef Banas, *The Scapegoats*, translated by Tadeusz Szafar, Weidenfeld & Nicolson, London, 1979.

Hand in hand with Sophie, tears blinding my eyes, I followed Auntie Maria and Mother along Krakowskie Przedmieście towards my new 'home'. It was dark, bitterly cold, a freezing rain began to fall and a biting wind lashed my face – the best weather for convicts to make their escape. With our noses buried in our collars, we felt almost secure. Nobody looked at us. Even Polish policemen on the beat, even the few Nazis braving the elements, seemed too overwhelmed by the weather to take any notice of the four awkward figures scurrying for shelter in the dark. A warm smell of freshly baked bread wafting from a gate we passed by almost made me faint. For the last eight days we had had nothing to eat but a handful of barley hastily cooked and swallowed night after night. It suddenly occurred to me that at the end of our route not only a roof but also a decent meal might await us. I smiled at the idea.

From Now Świat we turned right into Świętokrzyska Street and soon reached Marszałkowska Street. There, at the corner of the two streets, very close to the place where I had spent my childhood, was the house we were heading for: a magnificent six-storey residence for wealthy people, very much like ours at Sienna Street. Luckily, there was nobody in the entrance, but the wide marble staircase with thoroughly blacked-out windows beamed with light. This was the shortest but the most dangerous part of our route: we had to climb up the stairs and slip into the flat unnoticed. Ours as well as our hosts' future safety depended on that. We were lucky again, we made our way up and rang the bell of the second-floor apartment without seeing a single soul.

The heavy front door opened instantly. 'Welcome, welcome, dear ladies,' a tall old man with a little grey beard and moustache greeted us warmly. 'Come in, come in from the cold.' His small eyes smiled amiably, he sounded as though we were his dear, long-awaited guests. He looked homely in his worn-out smoking jacket. Trotting around in excitement, helping us to take off our shabby overcoats, he chattered gaily to his dog, an ugly mongrel called Miki, that had jumped up and barked ever since we had entered the hall.

A plump old lady in a warm dressing gown emerged from the adjacent room to welcome us, too. She shook our hands wholeheartedly and gently stroked Sophie's long hair, saying, 'How tired you all look.' She begged us to call her simply 'Grannie' and her husband 'Grandad'. Leading the way through a number of spacious rooms furnished with antiques, she showed us to a smaller one which was to be ours. It was a long narrow room with three beds, three chairs and a table. A thick wall-to-wall carpet muffled our steps, the large front window was thoroughly screened with a heavy curtain. It was warm and cosy.

Grannie discreetly retired and for a while we were left alone with Auntie Maria who had to rush home very soon, since it would soon be curfew time. We could see and kiss each other at last. She brought us clean clothes to change into, and took away our rags to wash and properly delouse. She promised to be back first thing in the morning. Then she left in a hurry, leaving us numb in the middle of the room, uncertain what to do next, dazed by warmth, silence and hunger. We had nothing to unpack, nothing to put away, we did not dare sit down on the antique chairs without a thorough wash, let alone stretch out on the dazzlingly crisp, white bedding. We were not left to our bewilderment for long, however. Soon we heard a sharp knocking at the door, and it was flung open before we managed to answer. A spry, good-looking, portly blonde lady in her late forties, carefully dressed and made up, briskly entered the room and immediately took command of the situation. She introduced herself as Mrs Serbin, the 'grandparents' Sokolnicki's widowed daughter, our landlady. We were too tired, she said, to meet the other members of her household now or to talk over the details of our stay in her house. It could wait till morning. Instead, we should take a bath, have a meal, and go to bed. We gladly accepted her suggestion.

In the sparkling bathroom, in the tub full of warm water, inhaling the fragrance of real soap I had long forgotten, I sank into a blissful oblivion. The world in which I suddenly found myself bore no relation to my recent past, nor did it seem to foretell any meaningful future. But neither the past nor the future mattered any more, not for this one, timeless moment. Was I already dead? Was it the bliss of eternity?

Mrs Serbin's vigorous knocking at the bathroom door brought me back to reality and saved me from a tragic end in the bathtub. She announced that supper was served in our room. I can still remember the taste of those delicious noodles with cottage cheese and sugar – I gulped them down far too fast so as to prevent a single moment of hunger. Later, lying in bed in the darkness, I could not get to sleep: the bed was too clean, too soft. I was not used to such comfort. Fits of violent coughing which had plagued me recently drove all my sleepiness away. A torrent of bitter thoughts washed away the last trace of ecstasy. I was in an unknown place, facing an unknown future among strangers. My own cruel but familiar world where I belonged remained behind the walls. I had deserted it, running for my safety, for the luxuries of a fragrant bath and a soft bed. I had deserted my people, leaving them to their terrible fate. In the early hours of the night, flooded with tears of agony and guilt, I crept out of bed and stretched myself out on the carpet. There, cold and miserable, I finally fell asleep.

During the days that followed we learnt the art of survival in hiding. Step by step, we gained the knowledge and skills which paying guests of a large, well-settled Polish family needed and were expected to have. Step by step, we got to know each member of the family, their private virtues and vices, their daily habits and foibles. We learnt the rules we were supposed to comply with.

It was easy to get on with Grannie and Grandad Sokolnicki. They were both warm, understanding people, of deep culture and exquisite tact. Grandad Sokolnicki, born of an old east Polish gentry family, was a retired architect. Before the Russian Revolution he had studied, then worked, in St Petersburg. His designs were highly valued and gained him an accolade from the Tzar himself. There he had met his future wife, a Polish nobleman's daughter. Their three children were born in Russia, but brought up as good Catholics and Polish patriots. The family had fled from Russia soon after the Revolution began, settled down in Warsaw, and had lived there ever since. Just before the outbreak of war Grandad had retired at the end of a long and successful career, spanning two countries and two cultures.

The Sokolnicki's eldest daughter, Klara, was a frail middle-aged spinster, shy and quiet, a kind of grey little mouse. She and her mother shared the main tasks, catering for the needs of all the household. Both mother and daughter devoted their spare time to prayers. In fact, Klara reminded me of a nun and I often wondered why she had not chosen to live in a convent instead of slaving away in her busy family house. She was a gentle, lovely person always ready to help everybody, including us.

Of the youngest Sokolnicki, Andrzej, we knew very little. He came and went without telling anybody his plans in advance. We met him only three or four times during our stay at Marszałkowska Street. We never discovered what kind of activities kept him away, or what his occupation was. I felt rather attracted to that slim, pale man in his mid-thirties – he treated us with the charm of a real prince addressing full-blooded princesses. I liked listening to his laughter in the next room and enjoyed the old Russian romances he sometimes sang alone in his room. There was an air of mystery about Andrzej and I wished he would talk to me and tell me his secrets. But he seemed to be busy most of the time. When at home, he remained apart, his mind always miles away. Some time later I was surprised to learn that it was Andrzej who had heard about us first and had urged his sister to give us shelter.

It went without saying that the most important person in the household, its head and guide, was the Sokolnicki's middle daughter, Mrs Serbin. I never heard her Christian name. Her parents referred to her as 'the daughter'; Klara, respectfully and with a touch of awe, would say 'the sister'. It was not quite clear why this was so. I believe all members of the family depended on Mrs Serbin's financial support, but here again it was hard to guess where this middle-aged, unemployed widow obtained the resources to support so many of her relatives.

Mrs Serbin was quite unlike her parents, sister or brother, or even her own daughter. It was really hard to believe that she shared blood and ancestors with them. Sharp, fast, keen to live a good, cheerful life, she showed nothing of her kin's kindness or understanding of other people's souls. Instead of their subtlety she showed sheer verve and vigour. While her mother and sister worked and prayed at home, she spent most of her day at her hairdresser's, dressmaker, or in a café with friends. From the start we felt uneasy in Mrs Serbin's presence. Our dependence on her was humiliating.

The third and fourth generation of the family also lived in the flat – Mrs Serbin's only daughter, Musia, with her husband and their two-year-old child nicknamed Kizia. The Bachs were a sullen young couple, always harassed-looking. They worked too hard and earned too little. The husband could hardly support his family on his junior clerk's salary; Musia attended some underground courses, trying to combine her studies with her duties as wife and mother.

There was one other paying guest in the household. We learnt this only the morning after our arrival when the door flew open and my favourite once-removed Aunt Maryla rushed in in her nightie to embrace us at last. They had kept her presence from us till the morning out of fear we might collapse from the shock, exhausted as we were on that first evening.

The last member of the household, apart from the mongrel Miki, was 'The Woman'. That person we never met and we were not supposed to. She was just a cleaner and a kitchen help coming early in the morning and leaving before the evening meal. She might have been the most honest and magnanimous person in the world, yet the iron rule of the house was that the three Lubowicki ladies, which meant Mother, Sophie and myself, should under no circumstances, show their faces to anybody but the members of the Sokolnicki family. So, we were confined to our room for most of the day and could not even open the door when The Woman was around. We had to get up early to use the loo and the bathroom before anybody else, then lock ourselves in until dark. At about six, Grannie would gently knock at the door to break the exhilarating news that The Woman had gone home and we could safely go to 'the smallest room'.

The name 'Lubowicki' we acquired within the first week of our arrival on the 'Aryan' side, together with brand-new *Kennkarten* (Identification cards) showing our 'Aryan' faces and stating in black and white that we were born and baptised in an estate near Lida, a little town in the east of Poland, now occupied by the Russians. The documents were fake of course, the name was chosen for us by Grandad Sokolnicki because it sounded pure Polish and posh. We needed all this to be registered as residents of the house, just in case somebody noticed there were some lodgers living in the flat apart from the members of the family. Moreover, without our registration slips Mrs Serbin could not obtain extra ration coupons. By no means could those rough papers save us if we were caught by Nazis or the navy-blue police. * Some Jews hiding on the 'Aryan' side were lucky enough to possess genuine certificates of birth and baptism once owned by real people who were now dead. These were far more expensive and we could not afford them. Besides, we did not intend to go out anyway: with our typically Jewish appearance even the best documents would not have saved us. Maryla, for whom Grandad Sokolnicki procured an identification card of the same rough kind, was in a slightly better position: she had a 'better look' – was not as dark, not as 'typical' as we were. For that reason she could sometimes – very rarely – go out, was allowed to move freely around the house, talk to 'The Woman' if she wished to, go to the loo whenever she needed. She also had her meals together with the family, at the long antique table in the dining room, while ours were served in our room by Grannie Sokolnicki or Klara, three times daily.

From the very first evening I knew we would not starve any more, but at the same time I suspected we would not get enough to feel comfortable either. This was right. The portions of tasty, nicely arranged food

*The navy-blue police were built during the German occupation around a nucleus of veteran members of the pre-war Polish police force and reinforced by Poles of German extraction and Polish collaborators.

we received would not have fed a baby. Grannie and Klara were both well aware of this and always looked away embarrassed when they brought our meals. It wasn't their fault – we knew very well that they would have gladly served us a whole lamb if it had been up to them. They were in Mrs Serbin's hands, however – she kept the larder locked and the key in her pocket after she had given out the daily ration of food in the morning. Maryla claimed that the family and she herself were treated only a tiny bit better. But once she had peeped into Mrs Serbin's private room and had by chance seen her sitting at her dressing table. On it was laid out cold meat, cheese and caviar.

Two outsiders were allowed to see us, after all. Auntie Maria visited us twice a week and was our main link with the outside world and our loved ones. Stefan and Jadwiga were already on the 'Aryan' side, too, living in hiding. Their landlady was the divorced wife of Mr Richter, my grandfather's prewar chauffeur. Zina Richter hated her ex-husband and remained truly devoted to our family. She took care of Stefan and Jadwiga with zeal and self-abandonment. On and off, Auntie Maria would call on them, bring them whatever they needed, including news from us; then, twice a week she would call on us and we would receive from her anything we needed and hear all about Stefan and Jadwiga. Moving between the two hiding places, selling things and supplying large sums of money that had to be paid monthly to our respective landlords, Auntie Maria led an exhausting and risky life. She had never been an enterprising, bold woman. Quiet, faint-hearted, now in her fifties, fighting silently for the lives of the five people she loved, she suddenly grew heroic. Her hair turned grey, her drawn face bore signs of insomnia and anxiety. Her visits were for us the highlights of the week, the only events we desperately looked forward to, not counting the end of the war that never seemed any closer.

The second visitor from the outside world who would call on us from time to time, bringing with him a breath of fresh air and a spark of youthful hope, was Mr Staś Chmielewski. We had not known him before, he was Maryla's, or rather her absent brother's friend from before the war. Much later I understood it was something more than friendship that bound Staś to Karol, many years his senior. Whatever it was, Staś's wholehearted dedication not only to Karol's close family but also to his far-removed relatives, even to Jews as a whole since Karol was Jewish, proved total and amazingly constant: it survived Karol himself. When Maryla and her old mother escaped from the ghetto during the first *Aktion*, Staś, like a loving son and brother, took them entirely into his care. He lodged the old lady with his own mother and, being acquainted with Andrzej Sokolnicki and his family, talked them into taking Maryla under their roof. Then, in the winter, alerted by Auntie Maria who turned to him for help, he did the same for us, not even knowing us personally.

We got on well with Staś from his first visit, it was as if we had known him for ages. It was so simple. He was an easy-going cheerful and spirited fellow, not at all frightened by what he was doing for us and lots of other people. He claimed that being single, not bound up with anybody but his mother who managed well on her own, he could afford to take risks. So he said when we first met and Mother tried to thank him for what he had done for us.

At the beginning I felt enchanted by Staś. Cut off from normal life, deprived of young company, I was inclined to fancy anybody who was handsome, young and male. Staś was all these at once: he was thirty-two, tall and strong, blue-eyed and fair-haired (which I particularly liked), and had the open face of a country lad. He was dressed in the wartime fashion – long boots, breeches, tweed jacket, a funny little hat with a green feather – not in the least what my father or uncles would wear, but I did not mind it. Pleased with my new acquaintance, I talked myself into believing that Staś resembled Roman. In fact, apart from the blue eyes and the blond hair, they had nothing in common.

Staś did not care for me, however. It became clear after a time and I felt slightly disappointed. I thought that my indoor life had made me entirely unattractive. I confessed my doubts to Mother but she said I was wrong. Blushing a little, she gently explained to me that Staś belonged to the certain kind of men who did not feel attracted to women. I misunderstood her communication and felt sorry for Staś, thinking he was impotent.

Our life secured by the locked door, muffled by the heavy curtains and the soft carpet, ran uneventfully from the morning wash till the evening bath, from meal to meal; from one visit to the next of our two guardian angels. The time in between we spent talking to each other and reading. Grandad Sokolnicki took it upon himself to provide us with books he borrowed from a library. He had exquisite literary taste and a good understanding of what would take our minds off our plight. To him I owed my introduction to Russian literature. During my four-month stay at Marszałkowska Street, I managed to read most of Leo Tolstoy and Chekhov, fall in love with Pushkin and Turgenev, even get a glimpse of the Soviet writers like Sholokhov or Alexsei Tolstoi, whom

Grandad liked as well.

My idleness, uselessness, the emptiness of my days caused me much pain. From time to time I suggested to Grannie Sokolnicki that I might help her in doing some jobs around the house, but she gently refused: I was not supposed to leave my room during the day, and by the evening, when The Woman had gone, all daily tasks had been done. Sometimes Musia, oppressed by her twofold commitments, would hastily burst into our room, begging us to take care of little Kizia for an hour or two. I loved these short spells when the frail, helpless child depended on me, when I could feed and cuddle her, feel she was fond of me without any hidden thoughts. Yet, at the same time, I shivered at the thought of what could happen to that child if our presence under the same roof was discovered.

Tired of reading, I would often spend hours thinking about Father, Roman and my friends. I missed them all bitterly. Once Auntie Maria brought me good news. By chance, she had met Hanka's mother in the street. Forgetting all about safety precautions, the two women walked up and down the street together exchanging information. Mrs K. and Hanka had escaped from the ghetto just before the second *Aktion*. With their friends' help they had acquired relatively safe documents and found a relatively good place to live. They did not need to hide, they both looked like plain peasant women. Mrs K. found a job and earned some money; Hanka resumed her studies with an underground study group.

I was overwhelmed by the news, happy and envious at the same time, since I could not go out and join a study group myself. But Auntie Maria had some more news. Mrs K. was in touch with somebody who used to be Zula's nanny before the war. Zula had escaped from the ghetto alone: her mother was taken during the first *Aktion*. She went straight to her old nanny, who with open arms took her under her roof with loving care. But Zula would not sit quietly at home, she was too lively, too light-hearted to put up with confinement. After a week, ignoring her guardian's warnings and entreaties, she rushed out into the street to breathe the fresh air and see people walking in the sun. Frightened to death, the old woman followed her at a distance. Zula was not a girl who could pass unnoticed. Her fiery hair, her beautiful pale face attracted everybody's attention. There could be little doubt about her Jewish origins. After a short while she was spotted by three Nazis idly strolling along the street. They stopped her, talked to her for a while, then pulled her into a gateway. From there Zula reappeared stark naked. Roaring with laughter, the Germans stopped a passing tram, forced the naked girl up onto the front platform, jumped up after her, and waved to the driver to resume his route. Numb and helpless the old woman watched the white body and the red head fading away into the heavy traffic. Zula never came back.

Somewhere beyond the curtained window winter lost its grip, slowly pushed away by the brighter skies and the heavy rains of the early spring. Distressed and lifeless, tormented by an unnamed disease, I spent most of my days in bed. Mother and Auntie Maria wrung their hands not knowing what to do with me. Calling for a doctor was out of the question; besides, it seemed clear it was not a doctor but fresh air and freedom that I needed.

Throughout the years of the war Auntie Maria had kept in touch with Halina, my 'Aryan' aunt who always showed a keen interest in our plight and was willing to help. Hearing about my bleakness, Halina suggested I paid her a visit. Taking a great risk by maintaining close contacts with her Jewish husband Vładek, who lived on the 'Aryan' side but not at home and was involved in the resistance movement, hiding Grandma Viera in her single-room flat, busy making all sorts of illicit transactions to support her husband, mother-in-law and little son, she could not invite me for longer than a couple of days. Yet it meant a lot to me: to go out, walk in the street, stay in a different place, see people other than the usual ones seemed really exciting. The matter had first to be discussed with our hosts, though. Mrs Serbin was strongly against the whole thing. She claimed, not without justification, that my going out and coming back would endanger all of us, and was contradictory to the rules we had agreed to observe. To my great surprise, all the rest of the household proved to be in favour of my venture. Grandad Sokolnicki, Klara, Musia, even her taciturn husband managed to convince Mrs Serbin that there was nothing wrong with my going out, because – they said – unlike Mother or Sophie, I did not look strikingly Jewish, my hair being less dark, my eyes bright, my nose of a medium size. To be on the safe side, Grannie Sokolnicki brought me an old hat to cover my wavy hair, while Mrs Serbin, still grumbling, handed me her own sunglasses, because, she explained, my eyes, though bright, were still typically Jewish due to that sad, dreamy expression.

One Friday evening, accompanied by Auntie Maria who was frightened to death and evidently looked it, seen off to the front door by all the household, even blessed and crossed over by the hands of Grannie Sokolnicki as though I were embarking on an expedition to the

North Pole, I finally left my confinement. Days being already longer, it was still light, the air was fresh and fragrant. I had not been in the open for three months and at first I felt dizzy. We walked along the main streets of the city and I looked around in excitement, while Auntie Maria, toddling double-bent at my side, whispered nervously, 'Don't look at people, for God's sake!' Suddenly I caught a glimpse of myself in a large mirror displayed in a shop window. Was it really me? What I saw was a sexually undefined creature in a shabby, far too long winter coat of a horrible brown colour, with a stiff, grey man's hat on top and huge dark glasses screening half of its face, turning it into a bee's rather than a human muzzle. I recoiled with disgust and resumed my way upset, silently cursing not the Nazis but those who considered it safer to make a monster of me.

Against all odds, life at Halina's seemed to run smoothly. She was a radiant woman, good-looking, warm and courageous. Born in a working-class family, she had soon learned to cope with the hardships of daily life and bravely faced the hazards of wartime. Seeing me in my disguise, she burst out laughing, tears coming to her eyes at the same time. She hugged me heartily and made me change in the corridor before my Grandma could be shocked by my appearance.

I found Grandma Viera much older and thinner than six months before. She had deteriorated quickly from living in constant anxiety about her four sons, of whom Julian seemed to be her greatest sorrow.

The weekend passed smoothly and happily. I enjoyed the company of my cousin, Jurek, who was now a charming, clever six-year-old boy. He took to me instantly and kept bringing me sweets from his mother's cupboard, which for me was an unspeakable pleasure: for once I did not feel hungry. On Sunday evening Halina saw me off to Marszałkowska Street. She forbade me to wear the hat and glasses and encouraged me to feel at ease in the street. I felt much better this way.

My next visit to Halina's was fixed for Saturday 17 April. This time I went on my own, dressed in a new spring jacket brought for me by Staś from the stall he ran in the market. The evening was warm and clear, I felt young and attractive again. But something had changed in Halina's home since I was there a month earlier. My Grandma was no longer there. Halina had had to put her up with friends on the outskirts of town, since the neighbourhood was rife with rumours that her mother-in-law looked slightly Jewish. This did not, however, deter Halina from running the risk of entertaining me. On Sunday morning she took me to a café in the city where we met Uncle Vladek. He was almost a stranger to me, yet it was nice to talk to an uncle again. In fact, it was the last time I ever saw Vładek. A few months later he was shot dead by a Nazi squad together with many other members of the Polish underground. Like my father and Józef, he died not because he was Jewish, but as a Pole who fought against the Nazis.

On Sunday afternoon Halina gave a party for her friends: a middle-aged lawyer evidently in love with her, a cheerful young woman, a shy cousin who was a factory worker. She introduced me to them as her niece, not hiding who I really was. We had a meal cooked by Halina, and drank a lot of vodka. I felt like a real guest, no worse than the others.

The following morning I was woken by the sound of heavy explosions. It was the day after Palm Sunday and for a while, still half asleep, I wondered why somebody had chosen to announce the resurrection six days early.* But soon I realised that something else was afoot. Violent machine-gun fire could be heard. Halina rushed out in her dressing gown to see what was going on. She returned distressed. People in the streets already knew: there was a battle raging behind the ghetto walls.

Sounds of heavy fighting continued throughout the day. In the evening, when I left Halina to go back to Marszałkowska Street, the sky was clouded with smoke. The pungent smell of burning brought memories of the siege of Warsaw to my mind. I was in danger then, suffering with others. Now, shamelessly secure, I watched from outside my people's hopeless fight. When I arrived home, the Sokolnicki grandparents, Klara and the Bachs were all gathered in the parlour praying. Their faces were grave.

The following days, resounding with explosions and continuous machine-gun fire, brought more confusing news. Nobody knew for certain how it had all started, but the fact of the ghetto uprising was soon taken for granted. It was clear that it could not last long, that in a day or two the overwhelming German military power would smother the reckless outburst of a handful of desperados. Yet, the battle went on and on. The ghetto was in flames, the ghetto fought.

It was at least a couple of days before the Sokolnickis recovered from the first shock and, still looking grave, resumed their daily routine. Grandad went out to the library, Grannie returned to her dusting and ironing, whispering her Christian prayers for the souls of the Jewish fighters. Little by little the subject of Easter and obtaining food for the occasion crept into family conversations, alongside horrifying tales of people seen dying in the flames, women with babies in their arms

*A Polish custom of exploding fireworks on Easter morning.

jumping down from the windows of burning houses, scores of fighters dragged out from underground shelters and killed on the spot.

Our days were empty, our nights sleepless. Late at night, all the other inhabitants asleep, Mother, Sophie and I would steal into the dark parlour, open the balcony door and stare out at the sky. It was bright red from the blaze devouring the northern quarter of the city. Once in a while the sharp barking of a machine gun would break the silence of the deserted streets below. A sudden gust of north wind would litter the pavements with charred debris.

On Easter Friday Mrs Serbin asked me to help in the kitchen. The Woman was off for holidays and there was plenty to do, all work being delayed because of the recent events. For that reason, all female members of the household were busy in the warm, spacious kitchen under Mrs Serbin's command. Some other time I would have greatly enjoyed beating eggs, sorting out raisins, inhaling the sweet scent of vanilla from the freshly-baked cake. This time, however, my mind was far away from my busy fingers. The atmosphere of excitement, so natural whenever a team struggles to get a job done on time, made me sick. Yet, it was better this way than being locked in the room with one's own grief.

On Easter Day we were invited to take part in the family dinner. I did all I could to put on a good face and not be a killjoy. No one was cheerful around the table, but there was a silent agreement that the subject of the ghetto uprising should not be discussed that evening. I could hardly bear it, all my thoughts being there. Mother and Sophie felt the same, so immediately after the last course, we retired to our room.

Staś offered to spend Easter Monday with us and came in the morning, dressed in his best tweed jacket, well groomed and good-looking, yet clearly sick at heart. He chose to pretend he was not, and tried hard to cheer us up. He even brought his own gramophone and a few records to distract our minds from our sorrow. 'Rosamunda, you came with the northern wind,' sang a strong male voice. From the north, clouds of black smoke darkened the radiant sky. Dense soot kept falling and stuck to the walls and pavements of the festive city. 'Alleluia!' rejoiced the crowds inside the churches of Warsaw.

The ghetto uprising entered its third week.

Nazi posters hung up all over the city appealed to the Poles to denounce Jews hiding on the 'Aryan' side, recent runaways as well as those who had escaped earlier. A mounting sense of danger held us all in a firm grip. The security rules were now reinforced. My going out became out of the question.

Once, in the middle of the night, we heard an air-raid warning: the Allies' bombers were roaring high above the city. Soon heavy detonations could be heard from afar. The German air defence answered with violent spanking. Quickly, calmly our inmates rushed down to the underground shelter. We could not risk being seen by the neighbours, so we stayed in the apartment. The old Sokolnickis decided to stay with us. Grannie murmured her prayers, Grandad jokingly talked to his mongrel, and we were all in seventh heaven since we believed that long-expected help and retaliation was finally coming down from the sky. Next day we learnt that the Russian bombers had succeeded in damaging a German strategic base in Warsaw, but that there had also been many casualties among the Poles.

Soon after the air raid, the ghetto battle finally came to an end. On 15 May the Nazis blew up the synagogue at Tłomackie Street to mark their victory over the Jews of Warsaw. The hunt for survivors was gaining strength.

My nights were now tormented by agonising thoughts and horrifying dreams. Once I saw Roman in my dream. We were living together in a small room, hiding from both the Nazis and the neighbours, who might have discovered that we slept in the same bed. In my sleep I heard violent knocking at the door and woke up in terror. In the faint light of the dawn I saw Mrs Serbin. Three tall men in dark hats and black leather jackets pushed by her, making their way into our room. 'Your documents, Mrs Lubowicki,' shouted Mrs Serbin. 'The gentlemen wish to see your *Kennkarten*.' A sharp flash of recognition made my heart sink: Gestapo! It was the end, death was at my bed. Her hands trembling, Mother quickly produced the three identification cards that she always kept by her bed in her handbag. One of the men turned the light on, but did not look at the documents: he stared straight at Mother's terrified face while his companions scrutinised Sophie and me. 'Jewish,' they concluded. 'Get up at once, you are coming with us,' said the first man icily. He spoke Polish.

They gave us five minutes to get ready and left the room, taking Mrs Serbin with them. After a while she was back, her face flaming, her voice breaking. 'Money,' she panted. 'They are willing to leave you alone if you pay them. Mrs Lubowicki, you must do it, you must give them money for the sake of all of us.' 'How much?' murmured Mother in slight relief, 'I have no money on me.' The sum they wanted was 100,000 zloty, a fortune which we were unable to procure. Even if

Auntie Maria had sold all the remaining goods, which were already running low, she would not have been able to raise half the required sum. But it was clear now that the three men were not from the Gestapo. They were obviously blackmailers who, though dangerous, might be ready to negotiate. Pulling herself together, Mother bravely decided to face them. Once dressed and self-possessed, she addressed the chief blackmailer in her fluent German. He stared at her sheepishly; he did not understand that language. It gave Mother a better position to negotiate from. After a short while the demand dropped to 40,000. The conditions were settled: the men would return to collect the money in three days. They left in a hurry.

There was no time to waste: our shelter had ceased to be safe, for our own and our hosts' sake we had to leave at once, the sooner the better. Grandad Sokolnicki hurried to fetch Auntie Maria. She came immediately, shattered and sobbing. We sat with her and Mrs Serbin trying to find a solution. If only we could get out of the way, Auntie Maria could somehow raise the money for the ransom and Mrs Serbin would be able to cope with the rascals more easily alone. Sure, but where could we go?

It was soon clear that as Halina was away just then, the only person we could ask for temporary shelter was Zina Richter, the woman who was already sheltering Jadwiga and Stefan in her tiny flat. There was no way to ask her, though, not even to let her know in advance we were coming. We had to leave *now*.

The day was bright, the hunt for Jews at its peak, our frightened eyes more Jewish than ever. Deeply distressed, we wondered how to do it, how to get to Zina's place unharmed. Surprisingly enough, the best idea came from Klara. There were now many wounded people in Warsaw, she said; some were mourning their loved ones killed in the recent bombing. We got her idea at once.

From her capacious chest of drawers Grannie Sokolnicki dug out a black hat with a fine black veil that she used to wear when mourning relatives. Klara brought out the family first aid kit. Mother was the mourner, her face concealed behind the veil; Sophie was the wounded, half of her face, including the nose, tightly bandaged, only one black eye squinting out sadly from the dressing – it was all right to look sad in such circumstances. We quickly decided that I should go undisguised. Grandad went down and, since no taxis were available in occupied Warsaw, he summoned a hansom cab. Then we hastily said goodbye to the people who were the first to give us shelter, and left for the unknown.

6 On the Run

The horses clip-clopped slowly along the main streets. The old cabman high on his perch, his back turned to us, sighed heavily time and again. Passers-by glanced at us with compassion. Only now, sitting idly in the cab, did we begin to realise how grave our predicament was. We did not know (and we never learnt) how the blackmailers had tracked us down; it was far from certain that, satisfied once, they would leave Mrs Serbin or even Auntie Maria in peace. They might be shadowing us right now and thus be about to discover Zina's place, with Stefan and Jadwiga hidden there. Wherever we turned, we brought great danger to those who wanted to help.

Two slow and three quick little knocks. The front door opened slowly, reluctantly. A pair of beautiful eyes stared at us in bewilderment. Then Jadwiga gave a cry of terror. Looking as though she were going to faint, she instantly let us in and locked the door. Stefan, whom she called, looked no less terrified. Zina was out.

It was our first reunion since leaving the ghetto in January, so, for a while, emotion took over. Not for long though. Sitting in Zina's kitchen we listened to Stefan and Jadwiga's hair-raising story before we started to go into the details of our own recent experiences.

Yesterday morning Zina had gone out to her part-time cleaning job and had never returned. With growing anxiety Stefan and Jadwiga had waited for her in vain. When curfew came they realised that something serious must have happened to her. Besides, they were hungry, they were dependent on Zina's daily shopping. They began to search the kitchen, then Zina's bedroom for something to eat. Then suddenly, on top of the bedside locker, Jadwiga noticed a broken ampoule of morphia and a half-filled syringe. In a flash they understood. Zina was an addict.

Having lived with her for some time they knew she was somewhat unbalanced, her moods changing rapidly within a single day, but they ascribed it to her loneliness, her longing for a man, perhaps some indulgence in drinking. Now, knowing the truth, they were scared. Had Zina been arrested in the street, which happened daily to ordinary people in wartime Warsaw, she might be ready to do anything to get her morphia. She was an honest, tender-hearted woman, but craving for drugs could make her betray her lodgers in return for her own freedom. It was obvious that Stefan and Jadwiga had to leave at once. And the three of us too, of course. But there was nowhere to go. We were trapped.

Zina returned home the following evening. She looked haggard and miserable. Seeing Mother, Sophie and me she burst out crying. Kissing us all in turns, she kept saying, 'Sorry! Sorry!' then locked herself in her room. After a time she reappeared composed. She never said where she had spent the last sixty hours.

The following morning Zina went off to work as usual. We were not starving since Jadwiga had ventured out and bought some food the day before. But the growing suspense turned us all into a bundle of nerves. We all jumped to our feet when we heard knocking.

It was a special knocking, though, two slow and three quick little knocks: Auntie Maria was at the door. She was pale and tired, but she brought good news. Within a day and a half she had managed to sell all that remained of Grandfather's paintings and already had two-thirds of the sum demanded by the blackmailers. She hoped to borrow the rest. Meanwhile Mrs Serbin had got in touch with a man who was ready to take us to a new shelter later that day. The place and time of our meeting this man were already fixed. Auntie Maria did not know any details – who the man was, where he intended to take us, for how long and for how much. We just had to trust him, there was no choice.

With this problem settled for better or worse, we now had another needing an instant decision. We had no money left. The time had come to use the last thing which throughout all those years Mother had kept for a rainy day. It was a platinum ring with a heavy, bright diamond of great value. Though born and brought up in a wealthy family, my mother was a very modest woman. She had, of course, many beautiful little jewels – birthday gifts from her parents and aunts – but she hardly ever wore them. Her wedding ring and a little golden watch were her only adornments. She would never wear a thing as ostentatiously expensive as this diamond ring. It was not meant to be worn, anyhow. With war approaching, Father had decided to invest all the savings of his long years of hard work in this single jewel, since he believed it would provide his family with more security than money. He was right. Now the rainy day had come and Mother took the ring out from a little linen bag she always kept inside her bra, and handed it to Auntie Maria to sell.

Poor Auntie was still fumbling with the precious thing, deadly anxious to hide it safely in her own bra, when she heard that Stefan and Jadwiga urgently needed a new hiding place, too. She looked as though she were close to heart failure. Then something extraordinary happened: a guardian angel suddenly appeared out of the blue. We heard two slow and three quick little knocks and in a moment a friendly-looking woman we hardly knew was cordially shaking our hands. She introduced herself as Mrs Koterba, Zina's elder sister. She looked a little puzzled to see so many people in the flat, but she guessed at once who we all were.

Wasting no time, Mrs Koterba told us what had brought her there. Zina had recently started a love affair with a fellow who happened to be a good friend of the Koterbas. Last night he had come uninvited to talk to them. He had been very upset by discovering that Zina was an addict. Naïvely, he had tried to cure her himself, he said, by keeping her off morphia. He had locked her in his flat for two days and nights, and had done his best to bring home to her how perilous addiction was. Zina was in a terrible state, she had kicked and bit him, moaned and talked nonsense. She had said something about hiding Jews in her flat, they might die from starvation if he kept her locked in. She told him to go to her place and see for himself that she was not lying. She even instructed him how to knock in order to be let in. The man had not gone, but when Zina had eventually calmed down he let her free. Then he had come to see the Koterbas to ask them for help.

All this was news to Mrs Koterba. She hardly knew about Zina's addiction, or about her giving shelter to Jews. She suspected the latter since she knew how deeply Zina was devoted to our family. But she had not said a word about her suspicion, and had cheered the man up by promising to take care of Zina. Once the friend had gone, she and her husband had spent all night thinking what to do. In the end, she had decided to go and see whether there really was someone hiding in Zina's flat.

And here she was, keen and efficient, conjuring up a solution. Zina must go to hospital and be cured of her addiction, she said. Even if she stayed at home, hiding under her roof would be most dangerous since she was no longer reliable. Mrs Koterba and her good old husband were ready to take over and offer hiding, but only to one couple. They never expected to find five people here. Surprised and moved, we quickly explained that only Jadwiga and Stefan needed her help, at which Mrs Koterba heaved a sigh of relief.

The details were settled at once. Zina must know neither about her sister's visit nor about Stefan and Jadwiga going to her place. When she came back from work we must lie to her, saying that we had found a shelter for all five of us and preferred to hide together, which was impossible in Zina's tiny flat. For safety's sake, Jadwiga and Stefan should wait an hour after our departure, then go straight to the Koterbas. This settled, Mrs Koterba left, wishing us good luck.

If the residents of Walicòw Street had looked down from their windows at six o'clock that evening, they would have seen a Black Widow, a Wounded Child and a young girl of slightly Mediterranean appearance emerging from a gate and speeding towards the corner. Maybe somebody noticed them and wondered who was hidden behind the black veil and the white bandage. Yet the three dreary figures made their way unhindered. A hansom cab was waiting round the corner, a fashionably dressed man sprawling on the passenger seat. Seeing the women he was waiting for, he made a quick inviting gesture.

We jogged down town towards the river. The man was stand-offish, reticent, probably scared. He spoke just once to whisper the address where we were going and to instruct Mother that she should introduce herself to the landlady as a Polish major's widow. He did not even say what the landlady's name was. 'Does she know who we really are?' whispered Mother anxiously. 'No need to talk with her about it,' snarled the man curtly, then stopped the cab and stepped out.

We jogged along for the next few minutes. By the Poniatowski Bridge the cabman pulled over: 'Here we are, ladies.' Mother paid him, he touched his peaked cap, cracked his whip at the horse, and slowly wheeled away. We were left on our own, dazzled by the glittering river so long unseen. A long row of high modern houses built just before the war for very important people ran along the riverside facing the bridge. One of those houses was to be our abode.

The lift took us smoothly to the seventh floor. The person who answered the door was an ageless, colourless little woman with restless eyes. She greeted us effusively, looking quite at her ease. Locking the door behind us, she instantly started telling us about her bad cold, the weather being not as warm as it should be in May, and about her brother who would not meet us till Saturday, since he worked as a railwayman away from home, and slept at home only at the weekends. Showing us to 'our' room she managed on her way to pick up some clothes from the corridor floor, dust a shelf with her fingertips, and scrutinise a pimple on her nose in the mirror. There were no questions asked, no answers necessary. 'It's cold, cold, dears, the central heating never works these days, as you know. Make yourselves comfortable, dears, dears, feel at home, please. You go to bed late? No? Fine, dears. It's good for you to go to sleep early. I stay up late at night and sleep instead in the morning. You won't mind it, dears, will you?' Bewildered by the flood of words, we listlessly examined the large, half-empty room with a bare window overlooking the bridge. The beds were only half-made, the sheets looking as if somebody had already spent a night or two in them. There was hardly any other furniture besides. The kitchen also looked seedy, uncared for. The landlady, who meantime managed to introduce herself as 'just' Lily, encouraged us to use the kitchen whenever we wanted to, since she hardly ever needed it herself. She preferred to eat out and cooked only when her brother was around. Shyly, anxiously Mother asked whether she would mind doing shopping for us. Lily giggled. 'I'm a lousy shopper, dear,' she said. 'But if you wish . . . Lily will do everything for people she likes. And I like you, dears, I really and truly like the three of you.'

She went out soon afterwards, leaving us locked in the flat. Having nothing better to do we explored our new surroundings. It was a big apartment, two of the rooms locked, the other two furnished with a petit-bourgeois plush cosiness: deep soft armchairs and sofas covered with dozens of hand-embroidered pillows and rag dolls; crochet doilies all over the little tables and cupboards; exotic plants in pots; gold-framed pictures showing bloody sunsets or stags in the forests; scores of shells, faience figurines, thick glassware balls. 'How on earth have people with this kind of taste got hold of an apartment in these blocks?' wondered Mother.

We could not turn the light on in our room because there were no curtains or blackout blinds over the window, so, overcoming repulsion, we slipped into bed and somehow managed to fall asleep. Late at night I woke up with a fit of violent coughing. I shivered from fever, I was obviously ill. Noise coming from the other rooms meant we were alone no longer. I listened carefully. A hilarious party was apparently going on next door – I could hear loud tipsy prattle, female giggles and ribald male laughter mingled with a very hoarse 'Rosamunda' coming from a faulty gramophone. Soon I made out that there were two women taking part in the fun, one of whom was Lily, and at least three men. Now, holding my breath, I was all ears. Yes, I had no doubt, the men were speaking German. I heard quick soft steps in the dark: Sophie was locking the door. Mother sat on her bed stupefied, she was no longer asleep, either. We all knew: we were trapped in a German brothel or something of the kind.

We did not say a word about what we knew when next morning, just before noon, Lily emerged from her bedroom, as friendly and restless as the day before. Her nocturnal visitors had disappeared much earlier. I had peeped through the keyhole when they were leaving and caught a glimpse of the field-grey uniforms in the corridor.

Lily got ready and, without being reminded, went out to do some shopping for us. She returned happy, with a five-kilo bag of fresh spinach, then sipped some black coffee and went to bed again.

Three days passed before Auntie Maria received our new address from Mrs Serbin and came to see us with money and news. We could hardly wait to see her, we badly needed her help again. The orgies in the adjacent room went on night after night; once somebody tried to force our locked door open; we could not stay in Lily's place much longer. Besides, I was really ill with fever and coughing at night, exhausted in the daytime. I obviously needed a doctor.

Auntie Maria sank in despair at hearing all this. She had brought good news and had hoped for a spell of relaxation in her life and ours. The blackmailers had taken just 22,000 and promised never to come back. Jadwiga and Stefan were safe with the Koterbas and had settled down all right; the diamond ring had been sold at a reasonable price and we could go on living in hiding for some time, perhaps till the end of the war. 'Oh Jesus, my Lord,' cried Auntie in a helpless prayer. 'What shall I do now, who shall I turn to next to save you, my poor, poor girls!'

The weekend came and Lily's brother showed up. He was a rough fat man, about fifty, speaking harsh, foreign-sounding Polish. He was German-born, *Reichsdeutsch*, he proudly told us immediately we met. Strangely enough, he seemed to be glad to see us and seemed to be trying to please us. We sat with him and Lily in the plush armchairs eating German sausages with stewed sauerkraut and drinking beer we detested. We hardly could reject his hospitality. Warmed by food and drink, he told us all about his job. Once, when younger, he had worked as an engine-driver's mate, but since the war his work had become far more rewarding and responsible. He was an armed train guard now, serving on the Warsaw–Berlin railway, searching for smugglers, partisans and Jews. He told us a few funny stories of some of his exploits; how he succeeded in catching or killing some of those bandits.

More and more excited by his tales, he suddenly grabbed my hand, pulled me to the sofa, and forced me to sit next to him. He put his heavy arm around my shoulders. 'Shall we go dance tonight, my pretty Fräulein?' I sat stiff, horrified, trying to avoid his breath which smelt of beer and sauerkraut. I did not know what to answer. Instantly, Mother came to my rescue. 'Sorry, Herr Schmidt,' she said resolutely, 'I won't let her out tonight. She's ill, poor thing, look how pale she is. She's got fever and a bad cough.' It was true, and Lily confirmed Mother's words with an understanding nod. '*Schade, Schade*,' ('Pity, pity') sighed Schmidt, greatly disappointed. 'Let's do it next Saturday then. I'll take you to *einen fabelhaften Nacht-Klub* ('to a wonderful night-club') Fräulein. You'll dance with the highest rank *Offizieren, mein Schatz,* ('my treasure') but first of all with me.' He squeezed my shoulders with a bear's tenderness, making me almost faint. Suddenly feeling sleepy, he shuffled along to the bedroom, pulling Lily with him. Obviously he was not her brother.

Sick and scared, I counted the days with rising anxiety. We had to run away from Lily as soon as possible, but for me Saturday was the deadline. Monday, Tuesday, then Wednesday went by. I spent long hours glued to the window, greedily watching the river, the street, the bridge. For once I could do it safely: nobody would notice or recognise me at this height. The weather was brilliant, spring at its peak. Young couples walked leisurely along the bridge holding hands. The colourful dresses of the girls streamed in the light breeze. An old woman sat on the pavement selling lovely big bunches of fresh lilac, white, purple, bluish. A crippled street singer plaintively sang 'Rosamunda' out of tune.

Auntie Maria turned up on Friday morning. She had found no hiding place for us so far, but Staś had something in mind and begged her to tell us to wait patiently till the end of the following week when, he hoped, somebody he had been in touch with would be ready to take us. But in my case patience was impossible: I had to leave before tomorrow.

When she had heard my story Auntie Maria thought for a long while. She had come to take me out that afternoon, anyway. She had made an appointment with a doctor for me. Come what may, she would not bring me back to this den of vice, she would hide me, cram me in safely somewhere . . . where? She did not know yet.

I got ready and left with Auntie Maria, my heart heavy as lead, since I was leaving Mother and Sophie without the slightest idea when, where or whether I would see them again.

The doctor, an elderly woman, was a pediatrician. I was a child no longer, but for Auntie Maria what mattered most was that she knew she could trust her. Indeed, she was a sweet, caring person. She knew who I was at first glance, but did not say a word about it. She took a long time to examine me and did it thoroughly. Her verdict came as a shock: I had TB, both lungs were affected.

The doctor explained that there was no need to despair because the disease was in its early stages, and since it was the first case in the whole family, and no hereditary tendency was suspected, I stood a good chance of recovery, provided I ate well and had plenty of fresh air. Living in the country or mountains was the only thing she could prescribe, apart from medicine for the cough and fever, and calcium tablets. As I put on my clothes again, I caught her sad, compassionate glance. She refused to accept money.

From the doctor's Auntie Maria took me to her sister Helena, the midwife. Though a person of high principles and dedicated like Auntie Maria, Helena could hardly conceal her anxiety when she saw me on her doorstep. She silently pulled the two of us into the bathroom and locked herself in with us. Deeply embarrassed, she said she did not want her son to see me. Antoni, she explained, was an impeccable, brave man, she could only be proud of him. But he would be terribly angry to see me in his house. Not that he was a coward, far from it. Feeling guilty at letting us into a deadly secret, Helena explained that Antoni was a high-ranking member of the underground movement, the commander of a military unit and a link with the West. His house had to be clear and above all suspicion.

Helena did not send me away, though. She put me up, first for a single night, then as I still had nowhere to go, sheltered me for two more days and nights. Keeping me out of his sight, she told her son that I was a patient of hers who had miscarried and had to lie still until I stopped bleeding. She put me to bed in her own room and there I lay day and night. Ill and exhausted, I dozed for most of the time, my face hidden under the blankets, since Antoni would pop in from time to time to pick

Maria Bulat – Auntie Maria

All these photographs show the Warsaw ghetto as I remember it. This one shows the wall: the 'Aryan' side is on the left (Photo: Institute of Jewish Affairs)

Above: The bridge linking the main area of the ghetto with the 'Little Ghetto'. Before it was built we had had to cross the street through busy traffic. And this was exactly where Sophie had been knocked down by a German lorry. (Photo: Institute of Jewish Affairs) *Below:* Jewish policemen – Julian or Daniel could have been one of them (Photo: Yad Vashem Archives, Jerusalem)

People were crammed into the ghetto by force. Thousands of refugees and the already destitute lived in the streets (Photo: Yad Vashem Archives, Jerusalem)

1946: helping to clear up
what remained of the
Warsaw ghetto. I am in
the middle passing bricks

Stefan in the summer of
1939

Jadwiga, 1942

Sophie, aged 11, soon
after her accident in
1941

My mother, 1941

Sophie and I
immediately
after the war

up some of his belongings. On the third day Helena begged Auntie Maria to take me away: Antoni needed the room for a secret meeting in the evening.

I do not remember where I stayed for the following three or four days. Dazed by fever, only half-conscious, I wandered with Auntie Maria along some unknown streets on the outskirts of the city, or sat on packed trams curiously watched by strangers. I slept in some strange places: in somebody's cousin's flat, in somebody else's friend's flat . . . At last the day came when Auntie Maria could take me to the new hiding place promised by Staś, where I saw Mother and Sophie again.

Of all my hiding places I liked that one the best. Nowy Świat, the main route linking the old town with the city centre, had always been a smart and fashionable street before the war and remained so after. During the Nazi occupation it was mainly used by the Germans. The house in which we found shelter had been badly damaged during the siege. Only the ground floor survived intact and now housed a German trading company. The first floor was partly destroyed and for that reason not used by the company, its paneless windows thoroughly boarded up. But its walls, floors and ceilings held fast. There was nothing above the first floor but charred stubs, all that remained of the upper storeys.

The German company downstairs worked daily from 8 a.m. till 4 p.m., after which time the staff left and the janitor locked the front gate, unlocking it only the next morning. The janitor was Polish. He lived with his mother in the building, in a little ground-floor tied flat next to the company office. A tall, swarthy, sullen man in his thirties, Kazik seemed far more intelligent than his job required. He did not talk much, a man of action rather than words. His work for the firm was just a smoke screen to hide secret activities of various kinds. One of those secret activities was hiding Jews. Not just two or three of them, but dozens. The whole spacious first floor of the building served as a shelter. Two large rooms and a kitchen, rough and sparsely furnished, served as the main living space during the day and was turned into bedrooms at night. The access to this area was through a small hatch in the wall just above the floor. It could be easily camouflaged and locked from the inside if necessary. An alarm device with a press button concealed next to the peephole in the front gate downstairs went off softly upstairs if Kazik was forced to open the gate to a stranger.

On my arrival there were fifteen people squatting in the shelter, families, couples, single folk of all ages. Another eight people had left only a day before, thus making room for us; all the rest hoped to leave soon. It was some time before we learnt where they were going.

During company working hours we had to keep to our living space and make no noise, but after four we were free to use all the floor and feel at ease. Nobody could see or hear us – unless of course we were too noisy, as there was a German sentry situated just opposite our house, at the corner of Nowy Świat and Świętokrzyska Street. Kazik and his mother did all our shopping and delivered it daily after four. Only then could we cook and eat: a smell of cooking coming from the supposedly deserted upstairs floor would have aroused the suspicions of the German clerks working downstairs.

It was quite a pleasant life compared to how we had lived before. Though sharing days and nights with strangers, sleeping next to them, having no privacy at all, was not what we particularly liked, we nevertheless felt much better with them than on our own. My health improved greatly too, due partly to the medicines prescribed by the kind doctor, but mostly because there were other people to talk to.

I have long forgotten the names and the faces of most of the people with whom we briefly shared this hiding place. But there was one man who left a strong impression on me and whom I still remember. Mr Lusternik, a writer, spent most of the day crouching on his mattress, scribbling non-stop in the semi-darkness. In the evening he would read his new story aloud to anybody who wanted to listen. I always did. I was very moved by his stories. They were all about the tragic events of the past two years, about the people from the Warsaw ghetto. One morning I crouched on my mattress and wrote my own short story which I give here in abbreviated form. It was based on an incident that I had heard from an eyewitness:

A lonely teenage boy was caught in a roundup and dragged to the *Umschlagplatz* together with a crowd of screaming, lamenting people. The boy did not scream but walked silent, aloof, holding his only property: a violin. In the *Platz*, swollen with human misery, resounding with cries, shots and hoots of the train leaving for the gas chambers of Treblinka, he was noticed by Commandant Brandt, the chief of the *Umschlagplatz*, well known for his cruelty as well as for his occasional fits of benevolence that sometimes saved someone's life. This time Brandt was in just such a mood. He stopped the boy and ordered him to play. An uncanny silence at once superseded the uproar. People huddled together to make room for the field-grey uniforms that pushed their way through the crowd, eager for entertainment. In the middle of the little clearing, the slim, pale boy with the violin shivered from fear in front of the bulky Nazi. For a while he could not bring himself to start, his fingers trembled. Then, suddenly, he played. It was a subtle, inspired music which sounded like a prayer, like a mighty call for help to God himself. The condemned and the butchers held their breath. They all believed the life of the gifted child was going to be saved. The boy knew it, too, and smiled. He finished with rich powerful chords of thanksgiving. There was silence again. The boy waited. The listeners waited, too. Commandant Brandt stood numb, spellbound. Raising himself, he glanced at his watch and pointed at the boy: 'Same time tomorrow,' he said with a spark of amusement. 'He'll play in Treblinka.' And, as if to himself, he added, 'Pity!'

This story might sound mawkish today, but it was true. The war, the holocaust saw such stories by the hundreds, day in day out, hour after hour.

I let Mr Lusternik read my story the same night. He sat silent for a long while, then said that I should start writing about everything I had seen and heard in the ghetto, since it was very important to record what had happened and leave a written testimony behind in case we did not survive.

We were sitting together on the edge of a vast wooden box full of books in one of the deserted rooms. Mr Lusternik smoked and offered me one of his cigarettes. This is how both my writing and smoking started.

Soon after that Mr Lusternik vanished from my life. He left the shelter. Most of the remaining inhabitants were getting ready to leave, too. By then we knew where they were going. They paid fortunes, and were prepared to pay much more, to be transferred to a camp in Vittel, a spa in the Nazi-occupied part of France. They had been assured that in this camp they would live safe and in some comfort till the end of the war. The secret partners in the deal were Nazi officials.

The transit point where the volunteers gathered and waited for a few weeks to be transferred to Vittel was Hotel Polski in Długa Street. The people who had left the shelter just before we came were still waiting for their transfer. And with Kazik as a go-between they kept sending messages to their former inmates urging them to come. Apparently life in Hotel Polski was like a holiday camp. People were well fed, free to do whatever they wished; in the evenings young girls and boys walked freely in the street, safe with special permits.

This picture made Sophie and me long to join the lucky party and go to Vittel. Mother was no less excited but afraid that the price might be too high. Besides, she wanted Stefan and Jadwiga to go with us. She sent them a long letter via Auntie Maria. Stefan's answer was a blunt: No! Even if he could afford the money, he would never trust the Nazis. He smelt a rat. And right he was. Only after the war did it emerge that the Vittel affair was a German death trap. Instead of going to Vittel, all the victims of the hoax were sent to concentration camps and murdered.

When most of our inmates had left, we felt suddenly deserted. Only three people were still left: Mr Lusternik's aged mother who had to wait until her son raised more money for her to join the party, and a middle-aged couple, Ralf and Olga. Ralf was bedridden with rheumatic fever. We hoped that Stefan and Jadwiga would come and live with us in Nowy Swiat. They felt they should leave the Koterbas in peace: Mr Koterba, good, honest man as he was, was terribly anxious with them under his roof. He kept praying day and night and was about to fall into religious mania. Their coming was easily agreed with Kazik and a date fixed.

On the evening of Stefan and Jadwiga's expected arrival, we were out of our wits with excitement. I still remember how I prepared a special treat for them: hard-boiled eggs doused with sour cream and sprinkled with chives. We waited in vain, however. The curfew came and they failed to turn up.

We heard their story from Auntie Maria a few days later. They were walking arm in arm along Nowy Swiat, Stefan's nose partly shaded by a black eye patch. They were just about to reach our place, when two strangers stopped them and accused them of being Jewish. Since Stefan flatly denied this, they demanded he prove he was not. They pulled them both by force into an open gate next to ours. When Stefan refused to unbutton his trousers, they threatened to call the German guard from the opposite corner. This made Stefan change his tactics. He asked the scoundrels what they wanted to leave him alone. They wanted everything they could lay their hands on. They robbed Stefan and Jadwiga of their wristwatches, fountain pens, cash. Then disappeared.

Going to Kazik's place was now out of the question: the brutes might still be around. For the same reason it would be risky to go straight back to the Koterbas. Stefan and Jadwiga entered the nearest church and hid in a dark aisle. Soon the sacristan, unaware of their presence, locked the church for the night. There they stayed till the morning, when they went back to the Koterbas.

With all my recent hopes brought to nothing, I lapsed into brooding. There was hardly anyone to talk to. Mrs Lusternik was not the kind of sweet old lady one could cuddle up to. Ralf and Olga, bright and amiable, were far too concerned about Ralf's disease to take interest in anything else.

I was now in charge of our security arrangements. Kazik told me exactly what to do if the alarm went off, and on the same evening tested me, pressing the button in the gate. We were not frightened because we had been warned of a rehearsal. Leaning out of the hatch I took hold of a special loop attached to a big, heavy sack of coal left outside our hiding place and swiftly pulled it over tight to the wall; then I barred the hatch from inside. When, after three minutes, Kazik came upstairs to check my performance, all he could see were deserted rooms littered with wooden boxes and heavy sacks. It was dead quiet around, nobody would have guessed there were six souls hiding next door, or even that 'next door' existed at all. Kazik praised me in his curt way, making me almost happy for a while.

Since there was now plenty of space, we could move from our mattresses in the middle of the room to the beds next to the boarded window, which gave us more light and a glimpse of the street through the gaps. From my bed I could see the German sentry opposite and the Cedergren, one of the highest buildings in prewar Warsaw which housed the telecommunications company. Time and again I caught glimpses of German soldiers marching along Nowy Swiat in the roadway singing *Heili Heilo*. This hideous song was my only musical entertainment; my sole visual pleasure was gazing at Roman's photograph, already crumpled and worn. A year had just passed since I had fallen in love with Roman. It seemed hopelessly long compared to the mere three weeks we had spent together.

Our one consolation were books that Kazik had stacked for his lodgers in a large wooden box. There were books of all imaginable kinds piled up at random for readers of various tastes: Shakespeare buried under trashy love stories, westerns mixed up with odd volumes of Proust. Mother, Sophie and I would browse among them for hours in the faint light from the cracks in the boarded windows, pick up two or three at a time, read them through during the day, and start browsing again the following evening.

Days were long now. Having nothing better to do we went to bed early. One day, on the last night of June, I lay in my bed trying in vain to fall asleep. It was hot; dim light from the dwindling day still crept through the cracks in the boarded windows; my neighbours breathed steadily, only Ralf moaned in his sleep. Suddenly in this weird stillness the alarm went off, peep . . . peep . . . peep . . . I jumped out of bed and swiftly, smoothly did all I was supposed to do. Instantly awakened, my neighbours sat up, petrified. At first we all thought it was just another rehearsal, this time without previous warning. Three, five, eight minutes went by, however, and there was no sound of Kazik. At last we heard steps behind the wall. And voices . . . Yes, there were loud male voices, none of them Kazik's voice. I felt my blood run cold, Sophie was trembling next to me. The shuffling sounds of heavy objects being pushed away left little doubt that the strangers were searching for our hiding place. They quickly cleared the wall of sacks and boxes and, unaware of the hatch just above the floor, started banging at the wall with something sounding like spade handles or gun butts. They were making an awful noise.

Deadly scared yet composed, I tried to think what to do. My mind was sound and clear. Somebody knew about our shelter. They knew exactly where it was. Sooner or later they would force it open and get hold of us. If they were Nazis we were lost. If they were only blackmailers we still stood a chance. But the terrible noise they were making might attract the attention of the sentry on the opposite corner, in which case we were lost again. The first thing to do was to stop the noise. 'We have to let them in,' I whispered. Nobody said a word. Barefooted in my nightshirt, I moved close to the wall and shouted, 'Stop banging. We're letting you in.' The turmoil stopped at once.

I bent down, shoved the iron bar away, pushed the hatch door open. Instantly I was seized by my hair and dragged out. Dazzled by the sharp light of a torch, I could vaguely see the man who held my hair in a firm grip: he was short, wore a German uniform, and pointed a gun straight at my head. Another man, tall, dressed in civilian clothes, lit up my face with the torch and stared at it closely. There was a third figure crouching in the dark whom I recognised as Kazik's mother.

'How many are there of you all together?' asked the civilian sternly. He spoke in Polish. '*Beantworte, schnell, schnell, du verfluchtes Schwein*' ('Answer, quickly, quickly, you damn swine') yelled the German pulling wildly at my hair and pressing the gun to my temple. 'Six,' I said. '*Luge!*' ('Lie!') roared the German. 'How many men among you?' 'Just one.' '*Luge!*' 'What kind of weapons have you got?' the tall man sounded less stern this time. I recovered my wits: they were afraid of us. 'Go in, check yourself,' I answered boldly. In response I received a hard kick from the German. For a while the two men whispered over my head. I managed to catch the German words for: 'You go, I stay,' 'No, you go.' Finally, I was handed over to the Pole in return for the torch. Holding both the torch and the gun, the man in uniform crept into the hatch and disappeared from sight.

As a hostage, I was left in the dark with the tall man who firmly pressed me to his side, as if I might try to run away. He was silent. Little by little I could feel his grip slacken. Gradually it became less hostile, more like a love embrace. Only now did I realise I was just in my nightshirt. Panic-stricken, I groped with one free hand for the old woman. She was sitting on the floor next to me, dead quiet. I felt a little better.

Soon the short man reappeared in the hatch summoning his companion to join him inside. I was pushed into the hatch followed by my oppressor, Kazik's mother left behind in the dark. The candles we always kept ready in our rooms just in case were now lit. The two men started searching Ralf's bed, causing him severe pain. They found nothing under the mattress nor under the sore body itself. They ordered us to sit down on the edge of the bed one next to the other and launched a thorough hunt, turning over other beds, drawers, bundles of our clothes. They looked much more relaxed now. For no visible reason, the German would now and again utter a wild roar, while the civilian smiled and seemed quite friendly. It dawned on me that they were playing a 'bad guy–good guy' game as if they expected to gain something this way. This could mean that we were not yet lost.

My guess was soon confirmed. While the bad guy was busy searching the kitchen, the good one came over, sat on a little table, lit a cigarette and began to talk 'privately'. He asked what our names were, what kind of illness kept Ralf in bed; he even said he was sorry for him. Then, with his eyes he pointed at the kitchen. He whispered, 'Be careful with him. He's a dangerous man.' It was the starting point for negotiations. Mother took the chance immediately. 'What does he want?' she whispered too, falling into line with the game. The tall man pondered a long while. 'Well . . .' he said at last with a false reluctance, 'I'm very much afraid he intends to take you all to the Gestapo, and there is nothing I can do to stop him, unless . . . unless . . . you can collect between you a sum of money large enough to satisfy him.' He stared at us with an expression of deep concern and pity. 'Think it over,' he added. 'I'll leave you for a while to let you discuss the matter on your own.' He stubbed out his cigarette, got off the table and came close to me. 'I'd like a word with you,' he said sternly again. 'Let's go outside!' I shuddered in my nightshirt and was just opening my mouth to say 'No' when the bad guy turned up from the kitchen. He heard his colleague's last words and shrieked out, pointing his gun at me, '*Raus, raus!*' ('Out, out!')

Shivering with cold and fear, I found myself with the tall man in the darkness again. Returning to his good-guy part, he gently pressed my hand. 'I'd like to make you an offer, my dear,' he said softly. 'I can see you're a nice girl, good-looking as well as brave. I have decided to help you. I'll take you with me to my own villa. You'll live safe with me there till the end of the war, or maybe for ever. Do you accept?' 'No!' I screamed spontaneously, but, controlling myself, instantly changed my tone. 'No,' I repeated gently. 'I appreciate your offer but can't accept it. Never in my life would I part from my mother and sister.' 'Think first of yourself, my girl,' insisted the man coming close and putting his arm around my waist. 'You can still change your mind.' His face was now touching mine, his hands wandering over my unprotected body. He was trying to push me away from the hatch to the darkest corner of the room. I began to struggle wildly with him. In vain – he held me in a firm grip, pressing me down to the floor. Unexpected help came suddenly from the dark. 'Leave that girl alone, sir,' said the old woman in the way peasants address their juniors. 'Can't you see she's just a child?' The tall man jumped aside as if ashamed of being caught red-handed. Furious, he forgot all about his good-guy part. 'Get off, you old hag,' he roared, and groped for Kazik's mother crouching in the shade. He slapped her face and forced her into the hatch. Calming down, he came back to me. But the precious seconds of delay were all I needed to collect my wits. 'Sir,' I said gravely, 'you were kind to me and that's why I feel obliged to warn you. I'm ill, you see, with this worst kind of disease . . .' He stopped dead in his tracks, his arms still stretched to seize me. I expected a blow, but it did not come. He stood thinking, uncertain what to do next. I felt he did not believe me but was too cautious to take a risk. All the tension gone, he icily told me to go back to the shelter and followed me in silence.

The whole incident did not last more than ten minutes. Meantime, Mother, Olga and Mrs Lusternik, the latter sick from fear, managed among them to pile up quite a few bank notes on the little table. The bad guy was back in the kitchen gulping vodka from a flask he had apparently brought with him, and munching our pickled gherkins. Without a word the tall man started counting the bank notes. Over his shoulder Mother was looking at me in agony. I answered her unasked question with a reassuring wink. 'Well,' said the good guy, tucking the bank notes into his pocket, 'not bad for a start, but I bet he'll say it's not enough. There are six of you, after all. He can get as much as that if he turns you over to the Gestapo.' 'That's all we've got,' said Olga bluntly. 'Any gold, silver, precious stones?' the man gripped Olga's hand. 'You've got a nice ring, my dear! Each of you must have something of the kind.' Olga had also a string of pearls on her neck, her husband a gold fob pocket watch on a gold chain. The old lady quickly produced her gold-framed spectacles and an antique brooch. Sophie and I had nothing, but Mother could hardly conceal her favourite watch and wedding ring. Urged by the man's stern gaze, she took them off reluctantly and put them on the table next to the other jewels. Good guy took out his handkerchief and raked them all into it. While he was busy fastening the knot, Mother suddenly asked him to leave her the wedding ring. She did not implore, she was far from humiliating herself by begging, she only said that the ring was of a great sentimental value to her. Was the tall man so deeply concerned with his good-guy role, or was he not completely rotten, after all? I did and do not know. Anyway, with a big gesture of magnanimity he dug out the wedding ring from his handkerchief, looked around, then flung it high up onto the top of the tiled stove. Pleased with himself, he winked at Mother, which meant that he and she were partners in cheating the bad guy.

The man in the uniform had finished his feast and came back from the kitchen, drunk and noisy. After a brief exchange of whispers with his 'assistant' he roared at us to get '*raus*', which the tall man translated as an order to go down to the ground floor and stay there until further notice. Since Ralf was unable to move, they ordered him to lie still on his bed facing the wall. They forbade us to get dressed or take anything with us.

So we left the first floor as we were, in our nightshirts and bare feet. Kazik's mother led the way. She took us to her own flat. Evidently someone else lived there apart from Kazik and herself: a young woman of unusual beauty was just suckling her newborn baby. She looked frightened to death. There was little doubt she was Jewish too. With her and the old woman we sat for hours, while the night wore on. There was no sign of Kazik. We believed he must be hiding somewhere very near. We also knew without asking that the baby was his.

At dawn the good guy turned up to take the key from the front gate. Soon we heard muffled sounds of heavy loads being dragged down and shuffled along. Then the key rasped in the lock, the gate creaked, groaned and banged. They were gone.

When we went back upstairs the rooms had been neatly cleared of anything of any saleable value, all our clothes, shoes, even towels gone, Kazik's pans, cups and cutlery taken, only the meagre furniture left. Mother pulled a chair to the stove, climbed up and groped for the wedding ring. Amazingly, it was there. We took it as a good omen.

Later Kazik showed up, more taciturn than ever. He knew everything that had happened last night, which only confirmed our guess that he had been hiding in the same building. Without a word he examined the emptied rooms, then said that he would make sure we left the place safely within hours. Our cover was blown, nobody could hide here any longer.

In our nightshirts and barefooted we waited till the afternoon. Just after four, when the company staff had left, Kazik turned up again bringing us money from Auntie Maria and some clothes to put on. He also brought a new black hat with a veil and bandages. Mother, Sophie and I were going to a temporary shelter. Kazik had already fixed it for us with a friend. Ralf, Olga and Mrs Lusternik had to wait a little longer until a fake ambulance would take them to Hotel Polski. We wished them good luck and went away.

Our new shelter was in the Old Town. This time we walked, it was near. When we reached Plac Zamkowy – the Castle Square – an inconspicuous figure in a grey suit moved off from King Zygmunt's monument and began to follow us. Without speaking a word, the man overtook us and led us through the tangle of narrow old streets.

In an ancient house coated with the grime of past centuries, in a bleak ground-floor room, a young woman called Krystyna was already waiting for us. She and her husband Tom, who had just led us there, were used to unexpected visitors, she said – people on the run often stopped here for a while. We were welcome to stay until we could find something better than their shabby place.

The place was really sordid, dark and damp. The two windows of the large single room were right at street level, passers-by could easily peep in, which they did from time to time. The only way for us to keep out of sight and avoid strangers who visited our hosts on business was to sit still on the sofa screened by a wardrobe at the back of the room. This we did, day after day, from early morning till dark when the windows were blacked-out for the night. Krystyna would bring us food there and talk kindly to us. Both she and Tom were fine, brave people. Having no children, they were engrossed in their work. Tom worked somewhere as a printer. Once home, he disappeared into the cellar which belonged to the flat and stayed there till late at night, printing underground leaflets and bulletins. Krystyna helped him with all fervour. We were let into this secret on the first day, since they trusted us as we trusted them. Besides, we could see their crude printing device each time when at night – and only then – we went down to the cellar to wash and use the rough toilet fixed next to the secret workshop. Recklessly, Krystyna confessed to us that the cellar also housed many weapons buried under the floor, as well as piles of forged documents and bank notes.

It was obvious that our living on this volcano was very dangerous both for us and for them, and for this reason it could not last long. We waited for word from Auntie Maria who knew our plight but for security's sake was not supposed to come there until she had found another hiding place to take us to.

For six or seven days we sat dumb behind the wardrobe unable even to read since it was too dark there. At night we shared the room with Tom and Krystyna, sleeping on the floor. One morning, soon after Tom had gone to work, someone banged abruptly at the window pane. Krystyna rushed out to see what it was. She returned shattered. A friend had brought news that Tom had just been grabbed by Gestapo men on the doorstep of his works, bundled into a vehicle and driven away. The friend warned her that she should expect a house search any moment, which Krystyna was well aware of herself. She begged us to leave at once, and ran down to the cellar to hide the printing machine.

The Black Widow, the Wounded Child and the Mediterranean-looking girl were in the street again, under the blazing sun of a hot summer day. Shocked by the speed of events, bewildered by their disguise, Mother and Sophie could hardly think. It was I who had to make decisions. But I was shocked too. Petrified, we stood next to the gate not knowing where to go. Strangers gaped at us in amazement. Something had to be done at once.

A hansom cab suddenly came round the corner and clattered slowly along the cobble stones. It was free. On a sudden desperate impulse I stopped it and we got in. 'Where to, Miss?' asked the cabman. My mind went blank. 'Where to?' repeated the man, staring at me apprehensively. Then, from the void, a well-known, much-loved place jumped into my mind. '5 Sienna Street,' I ordered. The cabman smacked at his horse.

We were now swinging through the city centre, making our way to the house of my childhood that had lain in ashes since the siege. In a while the old man would ask me, annoyed, 'Where are we going from here, Miss?' We turned into Świętokrzyska Street and were about to reach Marszałkowska Street when, in a sudden flash of recognition, I asked the man to stop. I paid him the full fare, muttering something about the beautiful weather and our desire to walk. Two cheerful ladies barged into the vacated cab taking it away. From where we stood the familiar gate was already visible. We had just a few steps to walk.

Tears filled Grandad Sokolnicki's eyes; I could see them glitter as he called to his wife to come and see who was here. She came tripping along, shadowed by Klara. They both burst into tears.

It soon turned out that we were particularly lucky: Mrs Serbin and the Bachs were away, spending July in the countryside. The Woman was off as well. Maryla had moved to another shelter soon after our blackmailing last May. So there were just these three at home, not counting Miki, the mongrel. We could stay with them, of course, and rest, and forget all about our hardship for a while, they assured us keenly. So we stayed.

When the tears had been wiped away, we soberly talked the whole matter over. It was decided that we would have to leave before Mrs Serbin came back from her holidays. She would never have us back again, and would bitterly reproach her parents for exposing her home to such a risk. She should not even know we were here. Auntie Maria and Staś were called and both came almost at once. Since 1 July they had been looking for a new 'place' for us anyway. They promised to do their best.

In the meantime we were caressed and spoiled by the three Sokolnickis who refused to hear about money, even for our keep. And they did all they could to make up for the paltry meals we had once endured under their roof. It was like basking peacefully on a safe, warm island amidst a roaring sea. For a while, just for a while . . . Soon a day came when we had to say goodbye again and leave for good.

The well-dressed lady whispered all the way. She told me all about her relatives who had generously agreed to have me with them. Her brother-in-law, she explained, was a talented pianist who, because of that awful war, had to earn his living by playing in a Warsaw club night after night. Her sister was a wonderful woman, I'd soon see for myself. And Mirka, her niece, was a lovely, lovely girl, exactly my age, pining for a friend, impatient to meet me. To the neighbours, acquaintances and anybody else I would be introduced as Mirka's close friend who had come to spend the summer holidays with her. Nobody would be suspicious, the lady was pretty sure, because my Polish was so perfect, no accent, no sound of the you-know-what in it. I would enjoy myself and breathe fresh air till the end of September – my stay had been paid for in advance up to this date. Later we would see.

The little suburban train rolled slowly along through fields and woods. Despite my guide's enthusiasm, I felt no excitement. All my thoughts were with Mother and Sophie who, in disguise, were now making their way in a different direction. We had had to separate, goodness knows for how long, because Danka, Zina's and Mrs Koterba's younger sister, who had decided to take Mother and Sophie, had room only for two. Besides, due to Auntie Maria's endeavours, I had got the unique opportunity of going to the country to an inconspicuous holiday resort in the woods. This was sorely needed as my health had deteriorated again.

The ancient train, panting and coughing, rumbled into a grubby place that hardly could have been called a 'railway station' had it not been for the board announcing *Radość* (which in Polish means 'Joy'). It came to a halt. My companion jumped to her feet. We had arrived.

The picture of the Majewski family that had been so beautifully painted by my guide had very little to do with the people I met in the little wooden cottage which was going to be my new 'home'. The father was a dreary fellow, peevish and quarrelsome. He spent his nights away, commuting to Warsaw. He returned early in the morning and slept till the afternoon. Then, unkempt, he would loll about in his pyjamas making a fuss about anything that came to his mind, senselessly bullying his wife and scolding his daughter. He looked at me as though I were transparent: I did not exist for him. He did not even bother to say 'Hello' when I first entered the house.

The mother was a harassed little woman, humble in her husband's presence, sour and nagging when he was away. If she ever addressed me it was just to tell me what I should or should not do.

But the greatest disappointment was Mirka, my 'friend'. Tall, slim with faded hair and a blank face, she looked rather silly. She dismissed my arrival with a neglectful nod, not even taking her eyes from her toenails which she was varnishing bright red. From the start I knew that I would have nothing in common with her. On that first night I felt lost and was about to beseech my travelling companion to take me back with her to Warsaw. When she and her brother-in-law left I did not know what to do with myself. Then I got the shock of hearing that I was going to have to share a bed with Mirka. By then I was already used to sharing a bed and did not mind sleeping with Mother or Sophie. But the very idea of Mirka snoring next to me seized me with horror. Luckily, she did not like it either, fetched herself a deckchair, and slept in it thereafter.

Despite the miserable start, my life in Radość was not all gloom. I was allowed, even encouraged, to go out and walk freely whenever I wished, to behave as an ordinary girl enjoying her summer holidays. So, instead of basking in the sun in the garden and listening to Mirka's prattle about fashionable clothes and boys, I walked into the forest and stayed there alone. It was as if all the dreams of my restless nights in the ghetto had suddenly come to life. Stretched out on the warm, fragrant moss, I watched the tops of the slender pines swaying in the wind, listened to their soft sighing and to sweet trills of birdsong. Nobody was around; sunbeams knitted their way down through the tangle of branches leaving long streaks of hazy brightness in the air; ants toiled laboriously building their hills.

Once on a rainy day, I ventured a walk to the tiny centre of the village and came across a small public library. Nothing in the world, not even the risk of being recognised, could have stopped me from entering. My pocket money proved enough to pay the modest fee. I left the place carrying two books. Now I could read in the forest, so I stayed there all day. I gave up my midday meals, reluctant to go back to the cottage even for a short while. I did not mind starving.

And starving it was. Mrs Majewski insisted on Mirka and me having our meals together, just the two of us. This meant that I had to share the meagre helpings with my friend. Brazen and callous, Mirka would eat at such a speed that, as a rule, there was little left for me. I could have tried to compete with her, have increased my own speed of eating, grabbed the sandwiches or potatoes one after another, and swallowed them without chewing. But this seemed undignified, I preferred to starve. The evening meals when I had to munch my tiny bits in the dreary presence of the father were a true ordeal. I loathed and despised that man, not only because of his rude behaviour, but also because he worked for the Nazis playing in their clubs. There was little doubt about this – there were no Polish nightclubs in occupied Warsaw.

There were some miserable days when I could not plunge into my green seclusion because of rain. On those bleak days I had to put up with Mirka's company, listen to her silly talk, often spend hours with her friends who were strangers to me. There was a cat in the cottage who I thought of as my only friend. Though not particularly fond of cats, I really liked that one. She was pregnant and soon gave birth to five kittens. It took place in the kitchen and was closely watched by Mirka, her mother and myself. We were all excited. For once I shared some feelings with those two. It was the first time I had ever witnessed the act of a creature coming to life. It was a weighty and warm experience.

Two days later, one rainy afternoon, I was left on my own in the cottage, all the family having gone to Warsaw to buy a dress for Mirka, a gift for her approaching saint's day. I went to the kitchen and, undisturbed, watched the bare blind little creatures tumbling helplessly and sucking at the cat. It was quiet, the kitchen was thoroughly cleaned, the freshly scrubbed floor covered with old newspapers. Idly, unconsciously, my eyes turned away from the kittens and wandered along the papers. Suddenly a flash of recognition struck me like a thunderbolt. I saw my father's name and surname printed in a long column of other names and surnames. I seized the paper from the floor and desperately tried to make out what this list was all about. There were pages and pages covered with names and surnames matched with dates of birth and military ranks. Sometimes just the rank followed the word 'Unknown'. The newspaper itself I easily identified as *Nowy Kurier Warszawski*, the only Warsaw daily appearing in Polish, which was known as a Nazi publication spreading Nazi lies and for that reason despised by Poles and never read by us. When I finally found the page with the beginning of the list, I made out from a brief introductory note that the names had been published daily for weeks or even months. The note said it was a list of Polish officers from Russian internment camps murdered by the Russians and recently discovered by German troops in mass graves near Katyń. Shocked, trembling, I read the list from the beginning and found my Uncle Józef's name too. Were they really dead? No, I could not believe it. It was certainly Nazi propaganda, one more cruel lie. The Russians would never do such a thing. Why should they murder those people? I knew from Stefan that they had treated them well. There was only one explanation, I thought, calming down: when the German Army had entered Russia and occupied the part of the country where the camps had been, they had seized the lists of ex-prisoners and now, cunningly, were accusing their enemy of committing these crimes. In fact, I comforted myself, Father, Józef and all the prisoners must certainly have been transferred by the Russians somewhere else when the Germans were approaching and were now probably working hard in a Siberian labour camp, or had joined the Red Army to fight together against Nazi Germany. The day would come when I would see them again, if only I could manage to survive myself. The only real danger were the Nazis. No one else in the whole world could match their cruelty, I believed. Then, suddenly, it dawned on me that the Nazis might have murdered the abandoned prisoners themselves and blamed the crime on the Russians. Horror wrung my heart like an iron claw. Sinking into despair, I went to bed to avoid seeing Mirka on her return. I had nobody to talk to. I was alone with my fear, my grief. I decided that Mother should not hear about the list: she would lose all her will to live if she thought that Father was dead. I promised myself never to tell her about my discovery if I ever saw her again. Later I kept my promise, until she heard about Katyń from someone else.

During the days that followed I kept silent, sharing my grief with no one. Both Mirka and her mother were now living for the saint's day party, and feverish preparations for the occasion were going on in the cottage. The great day came at last and a large group of girls and boys arrived for a festive meal and games. At the long table made up in the garden from all the small ones that neighbours could lend, I sat withdrawn, ignored by the others. I was served with an individual plate containing bits of everything that the other visitors had freely helped themselves to. But even my sense of humiliation was muffled by grief.

Soon after Mirka's memorable party my seventeenth birthday came. I kept this a secret, too; it was nobody's business. The day was bright and so I went to the forest early in the morning and stayed there till late afternoon. When I returned to the cottage, Majewski in his pyjamas was waiting for me in the garden. 'I have bad news for you,' he said, addressing me for the first time and staring through me at the wooden fence. 'There was a stranger hanging about all morning, asking questions about you. In these circumstances, you can't stay in my house any longer.'

It soon transpired that his sister-in-law had already been called to take me away. She arrived promptly and took me back to Warsaw the same evening. No friendly words were uttered when I said goodbye, no tears shed. On the train my companion said she had known a couple of days earlier that I would have to leave Radocść, and had already been in touch with Auntie Maria who would soon take care of me. She said nothing about the money that had been paid in advance for the remaining six weeks of my stay with Majewski. I had no doubt that Mirka's father had invented the nosy stranger just to get rid of me and keep the money. Clearly, my guide knew this too and felt uneasy. Actually she was not a bad sort. She took me to her home and put me up for the night in her own room. Auntie Maria appeared first thing in the morning and I travelled with her to Rembertów, where Mother and Sophie could hardly wait to see me again.

The six months I spent with the Bieliński family on the first floor of their plain, detached little house in Rembertów was the longest and the least eventful spell of my life on the run. We lived through those months quietly and comfortably enough, though in full confinement: not going out at all, unseen by strangers. Between my arrival and the day when eventually we had to leave this quiet place, we were seized by terror only once, about which I shall speak later. It was there that, undisturbed, I took to writing.

Rembertów was an ordinary little town near Warsaw which I had never seen before. Its only remarkable features were a big military firing ground and a factory, both converted by the Germans to their use during the occupation. The factory employed Polish workers and was the main source of livelihood for the local population. Mr Bieliński, our landlord, worked there too. Though a skilled worker, he earned far too little to keep a family of four. Danka, his wife, who was a midwife with no proper qualifications, tried hard to supplement the family budget by performing abortions, or travelling to the countryside, buying food there and selling it at a higher price in Warsaw. Both practices were illegal and severely penalised by the Nazis. Very exhausting, too. No wonder Danka gladly agreed to take us under her roof as a substitute for her risky travelling and a chance of a better life for her family and herself. We paid her far less than we had paid Mrs Serbin and in return ate no less than the members of the family, whose standards had improved with our arrival. We also had a well-heated room for ourselves, at least for most of the day. At night we shared this room with Danka and her eight-year-old daughter, Ela, while Mr Bieliński and his son Bogdan, who was thirteen, slept in the neighbouring room. At first Danka was reluctant to take three lodgers: there were not enough beds for three. But with great kindness she solved that problem by putting Mother and myself in the double bed, taking Ela into her own narrow one, and giving Sophie a baby's cot secured with a net, in which the little girl had slept before.

Two rooms, a kitchen and a small loft which housed a rough lavatory, were all the space the Bielińskis had. The ground floor of the house was occupied by widow Pawlik and her teenage daughter. While at home on our own, we had to keep dead quiet: Mr Bieliński insisted on nobody knowing about us, not even the Pawlik women who seemed totally harmless. From our window, screened with a muslin curtain during the day, we could see the little garden, the gate and people walking in the street. If a suspicious-looking stranger appeared at the gate we were supposed to run up to the loft and hide there. There was a narrow gap between the loft ceiling and the roof, which provided enough space for us to hide. To get there we had to climb up a heap of timber, crawl through a narrow passage, then lie flat next to each other with no way of moving or even breathing properly. We had rehearsed it once or twice and found it terribly hard. Yet it seemed safe.

For most of the day we were in the house with just Danka, Bieliński being at work, the children at school. Usually she kept herself busy in the kitchen, engrossed in her cooking, happy to be free from dangerous travel and illegal trade. Sometimes she sang. She was a lively, good-tempered woman, very much like her elder sister, Mrs Koterba. Only occasionally did she attend to a patient who would secretly slip in early in the morning and leave before the children came back. On these occasions we had to stay dead still in our room while the abortion was performed just behind our locked door. To witness it without the patient knowing we were there, to listen to her moans and screams, to the sickening splashes and Danka's sober remarks, was a nasty experience. Fortunately it happened seldom. Usually I could write quietly till the afternoon when the children came back from school and ran in and out making a lot of noise. They were good children, though, reliable and understanding. We could trust them. They were trained not to speak to strangers, forbidden to tell anybody about anything that happened at home. Danka said so, when at the beginning Mother expressed some doubts. So we trusted the children. Of the two I liked the boy more since he was like his mother: smiling and friendly. Ela took after her father – she was plain, somehow faded, unappealing. Nobody seemed to love that child. She often cried and I was sorry for her, yet I could never bring myself to stroke her greasy hair or kiss her pale cheek. I felt guilty about it.

To Mr Bieliński we hardly ever had a chance to talk. He returned late from work, had his meal in the kitchen, and went to bed soon after. On Sundays he disappeared from home for long hours. He was not a talkative man, anyway, and looked uneasy in our presence. I always had the feeling that he could only just tolerate having us under his roof, while his wife and children he obviously could not even bear to be with. More of that later.

Nobody ever visited the family, apart from Danka's cousin Aniela. We never met her in person since, like everybody else, she was not supposed to know we were there. She usually came in the morning and sat with Danka in the kitchen drinking ersatz coffee and talking a lot. Danka always looked rather upset after her cousin's visits. Once we saw her crying. Since we had become very friendly with her, Mother summoned up the courage to ask her what had made her cry. We were all in bed when this happened, Ela asleep, the light out. Then in the darkness we heard the story of Danka's wretched life.

She was twenty-two when she married Bieliński, who was eight years her senior. It was the real thing, not just a marriage of convenience as happened to many a girl. She was pretty then, dark, plump, keen both to work hard and to enjoy herself. He, though plain, seemed to Danka most desirable. She loved him, and he loved her, and at first they were very happy. But soon after Bogdan was born something suddenly changed. Bieliński cooled down, became irritable, unfriendly. He would not stay at home in his spare time and hardly ever talked to her. Finally he moved from their double bed to a couch. Not long after she learned that he was involved with Aniela, her own cousin. Aniela confessed it to Danka herself since they had always been close friends.

Aniela was Danka's age, resembled her like a sister, and was already married too. It was hard for both of them to understand why Bieliński had fallen head over heels in love with Aniela when he had Danka at home. And love it was, a devouring mutual passion, that had burnt for years and took Bieliński's heart away from his wife. Aniela had left her husband and settled down on her own. She spent all Sundays and holidays with her lover.

At first Danka had fallen into despair, wept her eyes out, wanted to kill herself. Then, little by little, she had stopped crying, had got used to her predicament, had finally given up. Somehow their shared life had returned to normal and lingered along from day to day, affection being replaced by daily routine. And when after a time Ela was born, it was due neither to a miracle nor to Danka's unfaithfulness: she still dearly loved her husband. The two cousins had never stopped seeing each other or ceased to be best friends. For Danka, Aniela became the only person to whom she could open her soul. Having lost her husband's heart, she needed her cousin more than ever. Years passed, the war came. Time and hardship dulled feelings and wore the two women down with fatigue: they were neither young nor attractive any longer.

At this point Danka sighed heavily in the darkness and lapsed into silence. We did not dare break it. But after a while she continued her story. Recently something had changed again.

We were already settled in her home, Danka said, when one rainy morning Aniela arrived, very upset. Restless and haggard, she was not her normal self. She did not even try to hide from Danka what had made her so miserable. She confessed that on the last two Sundays she had waited in vain for Bieliński: he had not shown up, nor had he sent her any word of explanation. It was unusual, it had never happened before and, alarmed, Aniela had come to her cousin expecting to hear the reason from her. Bieliński might have been ill or arrested. But he was neither. He had gone to work as usual, said Danka, and had spent the last two Sundays out, as he always did. The two women then began to wonder together about the strange behaviour of the man they loved. But they could not solve the riddle.

This state of uncertainty lasted for more than two months. Bieliński would leave home each Sunday, but fail to turn up at Aniela's. Gradually the two cousins came to the conclusion that he was involved in underground work. This seemed, however, impossible to believe: he was not that sort. There was no point in asking him directly; Bieliński would not tell the truth to either of his women. 'But the truth will out,' said Danka gravely, sighing again. In her despair, Aniela had begun to spy upon her loved one and had soon discovered his secret. That morning she had come running to Danka to sob her heart out in her arms: Bieliński had a lover, a young widow with whom he worked. The two cousins cried together all morning. There was no consolation for them. Now in bed Danka burst into tears again.

Hiding in other people's homes meant not only losing touch with the world outside, but also putting up with irksome restrictions and constant danger. Confined to a limited space, doomed to idleness, we seemed to have no life of our own. The men and women who sheltered us, even their children, wrestled with their daily problems, had their minor miseries and major dramas, their successes or failures, spells of joy or sadness. Our existence was blank, we just marked time. And having no life of our own, we lived the lives of others, sharing their joys and sorrows. Our concerns changed from one shelter to the next, according to what was important in the lives of our successive landladies and landlords. Some time and several shelters passed before I realised that for the people who sheltered us our presence also meant more than great danger, nuisance or extra income. Somehow it affected them, too. It boosted what was noble in them, or what was base. Sometimes it divided the family, at other times it brought the family together in a shared endeavour to help and survive.

It soon became clear that for Danka our silent presence was a blessing. For the first and only time in her life she had someone to talk to, to unburden herself to without any repercussions, someone uninvolved and ready to listen at any time of the day or night and for as long as she wished to talk. So she talked and we listened, patiently, compassionately. Mother was great at it, so full of understanding. She really knew how to comfort the wretched woman without moral preaching or high-flown words. It helped. Within a few days she had regained her balance. We could hear her singing in the kitchen again.

Danka's story made a strong impression on me. I did not say a word that night but listened greedily to her confessions and to Mother's thoughtful response. I think I learned a great deal from it and somehow matured.

I kept writing – it was for me a god-sent gift, an escape from present time and place. In the evenings I read my stories to Mother and Sophie. It helped them too. They never tried to write down their own memories. They preferred to read books that Danka borrowed for us from the local library, or do some mending for her. They were both far more patient than myself and bore the endless waiting and all the adversities of our daily life without grumbling, while I frantically rebelled to no avail. Though full grown, I still had a great deal to learn from my mother, and had never become as warm-hearted, forbearing and inwardly strong as she was. Sophie took after her to a far greater extent than myself. By then she was almost fourteen, no longer a child. With her slim body and masses of black hair worn in a long thick plait, her dark complexion and sad dark eyes, she grew womanly and attractive. Yet she was still the same silent girl, living mostly in her own inner world. Both she and Mother now knew about the Katyń list, but refused to believe in Father's death. We all trusted he was alive and well. This strong conviction had helped us to survive.

From Halina, who came to see us twice during our stay in Rembertów, we learned about Uncle Władek's death. She had heard it herself from an eyewitness and told us all about it on her first visit. After her husband was shot dead on the outskirts of Warsaw, she had had to take her little son and run away from home. For three months they stayed with her relatives in the country. This was why she had been absent when we had badly needed her help.

Auntie Maria visited us, too, at least twice a month. The news from Jadwiga and Stefan was sad. They had moved from the Koterbas and now lived with some other people. They were just getting used to their new place, when Jadwiga realised she was pregnant. Having a baby when constantly on the run was out of the question. There was not the slightest hope that the war would end before the baby was due. So Stefan and Jadwiga, two people so young and bright, who loved each other so much and were born to become the happy parents of a healthy child, had to quickly take a heart-breaking decision. Helena, the midwife, came promptly to the rescue so the problem was smoothly dealt with. But Jadwiga and Stefan had never recovered from the shock and lived in gloom, profoundly distressed. The news depressed me too and for a long while gave me sleepless nights.

The days, weeks and months of our uneventful life lulled our vigilance. It seemed that the rest of our lives would be as quiet and dull, that nothing would ever change, for better or worse. Winter came and covered the world outside our window with a thick blanket of snow, making our days even more peaceful and lonely. One day, on our own at home, we saw two tall figures approaching the gate. Pitch black, they stood out in sharp contrast to the snow-white garden, some strange, pointed objects protruding from behind their shoulders. They were making their way to the house. 'Gestapo,' murmured Mother, turning deadly pale. We shuddered in terror: without any doubt the most dangerous, the cruellest of the Jew hunters were about to seize us.

In the nick of time we found ourselves in the loft, and with the swiftness that only the greatest fear can beget, squeezed ourselves into the narrow gap under the roof, dropped flat and held our breath. No sound of banging or forcing of the front door came from downstairs, though. For a while we thought the butchers had gone. Then suddenly there came from the top a dreadful noise, as though a horse's hoof was striking straight on our bare brains: they were on the roof, apparently trying to get us that way. We lay numb, counting what we believed to be our last seconds. The noise grew unbearable. Now not just stamping but also some weird loud grinds and bangs pierced our ears, split our skulls: they were destroying the roof to grab us. In this pandemonium of sounds

I suddenly heard Sophie giggle. Quick-witted, she was the first to understand what was really going on up there. In a split second we were all stuffing our mouths with our fists, trying not to burst out laughing. We could hardly stop laughing long after the chimney sweeps had gone and when, swaying from exhaustion, we returned to our room. Later in the evening, all the family had great fun when we told them what had happened. The chimney sweeps' story became the highlight of our shared Christmas dinner, since the children begged us to tell it again and again, they liked it so much.

When, six weeks later, the real danger came we were not even frightened. Perhaps the human ability to live in great fear is limited, perhaps one can get used to living with terror. One way or another, we felt little fear when, all of a sudden, three strangers dressed in long boots and leather jackets opened the door and entered our room one Sunday. Sophie told me later that she saw a wide smile of nice surprise on my face when those three appeared. True enough I had not seen young men for a very long time.

As in the case of the two earlier incidents, we did not know and never found out who the men were and how they had come to track us down. Halina had just arrived on her second visit. It is possible they had followed her from Warsaw, since she was always involved in risky deals that attracted spies. Busy talking, none of us had noticed the strangers at the gate. Bielinski and the children were out, Danka had run downstairs to gossip with the widow Pawlik, leaving the front door unlocked. So, unhindered, they made their way into the house, entered the flat and found us in our room. Whether they knew in advance that we were hiding there was not quite clear. They had no doubts who we were, though, as soon as they saw us. They behaved politely, not even being particularly stern with us. They simply said that they were ordered to take us away and transfer us to a concentration camp, in which we might or might not survive. What a concentration camp meant we already knew only too well. Their threat sounded serious: the men spoke German and could have been Gestapo informers. It took Halina's pluck to offer them a ransom, which after a long hesitation they accepted, and which she gave them, starting with a large sum of Polish zloties and gradually adding to it American dollars and British pounds, until her handbag was empty. Luckily or unluckily, she had a fortune on her, that actually belonged not to her, but to her business partner. Danka on her way back up from the ground floor met the men already rushing down with their loot. A few days later we had to say goodbye to her.

*   *   *

We left Rembertów and went back to Warsaw in the middle of a bleak frosty winter. The blackmailers had left us entirely without money, since all that remained from the sale of the diamond ring had to be repaid to Halina. There was nothing else left to be sold. We would have gone under had it not been for Auntie Maria, who decided to sell a plot of land she had once been given by my grandparents. She sold it promptly so we could continue to hide and live for some time yet. But after this deal we stopped seeing Auntie Maria for a long time: she was terrified that she was being watched and dreaded the danger she might put us in. Staś now took us entirely under his care and became our only link with Auntie Maria.

It was hard to find a hiding place for the three of us and we had to separate again. The weeks that followed I spent with Maryla, who now lived with an elderly spinster. This lady did not mind in the least taking me in; she would not have minded having anybody though all she had was a single room and a kitchen. She was not concerned about money or even her own safety. Once a teacher, she had taken to the occult on her retirement and strongly believed in destiny. 'If I'm due to die tomorrow, I'll die, whether it's a tile falling off the roof or a Nazi shot,' she used to say. And being a sociable, friendly person she enjoyed having people around, provided they took care of their own daily needs. Engrossed in reading the stars and casting horoscopes, she despised all menial tasks and knew very little about things such as cooking. So Maryla and I did it all. It was great fun when, trying to outdo each other in being economical, we broke a record-producing fifteen pancakes from a single egg.

Maryla urged me to start learning English again. I was now particularly keen to learn. I thought that with a knowledge of English I could be useful to the underground which I had always wanted to join. There were so few people in the country who spoke the language. Imagine a wounded British parachutist having to be hidden and looked after by Poles? It sometimes happened, they said. Would I not be a godsend to him? Thus I daydreamed, earnestly repeating:

> I wandered lonely as a cloud
> That floats on high o'er vales and hills,
> When all at once I saw a crowd
> A host, of golden daffodils . . .

Only after thirty years did I realise that my wounded hero would not have understood me because of my dreadful pronunciation.

While I was enjoying my landlady's tales of spirits and Maryla's witty company, Mother and Sophie were going through terrible ordeals. For various reasons they had to leave one shelter after another, to hide in wardrobes and chests, often to walk along the streets in full daylight. One time, Staś, who was making desperate efforts to help them, had to abandon them in a church, while he rushed off to find a friend who, he hoped, might take them to her flat. The friend could not be found at that moment, so Mother and Sophie had to stay in the church for many hours. They were wearing their usual disguises and pretended to be praying all that time. The priest noticed them and took a deep interest in the two miserable figures. He must have guessed who they were and why they kept praying so keenly. When towards evening most of the congregation had left, he brought them food and drink which they badly needed. He also found a few words of Christian consolation for them. Soon after Staś arrived with good news and took Mother and Sophie to his old friend Vala.

'You're not exactly how I imagined,' said Vala when I first went to her place to be with Mother and Sophie again. 'I thought you were just a girl, nothing special. And now I see a young lady.' Her intensely blue eyes, reminding me of porcelain, stared at me in slight apprehension. Though short, round and fifty-two years old, she still looked attractive with her brilliant eyes and fresh rosy complexion. She seemed as excited by my arrival as Mother and Sophie. They felt perfectly at ease with her, though they had known her for only three weeks. All this made me feel at home from the very start and I even kissed Vala, I liked her so much. In her square room, which was also the kitchen and literally stuffed with furniture, a round table was laid for a special meal to celebrate my arrival: a roast chicken garnished with lettuce; an inviting pyramid of vegetable salad glistening with mayonnaise; home-pickled mushrooms; dainty shortcakes still warm from the oven; a decanter of purplish cherry liqueur, Vala's special pride. She told me at once that she was a perfect cook, which Mother and Sophie earnestly confirmed. Later I noticed that she loved to cook, to be praised for it, to watch people eating and to eat what she had cooked herself. That night, devouring Vala's delicacies, sipping her divine concoction, I learnt much more about her.

Vala had no relatives and only a few friends. Her only brother had been caught by the Gestapo in 1940 and she had never heard from him again. All that remained of him were a few books piled on her dressing table: works by Einstein, Rabindranath Tagore and Nietzsche. Vala had never read them herself, she had no interest in scholarly books. Besides, she worked too hard to read anything at all. She had worked like that for most of her adult life. Once, when young, she had been married to a station master. She had been a well-off lady then. But her husband, who was all that any woman could desire, died very young, leaving her childless in her early thirties. She had never remarried; nobody could equal her late husband, no man she knew was like him. She got used to living like a spinster, forgot what love meant. During the war, tired of solitude and pining to care for someone, she took in to her single room a nice Jewish couple and offered them everything she could: safety, warmth, good food. They were very fond of her and she of them, and they lived in harmony together for over a year. Then suddenly . . .

Vala, who was telling me this story at the festive table, stopped and blushed at this point, but prompted by Sophie, who already knew the story by heart, she went on. Last September, only six months ago, she had met at a party someone who told her she was sweet and good-looking despite her age. It came as a shock: she suddenly felt like a woman again, a feeling she had long forgotten. She liked the man: after all these years he was the first who seemed as good as her late husband. Very soon they became a couple. She was happy again. Only her lodgers worried her now. Though Edward had his own little flat, it was hard to keep their presence from him – he wanted to see her home, to pay her visits sometimes. But she knew him too little to tell him about these people – their lives were at stake, after all. The only thing she could do was to find another hiding place for them. She did this and they left bearing no grudge against her; they understood and wished her well. When, after some time, Staś, her brother's good friend, came in desperation to beg her for help in an emergency, she took Mother and Sophie under her roof without hesitation: by then she knew that Edward was a man of integrity, himself involved in the dangerous business of underground resistance. 'No need to describe him to you,' said Vala that first night. 'You can meet him on Sunday and judge for yourself.' The very thought of seeing Edward again, of introducing him as her man to anyone, made her happy. Her joyful mood and the cherry liqueur helped us to forget the squalor of our own existence. We went to bed with a strong belief that all was going to turn out for the best in the near future. How could we guess what was ahead?

Our daily life in Vala's single room in the attic where the other single rooms were occupied by many other lodgers of slender means was not in fact much fun. Vala worked in a factory as a canteen manageress, went to work early each morning, came back after dark. Day after day and for endless hours we were on our own, forced to whisper and move without making a sound in the narrow space between the beds and the cooker, between the round table and the kitchen sink. The neighbours were so close that we could hear them talking and coughing behind the thin walls or when they passed along the shared corridor on their way to the shared lavatory. They could equally well have heard us in our supposedly empty room if we had not been constantly on our guard when Vala was out. Only when she returned in the evening could we relax to some extent, but not too much, since everyone around thought that she lived in the room alone. Vala did the shopping on her way back from work and started cooking at once. She would not trust us to make the meal, she was convinced that we could not cook as well as her. She was right, of course. At table she usually whispered a lot, telling us all about her day and making plans for the next Sunday. Before going to bed we waited for all the neighbours to fall asleep. Vala would pop out into the corridor time and again, until there was no light coming through the keyholes and cracks of the nearest doors. Only then, one by one, could we steal to the toilet – during the day we had to use a rough substitute just in emergency. But emergency happened rarely: through our years on the run we had learnt to wait.

Sundays were different. Vala would be at home cooking from the early morning, making ready for her visitor with great excitement. Infected by her mood of joyous anticipation, we would also wash our hair, put on our better dresses, clean our shoes. Usually Edward turned up at breakfast time and stayed till after lunch. He was a tall handsome man, eight years younger than Vala. In his dark Sunday suit he looked a bit too solemn for my taste, yet his deep voice and gentle manners compensated for it. He was an ex-serviceman and now worked as a clerk at the Post Office headquarters. Being divorced, he lived alone and seemed to need Vala no less than she him. He was deeply devoted to her and lavishly praised her meals. To us he was kind and considerate. When coming or leaving he always kissed Mother's hand, shook mine earnestly and embraced Sophie in a fatherly way. After lunch Edward and Vala would go for a long walk, or perhaps to his place. She never said a word about her Sunday afternoons when she returned, full of cheer, just before curfew. So it went on for several weeks.

Easter was approaching and Vala decided to throw a party, to see good friends, and provide some distraction for us. Our guests arrived on Easter Monday: Edward, more solemn than ever; Staś, radiant and friendly, just as he had been a year before, with his gramophone; Maryla, my wittiest aunt; and, last but not least, Uncle Leo. We had not seen Uncle Leo since we had stayed with him for a while in the ghetto in the tragic days of July 1942. Meantime he had been hiding on the 'Aryan' side. Being an active, courageous man he never stayed long in hiding but moved boldly from place to place working as a doctor for the resistance. He had grown a long moustache to disguise his Jewish features, wore long boots and a leather jacket, and felt almost safe with his 'good' birth certificate which stated in black and white that he was the natural son of a prostitute and had been christened in a parish church as Konstanty Woźniak. In February, just after I had left, he moved in with the lady occultist, and was now living there with Maryla who, like my mother, was his cousin.

Vala had known both Maryla and Leo long before she had met us. She had sheltered both of them once or twice in the past. As with us, she did it because Staś begged her for help. So at her table everyone knew everyone else, apart from Edward who had to be introduced to the other guests.

The party lasted from lunch till dark and was a great success. We all sat squeezed tightly round the table, ate non-stop, drank cherry liqueur and talked. For once we were free to make as much noise as we liked: all the other lodgers in the attic knew that Vala was having an Easter party and they were having theirs, too.

At first, we talked a lot about what was going on in the world; since the Germans had been rapidly retreating from the east and an invasion from the west was expected any moment now, we fell into a hopeful, boisterous mood. The cherry liqueur was doing its job as well. Staś switched on his gramophone and we would certainly have danced had it not been for lack of space.

Feeling warm and safe with the people I liked, I got a little tipsy and, nestling blissfully between Edward and Staś, talked a bit too much and laughed a bit too loud. I thought no one had noticed it, but I was wrong. A pair of keen eyes had been watching me closely, as they always did. When the party was over, the visitors gone and Sophie and I had ducked under the fat, heavy feather quilt we shared, I suddenly heard from my gentle sister what she thought of me. 'It was disgusting,' she whispered passionately in my ear. 'I was blushing for you the whole time. You behaved like an idiot, cuddling up to that old man, making eyes at him. And he liked it, I must say, he grinned like a well-fed cat, the old fool.' I kicked her hard under the feather quilt and went to sleep.

Next morning I woke with the nasty feeling that something had gone wrong the night before. Vala had already gone out; from her bed Mother stared at me uneasily. 'I have to talk with you,' she said. And in her soft but compelling way she told me how stupid and unfair it was of me to flirt with Edward. Not just because I was seventeen and he forty-four, but because he belonged to Vala and meant the world to her. 'I know,' said Mother, 'that you didn't do it on purpose. I'm terribly sorry for you, my darling. I understand how you and Sophie feel, being deprived of young company, of everything girls of your age usually enjoy: boys, flirtation . . . Yet, you must think of other people, too, try to understand what they feel. Remember that being unhappy yourself is no excuse for making someone else unhappy.'

I felt ashamed, though I did not think that any harm had been done. I was wrong again. After the Easter party Vala's attitude to me changed drastically. She became cool and sarcastic when she addressed me, or looked only at Mother or Sophie when she spoke. She did not change in the least towards them, though. Nor did she stop inviting Edward each Sunday. Now our weekly meetings, which used to be pleasant affairs, became unbearable for all of us.

Edward had changed, too. He sat at the table tense, often silent and listless. Time and again I heard him sigh, or caught his shy, furtive glance when Vala had turned her back, busy at the cooker. I could not help blushing each time it happened and this made me feel even more awkward. I tried desperately to behave faultlessly, yet felt guilty all the time. I had a strong impression that Vala could see and hear more than there really was to be seen or heard. On the other hand, my flattered vanity, mixed with resentment which only increased the more harsh she was to me, prompted me to answer Edward's tender glances more and more often.

Spring beamed through the windowpanes of our attic room, the fifth spring of the war, the second of our life in hiding. Locked in the stuffy room, we were suffocating. Our hopes of a prompt defeat for the Nazis were fading. The invasion we were expecting never seemed to come. I was feverish again and coughed day and night, my head hidden under the fat feather quilt for fear the neighbours might hear.

Our safety in her home was one of the two or three things in her life that Vala took for granted, like her cooking; she boasted that it was perfect. She had her own elaborate way of making her neighbours believe that she had nothing to hide from them. When home from work in the evenings or on a Sunday, she would open the door and leave it ajar for an hour or so to let them see into the room as they walked along the corridor. We would sit still under the kitchen table covered with an oilcloth that hung down to the floor. I always had to take a cough tablet in advance each time it happened. Sometimes, on this or that pretext, Vala would invite one of her neighbours in and talk to them for a while, to let them see that there was no one but herself living in the room. Usually she chose nosy Stefa, a washerwoman who lived next door. 'The airings', as we called these sessions, seemed to work and Vala boasted that no one on earth suspected her of having lodgers.

But one day when Vala was out, I overheard Stefa gossiping about her with another neighbour. Due to the years spent in hiding my hearing had become so sharp that I could easily follow the conversation. 'She puts on airs,' Stefa was saying. 'She thinks she's a lady. Has she ever invited me for tea? Was she kind enough to introduce me to her lover who comes and goes each Sunday?' 'Right, she hardly ever talks to me, either,' agreed the other woman. 'She would rather talk to herself!' 'To herself?' 'Yes, I've heard her talking many a time when she was in her room on her own.' 'Really? I can't believe it! She must be mad or perhaps she's been hiding someone under that bulky feather quilt of hers. A spare lover, or a Jew perhaps?' The women giggled, the conversation ended.

I looked at Mother, then at Sophie, but deep in their reading they had heard nothing. I told them what I had heard and, very distressed, we wondered whether we should look for another shelter. Unexpectedly, Vala returned home soon after that: she had felt poorly at work and had taken the afternoon off. I repeated to her word for word the conversation I had overheard. Her response came as a blow: her face grew red with indignation. 'You lie, you brazen hussy!' she shouted, forgetting all about the neighbours. 'You lie, you lie, just to pester me!' She was panting heavily. I felt my face grow red too, my legs and hands shook. Never in my life had I lied to anybody and I was proud of it. Now my truthfulness was being questioned, my dignity challenged. I felt deadly insulted. In a desperate fury I ran mindlessly to the door, opened it and slammed it behind me. Down the six steep flights of steps I rushed like a lunatic until I found myself in the busy street, dressed in my indoor dress and slippers, with no money on me. Only then did I realise what I had done. But nothing in the world would have made me go back. People were stopping to have a close look at me as though I had run away from an asylum, so I had to move on and go somewhere. I could not possibly spend all the rest of my life in the street. I made up my mind very quickly: 'I'll go to Maryla.' I knew that Madam Occultist would not turn me adrift.

In fact she seemed rather pleased when she saw me on her doorstep and warmly invited me in. Maryla and Leo, however, were far less pleased. They were both enraged when I told them what had brought me there. They shouted that I was an idiot, and how had I dared put my own and other people's lives at risk just because I felt offended. 'And what do you think your mother feels like now?'

To my dismay, Staś dropped in and he, too, strongly disapproved of my behaviour. He offered at once to take me back to Vala. 'Never,' I said. 'It would be against my self-respect.' Staś got seriously angry. 'Your self-respect? You must leave your self-respect at home when your life is at stake,' he snarled at me. I really hated him for a moment. And I would have run away and gladly died rather than go back to a person who had insulted me, had it not been for a single thought that throbbed painfully in my mind and was spelled out by Maryla: I would kill my mother. So eventually I gave in and went back to Wilcza Street the same evening with Staś.

My life now became wretched beyond endurance. I never said sorry to Vala, nor did she apologise to me. We openly loathed each other. The subject of our quarrel was quickly forgotten: despite what they had said, the neighbours suspected nothing, or if they did certainly had no intention of betraying us. So we could safely stay on at Vala's place. Nothing changed outwardly. Vala was still very kind to Mother and Sophie and keen to please them with her cooking, but I could see them both withering in the constant tension.

Edward had never been told the reason for this tension but he clearly sensed it. He knew vaguely that something had happened between Vala and myself but, having no idea which of us was to blame, he assumed that it was I who deserved his compassion. His attitude towards Vala cooled from one visit to the next; he looked at her with resentment and even stopped praising her meals. Instead, he would often stroke my hair and Sophie's, sighing heavily and calling us 'poor little flowers deprived of sunshine', which made Sophie giggle. Since I had once told him I loved flowers and longed for them, he got into the habit of bringing primroses, then violets each time he came. He did not even bother to pretend that they were meant for Vala.

I tended these flowers when Vala was away and spent much time looking at them. There was nothing else I could bring myself to do. Depressed and listless, I lost all my zeal for writing. Now more than ever I wanted to join the underground, to make my senseless life useful. I asked Edward whether he could introduce me to the organisation he belonged to. He thought about it for a long while, then said he would ask his seniors. On the following Sunday he seemed to have forgotten all about my plea. Only when I insisted did he reluctantly say that my offer had been turned down. He did not say why. This failure made my existence even more blank. Once, listlessly skimming through one of the learned books that were left by Vala's brother, I came across a sentence which struck me as an awful truth: 'A man who sees his own life as a senseless biological process is not only unhappy but also unable to live.' This seemed to sum up my own life.

Something was wrong with Vala's health. She often returned from work early, complained of bad abdominal pains, and went straight to bed, too weak even to cook. She bled and, very distressed, blamed herself for having betrayed her late husband: she was convinced this was a punishment for her sin. She also blamed Edward and resented him, yet could not bring herself to stop him coming. Deep in my heart I was sorry for her but never said so.

One day in the middle of May, Vala did not return from work. In the evening Edward turned up to tell us that she had been taken ill and driven to hospital from work. He had received a message at his office and had immediately gone to the hospital. She was very poorly, he said, in pain and bleeding. She was going to have a major operation very soon. She asked him to take care of us for as long as she was away. But, he added, he would of course have done this without being asked.

So we now depended on Edward. He moved in and slept in Vala's bed, so as not to let us be alone at night. He introduced himself to the neighbours and told them about Vala's illness. They were all sympathetic and took his presence in Vala's room as natural.

In the morning Edward would go to work, taking with him some food that Mother had cooked for Vala on the previous day; he would then hurry to the hospital after work, spend some time with Vala listening to her troubles, do shopping on the way back. He never forgot flowers: day after day he brought me a bunch of fresh lilac carefully hidden under his coat from the inquisitive eyes of the neighbours.

Vala's operation went wrong. In fact there was little the surgeon could do. She had cancer and it had been discovered far too late to save her.

She was dying.

Locked in her flat, waiting for her lover, I felt guilty beyond repentance. There was no way I could make up for the harm I had done: she was dying unloved, disenchanted. I wanted to die, too. One hot stifling night I slipped noiselessly out of my bed and sat on the sill of the wide-open window. From the height of the sixth floor I peered down into the bottomless well of the narrow backyard. It was pitch dark, the only light being the tiny glimmer of an oil lamp burning before a statue and casting a faint gleam on the stony face of the Holy Virgin. Not long before, at sunset, a crowd of women had prayed there and had sung their song of praise which now haunted me:

> Let us praise green meadows and the hills
> That May adorns with flowers,
> Let us praise swift streams and shady groves,
> Let us praise the Holy Mother . . .

Deep in despair, I suddenly felt a light breeze and the scent of blossom coming from those green hills and flowery meadows. I knew that I would never jump, never end my life of my own free will, no matter how harmful and senseless it seemed.

Vala died at the beginning of June, on the day the allied forces landed in Normandy. Only Staś and Edward attended her funeral and both came to see us straight from the cemetery. We had to decide what to do next. The flat did not belong to Vala and had to be returned to the local authority once its only occupant was dead. Edward and Staś first had to dispose of Vala's belongings. We had to find a new shelter and leave the flat as soon as possible. Staś went to see Auntie Maria and ask her for help. Edward stayed and we sat with him at Vala's table, silent and mournful. It grew dark. Only then did he dare speak his mind. He said he was ready to take us to his own rough place, to hide Mother and Sophie there and marry me, so that I could live as his legitimate wife without having to hide. He stared at me tenderly, tears coming to his eyes. It took my mother's subtle skills to explain without hurt to this gentle, single-minded man that his offer could not be accepted.

Soon after that we parted from Edward for ever. He was killed six weeks later, when the Post Office headquarters, seized by the Polish insurgents to whom he belonged, were attacked by the Nazis, on the second day of the Warsaw uprising.

＊　＊　＊

I remember our last weeks spent in hiding as a time of raging hope. The defeat of Nazi Germany now seemed imminent. They were losing their fight in western Europe; from the east the Red Army was approaching the Vistula and was moving swiftly towards Warsaw. Though once again locked in someone's flat, we keenly followed the good news brought to us daily by our new landlady, Auntie Maria or by Staś. The town was in a turmoil, the Germans in retreat, deserting their barracks and offices, burning their archives. Long columns of vehicles full of wounded German soldiers were seen rushing westwards along the streets and bridges of Warsaw. It seemed that the underground resistance was getting ready to strike any time now to prevent the Russians from seizing power once they entered the capital. Young men and women began to disappear from their homes. The people of Warsaw held their breath in solemn anticipation.

Of those glorious days of July 1944 I remember little else. We stayed with one of Auntie Maria's neighbours, at 54 Złota Street, in the very centre of the city. Auntie Maria, with her sister Julia and her brother-in-law, lived in the same house, just across the courtyard. Far less concerned about our safety now that the war was clearly coming to an end, we would wave to her from our window to make her come and tell us what was going on. The days were hot, all windows stood open, and I could often hear someone playing the piano on the top floor just above my head. Auntie Maria told me it was a girl of my age, whose name was Urszula. I enjoyed listening to her music, though she was not a good pianist. She usually played waltzes by Johann Strauss, and went on and on with this trash for hours. Sometimes the music stopped and I could see her crossing the courtyard and going out with another girl. I felt deeply envious: she was free to walk along the sunny streets, breathe the warm air, see with her own eyes the Germans fleeing in panic . . . She might also be one of those who were getting ready to fight . . . Did she realise how lucky she was, I thought with exasperation.

On the night of 31 July, in her usual stumbling way, Urszula suddenly began to play Chopin's 'Revolutionary Etude'.

7 *Out of Hiding*

—————————

Commanded by General Komorowski (known as Bór), the
Warsaw corps of 50,000 troops attacked the relatively weak
German force on August 1 and within three days gained control
of most of the city. But the Germans sent in reinforcements,
forced the Poles into a defensive position, and brutally
bombarded them with air and artillery attacks for the next 63
days.

. . . While tens of thousands of Poles, including civilians,
were killed during the German suppression of the Warsaw
uprising, the Red Army, which had been detained during the
first days of the insurrection by a German assault, occupied a
position at Praga, a suburb across the Vistula River from
Warsaw, and remained idle . . .

The New Encyclopaedia Britannica
Vol. X: Warsaw Uprising

On 4 August, the fourth day of the uprising, we made up our minds,
packed our bags and slammed the front door behind us. There was no
way of getting back in since the landlady had as usual taken the key with
her when she went out in the morning. She never came back, cut off by
the battles in the city centre. Meanwhile, German attacks had reached
such a pitch that it was unbearable to stay where we were on the third

floor. It made no sense to die from a stray shell when freedom winked at us from round the corner and was, we thought, a matter of hours or days away. So, after our long months of hiding, we came out to face strangers, to hide with other people in the dark cellar of an unfamiliar house. The street and most of the district had been captured by Polish insurgents right at the beginning of the uprising, on that rainy afternoon when we first saw from our windows the small groups of armed people rushing down the street. They wore red and white armbands with the letters A.K. – the Home Army. They had already been fighting for four days and so far had prevented the Germans from recapturing the district. The Nazis could still take over again but it was too dreadful to think of. Besides, time was on our side: the Russians were just over the river.

The cellar was tightly packed, but somehow we squeezed in and settled down next to Auntie Maria, her eldest sister Julia and her husband Mr Urbański, who had once brought my gramophone to the ghetto. They welcomed us like a loving family and, nestling up to them, we survived our first air raid out of hiding. Nobody objected to our being in the narrow partitioned space that belonged to four or five tenants and their families. We caught some puzzled glances but no questions were asked. People were deadly scared, they prayed, preparing themselves for a sudden death. The walls swayed and cracked as they had during the siege of 1939, but with no anti-aircraft defence this time, we felt like sitting ducks. Young men and women with guns and red and white armbands ran up and down the underground passages: a large A.K. unit had its headquarters nearby. Towards evening we went up to Julia's flat to wash and eat. There was a little food in the larder and Julia made it clear that we should share it. She and her husband preferred to stay in the cellar and eat and sleep there. Like many others, they were too frightened to go upstairs, even for a short while. So at first we slept in their flat at night, and so did Auntie Maria, who did not want to leave us on our own: she felt we were safer when she was near. Soon we gave up sleeping in the flat, however: the heavy fighting went on after dark and roared throughout the night.

Once, on a quieter day, one of Auntie Maria's and Julia's nephews called into the cellar to see how his aunts were. I knew Tadeusz very well from before the war. Though three years my senior, he used to come and play with me when I was a child. Now he was an A.K. soldier, already an experienced fighter. He was overjoyed to see us alive. I thought my great chance had come at last and passionately begged Tadeusz to help me join the Home Army at once. He said it was a splendid idea and told me to get ready and wait for him; he first had to notify his commander. He disappeared for half an hour, then came back upset and confused. His commander refused to take me because I was Jewish. He told Tadeusz I should get in touch with A.L., the People's Army, which fought arm in arm with A.K. but, unlike them, accepted Jews. Tadeusz was deeply embarrassed and apologised as though it were his fault. There was no way of contacting the People's Army, they were fighting in a different part of town, cut off from our area by German troops. So I stayed in the cellar counting the explosions and idly waiting for death.

Days passed by. The sounds of the Eastern Front that had raised our hopes during the first days of the uprising could no longer be heard. Little by little the town was turning into ruins again; thousands of people were dying on the barricades or under the rubble. Yet the insurgents held on.

One day two A.K. soldiers burst into the cellar, shouting for volunteers to come out and build a street barricade. Sophie and I jumped to our feet and joined them at once. With several other volunteers we were making our way up to the street followed by the two soldiers, when one of them said, staring at me and Sophie, 'Aren't you ashamed, you Jewish girls, to sit idly in the cellar while other people are fighting?' It was like a slap in the face. Swallowing bitter tears of humiliation, we rushed to the heap of flagstones, grabbing them furiously, lifting and carrying them along. There was a heavy battle going on nearby, bullets whizzed over our heads; we paid no attention. In a fit of blind fury we went on with the job of raising the barricade. After a time, when it was high enough, the soldiers told us to go back to the cellar. 'You're brave girls, after all,' one of them said. We did not answer.

Bad news was coming from other parts of the town. They said the Old Town was razed to the ground. Strangers from bombed-out houses kept pouring into our cellar. Food was running out. German planes whirled low in the air from early morning, dived with a deadly whistle, dropped their bombs unhindered.

In the third week of the uprising a heavy bomb hit our house. We felt a powerful blast, the walls of the cellar quaked, it became pitch dark and huge pieces of mortar fell from the ceiling. Then a terrifying boom of the upper floors collapsing one upon the other could be heard, coming down, down, ever closer and closer. We were about to die or be buried alive under the rubble.

A long time passed before the tremors came to a standstill, the heavy dust settled and we could see each other again. We all sat numb, unable to believe we were still alive, waiting for the final blast to come. It did not come, though, and gradually convinced that the immediate danger was over, we all crowded to the exit to find out whether we had been cut off. We were not: it was the opposite wing of the house that had received the blast, the part where we had lived three weeks earlier. It lay in ruins now, just across the courtyard. Bewildered from the shock, and covered with white dust, the survivors bustled feverishly about dragging victims out from under the rubble. They laid them on the ground one next to another. We hurried to help.

Suddenly I saw Urszula again. She lay like a sack of flour among the other victims, lifeless, her face grey, her hair white from dust. Her life, which I had once envied so much, had come to a sudden end.

Some time later, at the end of August, an incendiary bomb fell down through the roof of our wing and the building caught fire. Tenants and squatters emerged from the cellars to fight the flames. As had happened once during the 1939 siege, a desperately brave man took up the command. There was a pump in the courtyard – the only source of water. Mr Tomczak ordered all buckets, watering cans, even pans and kettles to be brought to the courtyard. Two men were posted at the pump to do the filling, while the rest followed Mr Tomczak to the roof. The women formed a long line and passed vessels full of water from hand to hand, along the courtyard and up the staircase to the team working on the roof. We worked in this way from the afternoon till dark, ignoring the cannonade that roared quite close. But after a time it became clear that it was hopeless. The roof burned out, the upper floors caught fire, Mr Tomczak and his team gradually retreated to the lower floors. All hope of saving even a small part of the house was fast fading. Most of the people disappeared; they hurried to their blazing flats or cellars to collect their children or save some of their belongings and food from the flames. Auntie Maria, Julia and Mr Urbański, who despite their age had worked hard throughout the afternoon, finally gave in and ran to rescue their bits and pieces. Mother left her empty bucket too, and dived into the cellar to collect our bags. A moment came when I realised that of the crowd of women who had gathered to fight the fire, only Sophie and I remained – with one old woman at the pump and the desperate Mr Tomczak coping alone with the flames that had now reached the ground floor.

What happened afterwards, how the following days and weeks passed by, what came first, what next, which of the images and sounds I remember today are true and which have just come to me in nightmare, what I really saw and heard, and what was only told to me later, I honestly cannot say. Consumed by my illness that finally overtook me on the night of the fire, burning with fever, dazed, I followed Mother and Auntie Maria through smouldering ruins, along dark passages, up and down mountains of rubble. Next I was lying on a stony ledge in an unfamiliar cellar. In a faint light coming through the air vent, I could see Sophie's frightened face. Auntie Maria bent over me, tucking a rag under my shivering body. Mother was stroking my hair. Then darkness descended on me. Blank . . . Blank . . .

A flash of recognition . . .

The walls tremble again, bullets whistle somewhere . . .

> 'Holy Virgin, God's Mother,
> Pray for us who sinned . . . '

A huge underground hall full of people squatting in groups. Candles flicker here and there. The murmur of prayers. 'Where are we?' 'In a strange place, darling, just where there's some space to sit. They say it's Sienna Street.' 'Where are Julia, and Mr Urbański?' 'They've gone somewhere else to look for their relatives.' Blank, blank . . .

A fit of violent coughing. I writhe on the narrow ledge. I choke . . . 'Is there a doctor anywhere?' Something cool presses hard on my naked shoulders, wanders along my back, touches my breast. An unfamiliar face . . . The man's voice sounds cool, too: 'It looks serious, both lungs . . . There's nothing I can do . . . She should be properly fed!' Why is Sophie crying? . . .

A mighty explosion . . . Darkness . . . Flickering candles again . . . A sour smell of cabbage; someone's cooking in the dark . . . 'Mrs Kozłowska has sent this for the sick girl.' 'Who's Mrs Kozłowska?' 'I've no idea, darling. Please eat it before it gets cold.' The soup is blissfully hot, but I can't eat any more, I push the spoon away. A large tear drops from Sophie's eye straight into the bowl; she swallows it with the soup.

Is it night or day? It all looks the same. It all sounds the same, too. They say this deafening roar, which now goes on all the time alongside the gunfire and explosions, means the Russians are attacking again. Will we be rescued after all? Darkness.

Hot soup. Who's Mrs Kozłowska? No, not that tall lady who's bending over me, touching my icy hands and burning forehead. Is she a doctor? No, she's a sculptor, she says. She gives me some aspirin. The other tall woman is her maid. She knows what to do about the cough. 'Here you are.' She produces a set of cupping glasses, smack, smack, they cling hard to my naked back. I fall asleep and when I awake Mrs Kozłowska has sent a dish of hot pearl barley. Enough for all four of us to share. I can't see her face. She hides with her family somewhere in the cellar cooking on the top of a rough heater built from bricks. A little boy brings us soup or barley from her. Day in, day out.

'But madam,' the lady sculptor says, and she sounds truly concerned, 'your daughter badly needs some meat, some eggs, some fat at least.' 'Where can I possibly find anything like that?' sobs Mother in agony. Someone comes up from the dark. He has heard the conversation. He may be able to get a piece of bacon for us, no more than half a kilo, though, and he will have to pay for it. 'Have you got any money?' No, not enough. 'Any jewellery?' Yes. Mother takes off her wedding ring. The stranger disappears. 'Mother – how could you? Your wedding ring for   a   chunk   of   bacon . . . To   a   complete   stranger!' Blank . . . Blank . . .

Is it day or night? . . . No, no I won't . . . take this tin away . . . I'll walk to the latrine . . . When did Sophie grow so strong? I always used to lead her, I was the strong one, the helpful one . . . Now she leads me, she holds me tight, drags me out from the cellar to the courtyard and back. A few bullets burst nearby as we pass. The Eastern Front roars.

Some time, somehow the stranger reappears. He is terribly sorry, there's no more bacon left. He gives back Mother's wedding ring. I fall asleep happy.

The courtyard is blazing in the sunshine. Two heaps of fresh soil have appeared in the middle. Two rough wooden crosses are stuck in, one big, one small. 'Yesterday,' says Sophie, 'a little girl ran out of the cellar after her cat. Her father ran after her. Only the cat survived.'

There is no sound from the Eastern Front, it has stopped, it has stopped again. The German mine-throwers are now going day and night, mainly at night. First three or six powerful grinds, like a giant winding up an immense clock or a monstrous cow mooing. Then three or six powerful blasts. We call them 'cows'.

Somebody says, 'The corner of Marszałkowska Street and Świetokrzyska Street has gone. This big smart house came down in seconds, crushing the people in the cellars. Not a single soul has survived . . . '   The   Sokolnickis . . . Grannie . . . Grandad . . .

Klara . . . why them? Was Mrs Serbin down there? . . . Was the child? . . . No! No!

Refugees keep pouring into the cellar. Three people settle down next to my ledge. A couple and an older man. Jadwiga and Stefan? . . . Is that Henryk with them? . . . Nonsense, Henryk was murdered two years ago. The young woman had lit a candle and I can see their faces. They are Jews. The younger man and the woman cuddle up tight to each other. Oh, how she gazes at him . . . It's a great love, I can tell . . . 'My real name is Handelsman,' the older man says. 'We've been in a ground-floor flat up to now. Last night a dozen A.K. men and women burst in straight from the fighting. They were deadly exhausted, out of their minds. They dropped straight onto the floor and slept there all mixed up together. But before they went to sleep they started drinking. One of them went wild and shouted at us to clear out. He called me "you scabby old Jew" and pointed his gun at me.'

Dark night. Explosions. Soup. No sound from the Eastern Front. 'I'll go and try to find Helena,' says Auntie Maria. 'She may have some food.' 'For God's sake, Maria . . . Can't you hear what's going on up there? You'll be killed before you cross the street!' 'But I must, I must get food for her, otherwise she . . .' And she ties her scarf round her head, takes an empty bag. She is ready to go. 'Please, Auntie Maria, don't go, don't leave us, we need you so . . .' She hesitates, she thinks hard, she finally gives in.

Someone says, 'The Mirowski marketplace has been captured by the Germans. They have dragged hundreds of unarmed men out from the surrounding houses, locked them in the market building and set it on fire. They're burning alive now.'

> 'Lord, have mercy upon us,
> 'Christ, have mercy upon us . . .
> 'May they rest in peace . . .'

(We do not know yet that Stefan is one of those who are dying in the flames in the market. We shall learn this after the war.)

'When the insurgents surrender,' whispers Mr Handelsman, 'there'll be no chance of survival for any of us. We must run away now.' And he tells us how we could cross the Vistula in a boat and take refuge with the Russians. It has to be done by night, under fire from both sides. 'Terribly risky, of course,' he says, 'but I am trying to persuade my son and daughter-in-law to try. They can swim. I can't, I'm staying here. Can you and your daughters swim?' No, no . . . I hate cold water . . . I am shivering with cold . . . Let me die where I am . . . 'We'll go nowhere without you, father,' says the young woman.

It's all over. No gunfire, no bombs, no cows. Silence. Darkness. The insurgents have surrendered. The uprising is crushed. In seven days what is left of the city must be emptied. This is the German order: all survivors are to come out. Those who fought will go to prison camps. Civilians will be sent to work in Germany if they are young and strong, deported to the south of occupied Poland if unfit to work. Little by little, very reluctantly people start pouring out of the cellars.

What shall we do? We shall be killed if we stay, we shall be killed if we go. It is too late to cross the Vistula.

'We've been in touch with a squad of the People's Army,' says Mr Handelsman, coming back from somewhere. 'They are planning to escape through the sewers. If they succeed they'll hide in the woods and start to fight again. They have accepted the three of us. We're going with them.'

Mr Handelsman takes Mother to the commander to ask his advice. She returns excited but full of doubts. The squad is leaving behind a well-concealed underground bunker. We can go and hide there with other people who, like us, can neither face the Germans nor fight in the woods. There's a little food left in the bunker. The war is nearly over. If we are lucky we may survive.

The doctor who once examined me is still around. He is just getting ready to leave the cellar. Mother begs him to have a look at me. Does he think I could survive weeks, or months perhaps, locked in an underground bunker? Not even trying to disguise his irritation, the doctor takes his stethoscope, 'Your daughter is dying, madam,' he says. 'Without fresh air and good food she'll be dead by next month. Take your younger girl, madam, go and hide in the bunker, leave that one behind.'

The doctor has gone but Mother does not seem to have noticed. 'She's not dying,' she says. 'I won't let her die. There's a beautiful autumn outside. We'll go out into the fresh air and sunshine. We'll all go together. And all die together. Or maybe not.'

The lady sculptor and her maid are ready to leave. They come to say goodbye. They leave us a bottle of aspirin, a shawl, a pair of warm boots. A man I hardly recognise shyly approaches me. He has been in the cellar all this time, he says, just next to the pillar. Would I mind accepting a pair of trousers, his spare pair, and an anorak? I grin faintly at him. I accept. It is October now and I am still wearing the same summer dress I had on in August. Mother suddenly remembers Mrs Kozłowska. She must find her before she leaves to tell her how grateful we are. But Mrs Kozłowska has already left.

Daylight. An unfamiliar empty flat. Half of the big room is ruined. One leg of a piano dangles over the precipice. Auntie Maria brings a basin of water from somewhere. We wash ourselves, the first time in five weeks, or perhaps six. We comb our hair. We kill a few lice We are getting ready to go out. To face the Germans after all.

In the daylight, washed and dressed in trousers and anorak, I feel much better. My mind is clear. I have to decide what to take with me. We have very few belongings, but they are still too many when you've no idea where you're going. Roman's photograph I'll take, of course, but I have to leave my manuscripts: they would betray us if we were caught. No, I shan't burn them. There's a hole in the floor under the piano, just next to the leg which stands firm. I put all my copy books into the hole and cover them tightly with loose bricks. Perhaps someone will find them after the war.

'Now, my sweet, my dearest Maria,' says Mother, and her voice breaks, 'it's time for us to part. You go first. With a bit of luck you may find one of your sisters in the crowd, a friend, someone to go with. We'll meet again when the war is over.' Has she heard what Mother has said? She seems not to listen. She takes a sewing kit out of her bag and sews a loose button onto Sophie's cardigan, then cleans her own shoes. 'I'm not leaving you,' she says at last. 'We're going together.' For once this shy, tender woman sounds stern. No one will tell her what to do. She'd rather sacrifice her own safety than part from us.

The great exodus has now been going on for six days. Streams of refugees flow out from the wrecked buildings, merge into rivers in the streets, discharge into the broad highways. They swing along, moving slowly westwards. Like everyone else we swing along with the crowd. Rubble, craters, barricades block our way. Ruins smoulder here and there. At first there is no sign of Germans. We spot the first field-grey uniforms only when we approach the Mokotów allotments. Here they are, plenty of them. Spaced out densely along the road, neat, well fed, they watch the shabby mob closely. Now and again they pick out a young man and search him carefully, looking for arms, then take him away or kick him back into the crowd. Slowly, endlessly we pass by them, undisguised, helpless, scared. But why should they take any notice of three inconspicuous women as tattered and miserable as anyone else? They let us pass.

The open space, the dark, damp soil of the gardens welcome us with a rich crop of ripe tomatoes and onions. No one could reach these treasures during the fighting. Now we forget all about our plight. Thrilled by the sight of them, we push forward with the crowd, grab the glistening red tomatoes, plunge our fingers deep into the soil, stuff our mouths and pockets. The Germans do not interfere. They watch the bustling mass with scornful smiles; now and then one of them throws an onion at a good-looking girl or sneers, 'Look what your bandits have done to you!' It's like a lash in the face, but nobody cares. We revel in the unforgettable taste of cool raw onions dotted with fresh soil.

Then we plod on again, on and on, to the West Warsaw railway station. The day is fading, dusk comes on. I have walked for hours on my own, but now fever takes a grip on me, my legs give way, my body shivers. Mother and Sophie hold me up and drag me along like a heavy sack.

Then it is night, and we are lying on the floor of a vast hall in the railway station. Draught. Flickers of candlelight.

> 'Our Father which art in heaven,
> Hallowed be Thy name . . .'

Voices calling and echoing names of loved ones lost in the crowd or perhaps dead. Darkness.

The next morning we are herded to a train, packed in tight, and taken away. After a short journey we stop and they drive us out. Now we are in Pruszków, a small town near Warsaw used by the Nazis as a transfer camp. Here we must wait for 'selection' before continuing the journey. The local people hand out fresh bread and water to the deportees.

We spend a day and a night crowded on the floor of an empty store. Everyone around us is friendly. They understand. They are all equally distressed and despairing. They are all worried about the 'selection'. No one wants to be sent to Germany, ready prey for the enemy. Young men and women try their best to look old and unfit.

The crucial moment comes at last. In a big square under a blue early-morning sky, a score of Nazis with swastikas, and guns and whips, deal with the wretched mob. They work hard, sorting out the human bulk, neatly, quickly and efficiently: young, strong men and women to the right, old, unfit ones to the left. People obey in silence. When our turn comes, I feel a sharp push and suddenly find myself on the right-hand side of the square, Sophie clinging to my arm. Mother and Auntie Maria are being swept to the left. So the worst thing has happened, we have been separated, we shall never see each other again. Suddenly there's a little commotion on the left-hand side of the square and I see my mother moving forward and stealing over behind the Nazi backs to the right-hand side. Auntie Maria follows her. They join Sophie and myself unhindered. No one has noticed them: the guards are busy watching the people on the right in case they try to escape to the left. Great happiness overcomes my soul: we shall be together, we shall go to Germany together.

But no, Mother will not let us perish in the lion's den. She is determined to fight. She was never a gambler, but now she is ready to gamble. She pulls us along to the stocky officer shouting out his orders nearby. Tattered and haggard, she boldly approaches him, her dark Jewish eyes looking full into his face. She points at each of us and says reproachfully, '*Das ist ein Irrtum: die Dame ist alt; ich auch bin alt; das ist ein Kind; und das . . . das Mädchen ist krank, sehr krank . . . Lunge . . . Tuberkulose . . .* ' ('There's been a mistake! This lady is old; I am old, too; this is a child; and this . . . this girl is ill, very ill . . . lungs . . . tuberculosis . . .')

The Nazi is taken aback. No one from the mob ever speaks to him, let alone in fluent German. Nobody ever says there's been a mistake. Something must have gone wrong with the Nazi machine. He must correct the error. '*Ordnung muss sein! Entschuldigen Sie bitte!*' ('There must be order! I'm very sorry!') he mutters, like an embarrassed waiter accused by a customer of having served a wrong dish. Then, remembering his rank he yells, '*Links, links! Schneller, schneller!*' ('Left, left! Faster, faster!')

So we won't be sent to Germany. The Nazi hasn't noticed we are Jews, so perhaps there's just a chance we'll escape despite our sad eyes and long noses. Suddenly I see how beautiful the sky is, how golden the leaves on the trees, how cosy the barracks look. We settle down in one of them with the elderly, the children, the mothers and the infirm, waiting for a train to the south of Poland. Time passes. A day and a night go by. I fall into nothingness now and then, and come round again. On the whole I feel much better. There is a field kitchen in the camp. Like everyone else we collect our rations of soup and bread. At first Auntie Maria does all the queueing, alone. It's safer for us not to walk around or show our faces. But we can hardly live, the four of us, on single portions. So on the second day, Mother joins Auntie Maria in the queue. Sophie and I stay behind. The day is bright, most of our companions are outside sitting on the ground, enjoying the sunshine. We can't resist the temptation, so we go out too and sit down in front of the building.

It's too late to go back in when we see a German soldier approaching. He strolls along lazily, enjoying the beautiful weather and looking around. He stops in front of us, ready for a friendly chat. Suddenly his face twists in a nasty grin. *'Jude!'* he shouts, *'Sie sind Jude!'* ('You are Jews!') Petrified, we pretend not to understand. But the soldier knows the Polish word for Jews, *'Żydówki!'* he roars in a fit of fury. Everyone around us holds their breath. 'We're not Jewish,' I say, and it is the first time I have flatly denied my origins. 'We're Armenians.' Armenians, who look very much like Jews, are approved of by the Nazis, and the soldier must know this. He thinks intently for a moment, then in broken Polish orders us to show him our identification cards. We have none, of course, so quietly and patiently I explain to him that all our documents were burnt during the uprising. It sounds convincing. A woman next to us nods as if confirming the truth of my words. Confused, the German ponders again. 'Where are your parents?' he asks, calming down. 'They're dead,' I say. The woman sighs. Sophie confirms my statement. 'We're orphans,' she says. The soldier now seems fully convinced. Soon he will leave. But suddenly Mother, carrying a bowl of soup, appears on the path leading to the barracks. Seeing us with the soldier she hastens to help. Any fool would guess her relationship with us. *'Mutter?'* asks the German. *'Jawohl,'* she confirms. Dead silence around, people look at us terrified. The soldier goes berserk. 'You bloody liars!' he screams. *'Du verfluchte Juden!'* ('You damned Jews!') He grabs his gun and points it at us. In a moment we shall die. I close my eyes and squeeze Sophie's hand. But suddenly the man changes his mind. 'Wait here,' he shouts and runs off to fetch his superiors. He disappears round the corner. Only now do the people crouching nearby come to life again. 'Run away, ladies, run away,' they beg us. 'Hide somewhere, try to save your lives.' Yes, but where can we go? The camp is surrounded with barbed wire and guards. There's no place to hide. Out of the blue, a tall man in high boots comes to our rescue (what on earth is he doing here among the old and crippled?). He scoops up the three of us with his strong arms and makes us run with him. Auntie Maria follows, trotting behind. We stop at the far end of the camp away from the barracks, the crowds and the guards. There's a deserted barn here, full of rotting straw. The stranger tells us to bury ourselves in the straw and stay there till the following day. They may forget about us by tomorrow, he says comfortingly. Then off he goes. We shall never meet him again nor find out who he was.

The day ends, the night passes. We are cold and hungry but still alive. Then loudspeakers announce that all deportees going south must gather on the railway platform and wait there for the train. We cannot stay in the straw for ever, so out we come and walk to the platform. It is so over-crowded that it seems very unlikely our hostile soldier will find us here.

Now I am sitting curled up on the cool concrete of the platform, my head resting on Mother's shoulder, Sophie's head on mine. I doze off and wake again from a feverish slumber. It is night, a faint, blue light shines from somewhere. The guards walk up and down along the narrow gangway dividing the motionless crowd. Suddenly, opening my eyes, I see a uniformed figure bending over me. Is it a nightmare? No, it's real. He pulls me hard, he grabs Sophie's arm, orders us to follow him. 'Where are you going?' Mother cries, and jumps to her feet ready to come too. But the man stops her: he only wants the girls. He says we shall be back soon. He's not the one who wanted to shoot us, he's much older. And he looks odd, as if unstable. Oh yes, he's drunk. Pulling us across the dark deserted field he mumbles something in German. He calls us 'gypsy girls'. The thought that we shall die as gypsies not Jews comes vaguely to my mind. It's all the same to the Nazis. It's all the same to me. I am too cold, too ill even to feel frightened. I know what Sophie is thinking now: she is terrified he may rape us. Mother must be out of her wits for the same reason. But not I, no, I don't care. I am exhausted, fed up with the endless fear. If the soil were warm I would gladly bury myself alive, without German help.

We arrive at a solitary barracks. It's light and warm inside, the room swarms with guards off duty. They are lolling about half naked, lying on wooden bunks or cooking on an iron stove. They welcome us with ribald laughter and invite us to sit down on the floor. The man who has brought us here says something in German, too fast for me to under-stand apart from the words 'gypsies' and 'food'; then he lies down on an empty bunk and, still in his uniform and boots, immediately falls asleep. His friends do not pay much attention to us, they're busy eating. They all look old and tired. One of them brings us a bowl of scrambled eggs made from egg powder, some bread and ersatz coffee. He sits down next to us and stares at us, smiling. He has friendly blue eyes. At first I push the food away, I recoil from accepting German charity. But in the end I can't resist the smell of fresh bread, the long-forgotten taste of eggs, the hot drink. Sophie and I have not eaten for a couple of days. With a guilty conscience we start eating, trying not to look greedy or grateful. The German seems pleased. He talks to us while we eat. He says something about his wife and children waiting for him in a German village. 'The war is almost over,' he says and sighs wearily, but his eyes smile as he sighs. Two of his fellow guards join us now. They suggest we stay with them for good. We will be safe here, they promise, warm and well fed. In return we can do some washing and mending for the soldiers. But we decline their offer and the blue-eyed man takes us back to the platform. Before disappearing he bids us good luck.

Now it is morning again and an endlessly long train rolls slowly along the platform and comes to a standstill. The empty, roofless cattle trucks stand waiting to be filled. People push forward, hustled by the guards. The officers, spaced out along the train, black swastikas on their sleeves, stop people at random to check their documents. Somehow we push by unnoticed. The truck we have climbed into fills up in no time. More and more people are forced in by the guards, until we can all hardly breathe. Children are crying, men cursing and swearing, someone becomes hysterical. 'Let's throw these three Jewesses out!' a woman suddenly exclaims. 'We'd be better off without them.' A powerful hushing makes her hold her tongue. 'One more word,' a crippled man says sternly, 'and you'll be thrown out yourself.'

Now there's a long wait. At last the train jerks and starts rolling, still hesitantly. Little by little the barracks vanish from sight, replaced by the fields of the Mazovian plain. Slowly, infinitely slowly, the train crawls into flat open countryside. Half sitting, half lying, squeezed in by people's arms and legs, propped against someone's knees, I watch feathery clouds flying across the immense sky, chasing the train. The day reaches its peak, then fades away, and the sky darkens. Thick mist rises from the earth and wraps me in a deep chill. Now it is late night, no stars, no moon. The train pants and rattles, it stops, then starts again, rolls backwards, forwards, or breaks for a long while. Shall we ever arrive anywhere? The moans, sobs and cursing have slowly subsided. People fall into slumber or attend to their bodily needs: empty tins are passed from hand to hand and made use of in the dark. I say no when it comes to me, and so does Sophie. Never in someone's presence: it's a vow we've made, our own little piece of resistance against the war.

Sunrise greets us with a marvellous view: we have left the flat country far behind and the train is making its way through the beautiful hills and valleys of the upland south. The autumnal fields cheer our eyes with a rich green and brown patchwork sparkling with dew.

Morning is in full swing when we come to a halt. It has taken us twenty-four hours, instead of four or five, to arrive at Craçow. They let us out for a very short while, then cram us back into the cattle trucks. We wait again. The platform swarms with Craçowians who have come running to help. They shower us with parcels flung into the trucks. A neat little parcel drops straight down into my lap. It is an egg sandwich. Life seems brighter again.

We leave the hospitable city in the afternoon and start crawling along again through fields and forests. The sky darkens as on the day before, and the second night wraps the earth in shadows.

Some time, somewhere the train stops for good and they order us out. Jumping down from the high trucks we land in heavy mud. It is too dark to see where we are. In front of the railway station, in a square thick with mud, horses are neighing and harsh peasant voices can be heard in the dark. Everyone from the train is fighting their way through mud and darkness, groping for the carts that will take them away. The carts fill up quickly and set off at once. Somebody says there are not enough carts to take all of us. No one wants to be left behind. Panic-stricken people rush forward in a stampede. Bewildered, benumbed we are swept from side to side, not knowing what to do, too weak and helpless to fight. Whenever we find a cart it turns out to be already full. The human wave brings us to the edge of the square. And here, all of a sudden, we find ourselves next to a lonely cart quietly waiting in the dark. 'Room for four,' a faceless voice says harshly.

8 Winter into Spring

A pair of drowsy horses trotted slowly through night and mist. The soggy ground squelched under their hooves, the cart bounced and jolted on the potholes. The motionless driver, his back turned on us, seemed sound asleep; he had not uttered a word since we had set off. We did not talk either, sunk deep in our thoughts. With the crowds left far behind, we were now alone for the first time since the start of the uprising. To be no longer squeezed between tussling human bodies, no longer fighting for breath and weary of human din, was an enormous relief. I prayed that the night, the cold, the bouncing of the cart would last for ever. We were free and safe as long as it lasted. At the end of the muddy road some strangers in an unknown place would turn lights on, look closely at our faces and decide our fate. They might refuse to shelter us, and lock us out, afraid of the danger we carried with us. Or even worse, they might turn us over to the Nazis. Peasants were said to be greedy and the reward for denouncing a Jew was at least 500 zloties. Who knows what this numb, faceless figure may do at dawn, when he suddenly learns who he has taken into his care? These were my thoughts as I shivered from cold and fever. Then I fell asleep.

I awoke only when the cart came to a sudden stop. It was still dark and faint outlines of thatched cottages loomed in the blackness: we had arrived at a village. Only then did the driver speak. He said he was only going to have two of us in his house, the other two would have to go to his neighbour. Mother wanted to be with me, so the man took Sophie and Auntie Maria next door. Soon he returned and let us into his cottage. He did not follow us but stayed outside to unharness his horses.

We entered the house. It was totally dark in the overheated room except for an oil lamp flickering faintly on a holy picture and a bed piled high with pillows and eiderdowns. The room smelled of the cowshed and seemed deserted. We stood on the doorstep wondering what to do. Then, from under the heap of bedding, a shrill voice screeched, 'Praised be Jesus Christ.' 'For ever and ever,' we answered. We could not see who was speaking, but the voice seemed female, old and wasted. She could not see us either. Soon the driver came in and the woman, addressing him as Błazek, ordered him to fetch some straw. This he silently did, and spread the rustling stuff on the floor next to the warm oven. 'Lie down, poor things, and have a good sleep,' screeched the voice. We obeyed, stretched ourselves out on the straw and, overcome by stifling heat, instantly fell asleep.

Some time later, I woke choking with a cough. It was still dark. The fire in the oven had apparently gone out and it was now bitterly cold in the room. Coughing and wriggling, I was groping for straw to bury myself in when I heard the rusty voice again: 'Come on, my child, lie down next to me, you'll be warm and comfy here.' Surprised by myself, I walked to the bed and, with a vague feeling of remorse because of the lice I carried, dived in under the immense eiderdown.

Morning was well under way when I woke, pleasantly relaxed. Sunlight streaming through a narrow window shone straight into my face. A jumbled chorus of animal sounds – mooing, barking, grunting, the crowing of the cocks – came through the wall from outside. I was in bed alone. The bed stood in a spacious kitchen with a rough earth floor and a low ceiling. A huge earthenware oven occupied most of the space and glowed with bright flames. Next to the oven crouched a dark figure which in the light cast by the flames looked like a withered shrub. Her face was parched, bird-like, her back bowed with age, her arms and legs like leafless tree branches. She was peeling potatoes and throwing them into a cauldron seething on top of the oven. Mother crouched next to her, helping. A strong smell of smoke, mixed with that of melted lard, made me cough.

The ancient woman got up from the floor and stepped to the bed with unexpected swiftness. She was as short as a child and looked well over eighty. She gave me a long scrutinising glance. Her eyes were sharp and inquisitive. No secret, no sin could escape those keen eyes. Even if she had suspected nothing so far, staring into my sun-lit face, she must have guessed. My heart sank, I waited for her verdict. Motionless and silent, my mother was waiting too. The old woman said nothing and left the room, perhaps to bring the man to turn us out. Too scared even to talk, we waited in silence. She came back a long while later carrying a couple of eggs. She broke them into a mug and handed the mug to me. 'Drink it up, my child,' she said. I sipped the slimy stuff, beginning to believe that she had accepted us. My belief turned to certainty when the old woman said that her son Błażek would soon get a boxroom ready for Mother and me. Till then, she said, I should stay in her bed, since she could tell I was very ill.

Thus we began a new life in a village called Zielonki, with a peasant family called Pietrzyk, who intended neither to claim a reward for betraying us, nor to drive us out of their cottage. We had to live openly now, not hiding from people but also not telling them the truth.

Mrs Pietrzyk's eldest son, Piotr, and his pregnant wife also lived in the cottage. Piotr would inherit the farm after his mother's death. He worked hard in the farmyard all day long and only came into the kitchen for meals. When not working, he kept to his own room with his wife. The couple took our presence for granted, they were friendly but not really concerned. We were none of their business. The handsome, sulky Błażek, Mrs Pietrzyk's younger son, was even less interested in us. He counted for little in the family and was treated like a slave. He had no place of his own in the house and slept in the stable with the horses. Though old and wasted, the mother still played first fiddle and ruled unopposed in the household. On her order the boxroom was soon cleared for us, a big rough bed with a thick pallet and half a dozen blankets pushed in, and an iron stove with a long pipe installed. We were on our own.

Auntie Maria and Sophie were less fortunate. The family they stayed with was rude and unfriendly. The four teenage daughters of the house teased and mocked Sophie for being a town girl and knowing little about country life. They told her that rats might come at night and bite her ears off. Sophie did not believe a word but hated to be ridiculed. So she and Auntie Maria came to us each morning and stayed till late. Mrs Pietrzyk did not mind. She even offered them meals as she did us. But it was hard to accept her generosity for very long. On the other hand, we were almost penniless now.

Auntie Maria went to explore the village and returned with news. The place was swarming with evacuees, there was hardly a farmer who did not have some under his roof. R.G.O. – a Polish organisation that was helping refugees throughout occupied Poland – had already set up a cookhouse and was issuing free meals once a day. It was stationed in the centre of the village next to both the Polish and German police stations, said Auntie Maria with a sigh.

On the third or fourth day after our arrival, Mrs Pietrzyk decided that raw eggs and greasy dumplings were not enough to bring me back to health, and ordered Błażek to fetch the village doctor. The young, haggard woman who turned up in our boxroom instantly won my heart. She examined me carefully, found my lungs in a bad state, gave me some medicine, and advised an X-ray to find out whether I needed hospital treatment. She must have liked us, too, since she told us all about herself on that first visit. She and her husband, who also was a doctor, had lived in Cracow until he was arrested for his involvement in the resistance. She then ran away and settled in Zielonki. There had been no news from her husband since he had been locked in Montelupich prison long ago. She did not know if he was still alive. The doctor broke down as she told us this and on an impulse Mother stroked her hair. She obviously knew we were Jews but the thought that she might betray us was clearly preposterous.

The following day, Błażek harnessed his horses and took Mother and myself to Cracow. We could hardly believe how close we were to the town: the journey that by train and cart had lasted eight hours when we had first travelled to Zielonki, now took no longer than two. And how beautiful it was as we passed through dappled fields basking in the sun.

The hospital was on the outskirts of the city. Błażek helped us out of the cart and promised to wait. We did not have to wait long to see the X-ray doctor. Both Mother and I were scared when this middle-aged bald man eyed us intently up and down. 'You look so foreign,' he said at last. 'And so sad.' He smiled at us with a kind-hearted, reassuring smile. Then he gave me a thorough checkup again and X-rayed my lungs. When it was all done, the doctor said that my lungs were seriously affected by the disease but he would not keep me in hospital as long as there was a chance of recovery without any special treatment. Rich food and fresh air were all I needed, so living in the countryside might cure me. He told me to spend a lot of time outdoors as soon as I felt strong enough to walk. We left his surgery in high spirits. I felt happy, keen to live, fond of humankind again.

In the hospital hall I noticed a stand with sweets and stationery. Though we were very poor now, I couldn't resist the temptation. Sighing, Mother took a small bank note out of her shabby bag and I bought myself an exercise book and a pencil.

20 October 1944

So we are still alive. And together. It is so quiet around here
and feels so safe that I can hardly believe all our recent past was
real. Is the nightmare over? Shall we live like this till the end of
the war and finally survive? During the day, when the sun
shines in through the tiny square of our window, I think yes,
this is it, we've escaped. But when I wake in the middle of the
night, terrifying images come back in a torrent, fear creeps over
my soul and I can't go back to sleep. Then I start thinking about
our present life, how insecure we really are and how far from
safety. For *they* are still here, though we don't hear much about
them. They are here, ruling over this quiet country, over these
people who have taken us in under their roof. And we are here
only because *they* have ordered local farmers to shelter the
deportees, just as they order them to give part of their livestock
to the Third Reich. The Nazis may be losing battles in the west,
they may be bleeding to death in the east, but right here they
are still in full command. So, any day or night this quiet spell
could easily come to an abrupt end. Suppose someone in the
village hates Jews, or has a grudge against the family who
shelters us, or fancies a reward? I bet the old woman and her
sons don't realise who we are. Perhaps they don't even know
what a Jew looks like. I hope they won't be shot if the Nazis
come to take us; they are only doing what they have been forced
to do, after all: sheltering refugees from Warsaw. And that's
what we are, refugees from Warsaw.

I know that keeping this diary means taking a great and
unnecessary risk; it states in black and white everything we are
trying to hide. But I don't want my experiences to sink into
oblivion, so I'll keep on writing, if not for posterity's sake at least
for my own. Now I'll bury it deep in the pallet and go to sleep
on top of it.

21 October

This afternoon Auntie Maria came back from the village
beaming with joy. She had a jar with four helpings of thick
vegetable soup and a loaf of bread. The fact is, she has managed
to convince the R.G.O. people to register the three of us in our
absence, without having to show our faces or any identification
cards. She simply told them we were in bed with flu. They also

gave her a big can of a very strong vinegar which kills insects, a most precious thing that we have been dying for day and night. Our hair now smells like pickled gherkins and we are happy: at least this battle is going to be won. Mrs Pietrzyk popped in, sniffed once or twice and looked a bit puzzled. But she said nothing. I imagine she's far less squeamish about vermin than we are. Maybe for her lice are just living creatures like chickens or cows.

27 October

It has been raining for days. I can't possibly go out. Not just because of the rain but also because I'm still very weak. My bouts of fever come and go, and leave me sweating and exhausted. So I stay in bed and listen to the mooing and squawking. My sharp ears often catch human voices too, Piotr and Błażek squabbling in the farmyard. They call each other names: 'You ugly thing!' 'You nasty thing!' Not a single filthy word. I think that despite their apparent roughness they're kind, warm-hearted people.

The old woman came to ask how I was. She brought a bottle of thick, snow-white liquid and forced me to take a mighty gulp. 'It'll do you good, my child,' she said. 'Your lungs will heal in no time.' She gave me a lump of fresh home-made bread with it and a pinch of salt. The liquid was fatty but I liked it. She left the bottle and said I should finish it within a week.

28 October

I could *die* with disgust. I've brushed my teeth twice, but it doesn't help. This morning, after I'd taken a second gulp from the bottle, Mother asked Mrs Pietrzyk what the white liquid really was. The old woman was reluctant to say, but Mother insisted, so finally she said it was dog's fat. There's a clever man in the village, she explained, who disposes of stray dogs. He squeezes fat from them. It has great healing powers. It has already cured many people Mrs Pietrzyk knows from fatal diseases. Horrified, Mother felt obliged to thank her profusely for having gone to all the trouble of finding this miraculous medicine. Later, Sophie said she would get rid of the sickening liquid discreetly: she's going to pour it out in the bushes, just a little each day, because Mrs Pietrzyk comes to check that I have remembered to take my daily dose. Isn't she a darling?

29 October

I feel much better, so today I got up and explored the cottage with Sophie. It's larger than I thought. One room is always locked and when we asked Mrs Pietrzyk why, she gladly unlocked it and showed us in. I gave a little cry of surprise when we entered, it was so beautiful. It has heavy, almost black furniture daintily carved all over, standing out in sharp contrast against whitewashed walls; the room is full of brightness from holy pictures framed in gold; it glows with multicoloured paper cutouts on the walls, dried flowers in hand-painted pots, richly embroidered linen. They call this room 'the white chamber' said Mrs Pietrzyk, and they only use it on special occasions: when someone in the family is born, marries or dies. For most of their lives it stays locked, while the family crowds into the kitchen or works in the fields and farmyard.

At the end of the long dark corridor we came across another locked door. When we asked about it, the old woman looked solemn and said the room behind the locked door belonged to her youngest son, Jan. She was a bit vague about him. He lives in Cracow, busy studying, she said, and is soon to become a priest. In these dangerous days it is better not to talk about it, she sighed. Maybe we'll meet Jan some time, he comes home and stays for a while whenever he can. As she spoke of Jan her eyes beamed with love and pride. Now both Sophie and I are pining to meet him.

Days passed by, one by one, and we got used to our new surroundings. My health had greatly improved. At the beginning of November, the young doctor who called on me from time to time, told me to get up and go for a walk. Sophie could hardly wait for me to join her; she was fed up with her lonely rambling. After that we went out together whenever the weather was fine. We would certainly have explored the village had it not been for Mother's and Auntie Maria's grumbling. They flatly forbade us to go there and show our faces around. So we walked over the endless fields, all totally deserted at this time of year. Alone and happy under the immense dome of the autumn sky, we daydreamed and conjured up wonderful pictures of our future life in freedom. These walks, which meant the world to us, had to stop, however, when, after heavy rain, our muddy, worn-out shoes fell to pieces.

Stuck in bed again I spent my days brooding, while Sophie hung around trying to make herself useful.

One day, seeing me idle and moody, Mrs Pietrzyk brought me two books from Jan's locked room. They were religious books: the catechism and *Life of the Holy Virgin*. Starved of books for months, I fell on them greedily.

15 November
I've been reading *The Life of the Holy Virgin*. It's a beautiful book, deeply moving. A monk wrote it, I think. I had to stop when I came to the bit in which Saint Mary, alone under the cross, mourns for her crucified son. I burst into tears and could hardly pull myself together. Now, having calmed down, I'm wondering why I cried. I shouldn't be so moved by the story of a mother who lost her child 2,000 years ago. Not after what I have seen myself. Perhaps it made such an impression on me just because the account, every page and sentence of it, radiates with such a powerful Christian belief. Have I been infected?

Since we now had to pretend we were Christians, the catechism was just what we needed. I relearnt what I once had been taught at school, while Mother and Sophie had to start from scratch. Strangely enough, Auntie Maria had to do the same thing: though born and brought up as a Catholic, she had long ago forgotten her faith from living for years and years with our family. So we all busied ourselves learning prayers and dogmas by heart and reciting them under our breath, so as not to be overheard by our hosts.

Despite our changed circumstances, Auntie Maria still felt responsible for our wellbeing. It was she who wracked her brains to find a way of buying shoes for us. One morning when Błażek was getting ready to drive to town, Auntie Maria asked him to take her with him. She returned late, bringing us heavy men's boots, warm pullovers and a few little things we badly needed. She was a bit evasive about how she had managed to buy these, but the riddle was soon solved when we noticed that the little golden cross she wore round her neck and the silver watch from around her wrist had disappeared.

The following day – a Saturday – Sophie and I started out again on our solitary rambling – shod in our new boots. When we returned just before dusk, Mrs Pietrzyk asked us to follow her to the 'white chamber'.

Puzzled, we watched her unlock a carved oak chest. She took out two beautiful woollen kerchiefs: a white one and a blue one, both decorated with red roses and green leaves. The white one was for Sophie, the blue one for me. When we stared at them, wondering whether it was a gift or just a loan, the old woman said that we would need the kerchiefs tomorrow. 'You surely want to go to church, children, now you've got those decent shoes,' she chattered, relocking the chest. 'But you can't go to church bareheaded, can you? So take them and keep them for as long as you live here. But remember, only wear them on Sundays when you go to church.'

Mother and Auntie Maria were panic-stricken when they heard what Sophie and I were supposed to do. We spent half the night wondering how to prevent what we thought might be a disaster. Sunday services would certainly be attended by everyone from the village – farmers as well as refugees, Polish policemen, and maybe some Nazis too. Should we lie to Mrs Pietrzyk and say we had suddenly been taken ill? This would not work for long, however. Should we tell her the truth? We didn't dare do that either. The only thing we could do was to go to church. Having decided this, we started wondering whether Mother and Auntie Maria should come too. Sophie and I would certainly feel better if Auntie Maria came with us, but then Mrs Pietrzyk might ask why Mother had stayed behind. But if Mother went too, it would mean showing three instead of two forbidden faces. At last we came to the conclusion that Sophie and I should go alone and that Mother and Auntie Maria should keep away from church unless Mrs Pietrzyk prompted them to go.

On Sunday morning we put on our boots and kerchiefs and went to see Mrs Pietrzyk to show her we were going to church. She was very pleased and said we looked no worse than the village girls. She was getting ready herself but did not want to detain us, so we left.

I can hardly remember this first visit to church. We were so terribly frightened that we almost ran there, not looking around or taking notice of the beautiful view or the people we met on our way. When we arrived, the church was already tightly packed, the service just about to begin. Overcome by shyness, we did not dare go inside and mix with the crowd. Instead, we knelt down in the porch. Our heads bent low, we pretended to pray. As soon as Mass was over and people began to pour out, we ran back home. Later that day we heard from Mrs Pietrzyk that she had seen us kneeling in the porch. 'I didn't know you were so godly, children,' she said. 'The only folks I know who pray in the porch are nuns and monks.' Though she spoke with approval, we understood at once that we had made a serious mistake.

We spent the following week in great anxiety. The next unavoidable visit to church was fast approaching and we were terrified we might make another blunder. On Saturday night, when Mother and I were already in bed, we heard an unusual commotion in the cottage. Brisk steps could be heard in the corridor, a key grated in a lock, a door banged. It was too late to creep out and see what was going on. By the morning we had forgotten all about it. Sophie came over from next door, we got dressed up and went to church, meeting no one from the household. Despite our earlier misgivings, we were far more calm this time and noticed how beautiful the little wooden church was, perched on the top of the hill, high up in the cloudy sky. From its pointed belfry, a sonorous bell summoned the congregation to prayers. People were surging along the paths and lanes from all directions, greeting each other with 'Praised be Jesus Christ'. Some addressed us and we answered, 'For ever and ever'. The villagers were dressed in their Sunday best, wore high polished boots and neat sheepskin jackets. Men sported dark hats, women wide colourful skirts and flowery kerchiefs. The refugees could easily be spotted by their dull and shabby clothes. There were no uniforms to be seen.

Merging with the crowd, carried along by the stream of people, we suddenly found ourselves inside the church. The pews were already crammed, so we stopped in the aisle and like many others remained standing near the altar. Only then did I dare look around. The holy place was full of light, shade and colours. Red, blue and yellow shafts of daylight streamed in through the narrow stained-glass windows and shimmered on the heads and gowns of the touchingly simple wooden figures of the saints. A life-size carving of Christ on the cross, his body bleeding with red paint, hovered over the congregation; his wooden face bore an expression of such deep human suffering that, instinctively, my heart contracted with pain. The crowd murmured softly in solemn expectation. An elderly priest lit the tall candles at the altar and sank to his knees in silent prayer.

Soon the organ resounded with unexpected strength and filled the crowded space with the grave chords of Kyrie eleison. The people standing in the aisle dropped to their knees and we did the same. My head bent low, my eyes closed, I felt carried away by an unknown, powerful sensation. It was as if I had entered an utterly new realm of unearthly experience. Peace, love, hope flew into my soul with the powerful music and the pious whispers of the crowd. I felt united with the people kneeling next to me more than I had ever been with anyone else. I glanced at Sophie: her face was pale, inspired, her eyes half closed, she seemed transported and transformed.

At this very moment a strong scent of burning incense filled the air, a shrill sound of little bells could be heard and two small boys dressed in white surplices emerged in front of the altar followed by an *angel*. Yes, for a split second I thought a real angel had descended to earth, bringing with him the light of eternity. Spellbound, I stopped breathing. The 'angel' was tall, dressed in a white robe, its wide sleeves flowing like wings. His face was of great beauty, his fair hair shone like a halo in the candlelight. He raised his arms, silently blessing the congregation. The organ now played a sweet, peaceful tune. The old priest gave a little sign and the 'angel' sang out in a strong, manly voice. The crowd burst into song. The wooden walls of the church swayed from a mighty Sanctus. The organ roared, the dazing scent of incense grew stronger and stronger. Bewildered and enthralled, I prayed in ecstasy, 'Oh God, let me believe in you, let me believe in your Son and the Holy Spirit.'

The Mass continued, the young priest knelt and stood by turns, followed by the crowd. He sang, he prayed, he performed various rites at the altar, then he climbed into the pulpit and began to preach. The sermon was simple and clear. It was about the equality of all humankind in the eyes of the Almighty God and the sacred duty of every Christian soul to help those who were in peril, no matter which race they belonged to or which faith they espoused. When he finished, the organ thundered again and the crowd struck up Agnus Dei. Then the Mass was over.

We left the church entranced, oblivious of all that had troubled us before. Sophie was still very pale and it seemed to me she might faint. Somewhere on our way home we met Mrs Pietrzyk. 'So you've seen Jan,' she said. 'I bet you liked him.' She looked radiant. She winked at us and promised Jan would come and talk to us after his midday meal.

Wearing his ordinary clothes, Jan did not look at all like one of the heavenly host. But he was unusually handsome and radiated manliness. There was very little of the country lad in him – his manners and speech were polished by years at college. He sat with us in our little room, clearly at ease and very attentive. He confessed that the service he had performed that morning had been his first. It had been a rehearsal, in fact, since he was not yet a priest, his final exams were just approaching. If he got through, he said, he might replace the old vicar after the war. He begged us to tell him all about the Warsaw uprising and our own experiences. So we told him all we could without letting out our secret. He listened sadly, nodded gravely and sighed. He confirmed what we had already heard – that Warsaw had been razed to the ground by the Nazis as soon as the deportees had left. That same night Jan went away and life in the cottage returned to its normal pattern. But for both Sophie and me the strange sensations we had experienced in church were not yet over.

11 December 1944

A cool, bleak Monday. I've got a cold and have to stay in bed again. It's four o'clock and the tiny little square of sky I can see through the window is turning grey. A solitary twig from the bare tree outside cuts across the square and waves to me sadly. Now and again it taps on the windowpane and seems to form a black cross. And when I look at it intensely, forgetting where I am and who I am, it seems to grow bigger and thicker and turns into a real cross with Christ stretched out on it, staring at me in agony. For a short while faint memories of what I felt in church surge into my tormented mind – then quickly fade away. Now the twig has gone, the cross has vanished and, writing these words, I try to think soberly about what happened yesterday. It was as though my mind – or soul – that up to now has been closed was suddenly opened wide to let in an unearthly Truth. I yearned for God, for faith, for being one of those who believe. I rejoiced in the feeling, I was completely swept away with spiritual bliss and longed for it all to last for ever. It must have been the music, the incense, the simple beauty of the little shrine that bewitched me. It wasn't God who opened heaven to me – it was the man who played the organ, the man who built the church, Jan Pietrzyk singing and praying.

How can I believe in God, this callous God who has allowed the slaughter of children, the gas chambers, my people's martyrdom? How can I become a Christian? I don't belong to them, I can't, I don't even want to. I belong to the Jews. Not because I was born one or because I share their faith – I never have done. I belong to the Jews because I have suffered as one of them. It's suffering that has made me Jewish. I belong to people who have been murdered or who are still struggling to escape death. If some of them do survive the war, and if I survive myself, I'll join them. Our shared experience of this ordeal will bring us together. We'll build a home of our own, a place for all homeless Jews where we can live in peace and dignity, respected by other nations and respecting their rights in turn. That's what I believe and where I belong.

There was no way I could confess my thoughts to Mother. Living from day to day, worrying endlessly about our safety and daily needs, she had no heart to listen to purely spiritual dilemmas. I tried to talk to Sophie who I knew was still under the spell of the Sunday Mass. But Sophie neither wanted to talk nor listen. Absorbed in her own thoughts and more silent than ever, she spent most of her days wandering in the fields. In my bed, staring vacantly out of the window, I sometimes caught a glimpse of her, a dark lonely shape on the snowy whiteness of the plain. She seemed to be miles away even when we were together, smiling to herself and not answering questions. She was not with us. Some time had passed before I found out why.

19 December

Great excitement in the cottage: preparations for Christmas have been going on since last Friday. First they stuck a pig – in great secrecy, of course, as it should have been handed over to the Germans. Then everyone in the family worked hard to make the pig meat into joints, lard and sausages. We offered to help, but Mrs Pietrzyk said the sight and smell of the carcase was more than town folk could bear. So we kept to our room. Once they had finished with the sausages, they started whitewashing the walls. It was our turn yesterday. Błażek appeared with his bucket and brush and we moved into the kitchen. We sat there cosily as it was snowing like mad outside, and helped Mrs Pietrzyk peel vegetables, sort peas, grind poppy seeds with sugar, and mend Błażek's old trousers. The old woman first sang canticles in her rusty voice, then started telling us stories about her family. She had had eight children all together, she said. She had outlived three of them, as well as her two husbands. Her eldest daughter lives with her own family somewhere far away, the other one has given herself to God and lives locked away in a convent. That's why Piotr, one of her younger children, will inherit the farm. Błażek is not fit to be on his own, she said, he is far too daft. But to make up for Błażek's deficiency, the Almighty had blessed her with her youngest child, whom she had given birth to at almost fifty. Mrs Pietrzyk now went into raptures over Jan: how clever he has always been, even as a young child, how kind-hearted and handsome.

As she carried on like this, getting more and more excited and fetching photographs of Jan at different stages of his life, I happened to glance at Sophie and could hardly believe my eyes: her face was crimson. Later, back in our room, I noticed her take something out of her pocket and gaze at it stealthily. Caught red-handed, she had to admit that she'd stolen one of Jan's pictures. She was terribly embarrassed, didn't know what to say, how to explain why she had done it. But I don't need an explanation: I can still remember how it feels when one is growing up and suddenly meets a man with a pair of starry blue eyes and a head of soft blond hair. My poor, poor little Sophie, there's no hope for her. Why on earth did she have to fall in love with a Catholic priest?

Three days before Christmas Eve, Błażek brought two fragrant fir trees from the nearest wood. To our surprise, one of them was for us. We somehow managed to tuck the prickly thing into the gap between the bed and window and, truly embarrassed, wondered what to hang on it. But Mrs Pietrzyk had worked out the whole matter in advance. Soon she appeared with a roll of bright coloured paper, two pairs of scissors and a jar of flour-and-water paste: 'It's for you, ladies. Show us what you clever townsfolk can do!' We set about cutting up and sticking the colourful strips with true zeal. It was sweet to sit in the warm light of the kerosene lamp, breathe in the fresh scent of the tree and produce the rustling chains and fluffy balls. It brought back memories of childhood to all four of us.

Within a couple of days all the decorations were ready except for the most important one to go at the top of the tree. Our burst of creativity suddenly deserted us and we couldn't think what would be best and easy enough to make. At last I decided to try and make a star. Since I had never been good with my fingers, I took great pains with it. There was no gold or silver paper so I had to use blue. When I had finished, we put all the stuff away since, according to Polish custom, the tree should be dressed by dusk on Christmas Eve.

We felt very uneasy about the approaching festivities, fearing we might do something wrong and show our ignorance of Christian traditions. To make it worse, two ladies from Warsaw who had befriended Auntie Maria in the queue for free meals, insisted on spending Christmas Eve with her, but claimed that the place they lived in was not good enough for the occasion. Auntie Maria could hardly say no, which meant they would come, meet the rest of us and be able to watch us closely for hours. We really dreaded it.

On the morning of the crucial day we dressed our fragrant tree, and, very pleased with ourselves since it looked gorgeous, called Mrs Pietrzyk in to let her see and marvel at it. The old woman scanned the tree, nodding with approval, then stepped back and glanced at the top with special attention. Her expression changed, her jaw dropped, she clearly did not like what she saw. Taken aback, I followed her gaze to the top of the tree and shuddered: in full daylight against the background of the whitewashed wall stood a six-pointed blue star of David, the emblem of the Jews.

Mrs Pietrzyk said nothing and left, but after a while she came back with a golden cardboard angel of impressive size. 'This would look better, if you ask me,' she said flatly. We didn't quite know what she really meant.

Christmas Eve, which we had dreaded so much, turned out rather well. The two Warsaw women arrived in festive mood and seemed very friendly. One of them, a dressmaker, had lost her husband in the war, the other, a chiropodist, was a spinster. We had an almost traditional supper, since Mrs Pietrzyk presented us with borsch and noodles with poppy seed, and the ladies also brought some food to share. Before we began, all the Pietrzyk family came in for a while to break the wafers with us. Then we sang carols and really enjoyed ourselves: despite our earlier misgivings everything worked out fine.

Since they mixed with other people far more than we did, our two visitors knew quite a lot about what was happening far away from the quiet village. The Red Army was still waiting idly in the Warsaw suburbs across the Vistula, but rumour had it that the Russians had steadily advanced everywhere else, pushing back the Germans with breathtaking speed. At the same time, the Nazis were losing in western Europe and the Third Reich was clearly approaching its bitter end. The final victory of the Allies was now close.

As we parted from our visitors, the dressmaker warmly embraced Mother and said, 'Hope for the best, my dear. You've endured the worst, God will help you till the end.' 'It won't be long now,' chimed in the chiropodist. They had both guessed our secret.

At dusk on Christmas Day, sitting idly in the bleak seclusion of our little room, we suddenly heard loud joyful voices. A burst of youthful laughter, a lively accordion tune was nearing the cottage. A sharp bang on our windowpane made us jump to our feet. Her hands trembling, Auntie Maria cautiously opened the window. Hidden behind her, I saw a group of young villagers crowding round the accordion player. 'What do you want, gentlemen?' asked Auntie Maria, her voice shrill with apprehension. The accordionist stepped forward, banged the keys of his instrument in earnest and sang, echoed by the others:

> 'Two pretty girls live in this cottage,
> We long to go dancing with them'

Bewildered, Auntie Maria struggled with the window, trying to shut it, but the boy's round face was already inside. A pair of smiling eyes stared full into my face. 'Come on girls, don't be shy, we're waiting for you.' He moved back, letting Auntie Maria close the window, and waited in the dark, chatting to his friends. 'Let's get Mrs Pietrzyk,' said Mother. 'She'll know how to get rid of them.' 'Get rid of them?' said Sophie all of a sudden in a plaintive voice. 'Why should we get rid of them?' Dismissing common sense, I backed her up. 'Yes, why not go dancing with them?' And, as usual, I promptly found the right excuse for doing something I badly wanted to do, 'Isn't it better to behave as any other girl would under the circumstances? If we refuse they may think we've got something to hide.' There was nothing Mother or Auntie Maria could say against this argument and, very distressed, they gave in – especially as the impatient knocking at the window had started again. In a flash Sophie and I slipped out of our trousers and pullovers and put on our worn summer dresses, now neatly washed and ironed. Wasting no time to comb our hair, we flew off into the frosty darkness of the Christmas night.

The big, bright room of a cottage in the village swarmed with dancers, vibrated with the clamour of two fiddles, the thudding of heavy boots, the buzz of merry voices. The whole world reeled before my eyes – brightly coloured skirts, long pigtails, sweaty faces whirling in the air. 'Heigh, heigh, tra la la!' roared the accordionist, joining the fiddlers. The dancers chanted and tapped their feet. Little clouds of grey dust rose from the rough planks on the floor.

There was no time to think, to feel out of place or retreat. We were grabbed and carried away into the middle of the throbbing crowd straight from the doorstep. I spun in a waltz with a long, thin boy, bounced in a breathtaking polka with a broad-shouldered one, I wiggled, swung and galloped, lost in abandon, overwhelmed by joy.

The hefty arms of strangers held me tight, blue, brown and grey eyes staring boldly into mine. There was no chance to talk. Time and again, I caught glimpses of Sophie's flushed face, her long black plait flying in the air.

Soon Antek, the accordionist, passed his noisy instrument to a pimply youth and dived into the frenzied throng. I was dancing with a fat man when I saw him making his way in my direction. He clapped his hands to show he wished to dance with me and took me away from the fat man. So now I spun with Antek and enjoyed myself even more since he was a great dancer. We did not stop when, from the lively *krakowiak* (a popular Polish folk dance), the music turned into a sobbing tango, or when it brought us back to a frenzy with the murderous rhythm of *oberek* (a very fast-moving folk dance). Two or three times Antek refused when other dancers clapped their hands for me. We paused only for a little while when the orchestra stopped to have a drink. Antek then said that he had first seen Sophie and me in church, and ever since then had badly wanted to meet us, because we were so pretty, so ladylike, so different. He had never met town girls before, he said, and never realised they might be so nice. He made me laugh when he went into raptures over my miserable dress. He was a fine, open boy. I liked his smile and the gentle, gallant way he treated me. We danced again, but after a time Antek said he must go back to the accordion to let his friend have some fun too. The two fiddlers had already left their instruments and were prancing about like everyone else.

Now, feeling a little bored and tired, I was dancing again with the broad-shouldered Franek who seemed rather tipsy. I did not like the way he squeezed my waist and pressed his face close to mine. I did not like him at all and wanted to stop dancing. But he would not let me go. To make it worse, he pulled me to a poorly lit corner of the room and with his bulky body pressed me against the wall. No one paid us the slightest attention as a few other couples were leaning against the wall in similar fashion. I was struggling to escape from this unwelcome embrace when Franek whispered straight into my ear, 'Come to the barn with me, sweetie.' I sensed something threatening in his voice. His rough hands were now hurting me. 'Leave me alone!' I screamed. The music suddenly stopped and I saw Antek jump to his feet. 'Easy, easy, little girl,' hissed Franek, his face growing red. 'Don't cock your long nose at me. You come with me to the barn or I'll fetch the police.'

At this very moment a mighty punch landed in the middle of his sweaty face and, losing his balance, Franek dropped flat to the floor.

'Wait for me in the porch,' shouted Antek and I ran to the door, grabbing hold of Sophie. Before I slammed the door, I caught a glimpse of Franek clumsily lifting himself up from the floor. A little crowd of dancers was gathering around him. After a while, Antek came out to the porch and saw us home to our cottage. He seemed very pleased with himself.

We did not tell Mother or Auntie Maria what had happened that night. There was no point in adding to their worries. There was nothing we could do to escape Franek's revenge, anyway. Hiding or running away from the village was out of the question. Tormented by fear and guilt, we suffered in silence. It was too high a price to pay for a moment of mindless joy.

Three days later Antek knocked at our window again. He wanted a word with me. I went out and met him in the dark. 'Franek will never pester you again,' he said, coming straight to the point. 'The matter is settled. I give you my word of honour.' The moon sailed out from behind a cloud and in its light I saw two big plasters on Antek's face – one on his left cheek, one above his eyebrow. I really liked this boy and trusted him. Shyly, he suggested we might go for a walk and I said yes.

29 December 1944

I can hardly understand my own behaviour last night. I walked for two hours or more with this gentle boy and I told him nothing but lies. Was it necessary, I wonder? The truth is, when we left the cottage and plunged into the open, moonlit fields, he suddenly asked me to be his girlfriend. He sounded so keen but so shy in saying this that I almost burst out laughing. I could swear he blushed. I knew I might easily hurt his feelings if I trifled with them, so, very gently, I told him I already had a boyfriend. I could easily have stopped there: I had made my point and Antek accepted it. But no, I did not stop, I went on making up more and more silly stories. In fact Roman is my fiancé, I said, and we are going to get married as soon as the war is over and he gets back from prison camp. Before the uprising, I continued, I had a terribly busy and exciting life with Roman. We belonged to the resistance, we studied and went to forbidden concerts . . . The little flat in the Old Town where we lived together was always full of friends and people needing help . . . And after the war, I chattered away, when I meet Roman again, we are both going to try to make our life even

more useful and exciting. We shall travel all round the world to
see how other people live and what makes them suffer. Together
with our friends who share our beliefs, we shall fight all evil,
denounce all prejudice, oppose all injustice. How? We don't
know yet. Perhaps by writing books . . .

Antek listened to my prattle, enthralled and full of
admiration. When at last I stopped talking, he said his own life
was far less exciting, just hard work and a little fun; but he liked
it this way, and the only thing he really longed for was to be
better educated, know more about the world. But he sounded a
bit upset, so I let him kiss me goodbye when we parted.

I've been thinking now about this glorious future that I
dreamed up last night. Will it come true? Shall I ever live a
free, useful, happy life with someone I love and who loves me?
Will it happen soon, will a day come when the whole world
suddenly opens for me and lets me choose what I want to do.
I've been waiting so long, so long . . . I can't wait any longer, I
want to live *now*.

Just before New Year, Jan came back to the cottage. Kind and serene as
ever, he didn't seem to notice Sophie's languishing gazes, or the sprigs of
mistletoe she spread on the floor in front of his door for lack of fresh
flowers. Nor did he pay much attention to me, he seemed far more
interested in Auntie Maria. On New Year's Eve he invited her in to his
room. Auntie Maria spent twenty-four minutes and fifteen seconds
there, said Sophie later. She looked worried when she came out. She
told us everything that Jan had said, word for word. First he spoke about
the war. It would soon be over. Nevertheless, though we all lived in
hope of a swift Nazi defeat, people seemed to forget that the fiend still
held our tormented country in a firm grip. The terror had not stopped
yet, it was still raging as before. In the big cities hundreds of people were
being grabbed daily from their homes and streets, thrown into prisons
and concentration camps or killed on the spot. In our quiet village, Jan
went on, people lived in an illusory peace, unaware of danger. It was a
priest's duty to warn them, young boys and girls most of all, since they
were the most vulnerable. Here Jan mentioned myself and Sophie and
said we should be more careful and stay at home, rather than going
about and mixing with the locals. Auntie Maria thanked him and
promised to keep an eye on us, but left his room not really understanding why he had suddenly said all this. But Sophie and I knew quite well

– he must have heard something about what had happened on Christmas night.

On New Year's morning the old vicar made his yearly round through the village, calling on all the farmers with the crucifix. Mrs Pietrzyk had told us about this in advance to let us get ready. We felt completely lost, not knowing what we were supposed to do. I tried in vain to find some hint in the catechism, and Auntie Maria desperately searched her memory. We must have looked very sheepish when the old man entered our room, a broad benign smile on his fleshy face. 'Praised be Jesus Christ,' he said and pointed the big silver crucifix at Auntie Maria. 'For ever and ever,' we answered in chorus. At this very moment, Auntie Maria's eyes flashed with recollection. She bowed down before the priest and kissed the crucifix. The vicar stretched out his hands over her head and whispered his blessing. Then he approached Mother, myself and Sophie in turn and, obediently, we did as we were supposed to do. As I kissed the cold silver feet of the crucified Christ I felt a fraud.

The first days of 1945 brought gloom and unrest to our peaceful village. Jan received a secret message and disappeared from home at once. Soon after, two farmers were arrested and taken away by the German police for having failed to hand over their quota of cattle. The same day, Mrs Pietrzyk came to ask us a favour. She wanted us to foster her heifer which otherwise might bring disaster to the family. A thorough search for unlawfully kept cattle was now under way. But so far, she said, the rascals were not interfering with refugees. 'They won't touch her if you say she's yours.' We agreed, of course, and let the young cow into our room. Tethered to the bed, she occupied most of the scant space and performed all her vital duties in our company.

Some time later we were devastated to hear that our sweet young doctor had been arrested. The Gestapo had come from Cracow late one night and taken her away straight from her bed. We could hardly bear the news. Several hours before her arrest, she had called on us to wish us a happy New Year. She had beamed with hope, saying that this year would bring us freedom and very soon. She had brought a big wedge of homemade cake and half of it was still on the plate, waiting to be eaten.

Despite these sad events and the mounting tension, hope was steadily growing. The Red Army was now heading westwards with unbelievable speed. On the day that the long-awaited battle of Warsaw finally began, we also heard the first sounds of the Eastern Front approaching Cracow. The familiar, welcome roar grew stronger from day to day and then from hour to hour, until it was so close that the inhabitants of our little village, unaccustomed to the sounds of war, ran for their lives in panic and hid in their cellars.

For us the war came to an abrupt end at 8 a.m. on Friday, 19 January 1945. After a sleepless night echoing with cannon-fire, heavy with great expectations, we saw in the faint light of the wintry dawn the weird, grey hunched outlines of the first Russian soldiers. Stealthily, they scuttled, one by one past our window, their guns at the ready. By noon the sounds of heavy battle subsided and were replaced by a steady rumble of heavy vehicles coming from afar.

Just before dusk I went out to fetch some wood. In the semidark shed, crammed with logs and tools, something stirred. I sensed a human presence. I pushed the door wide open to let in more light. Only then did I notice a flap of field-grey military coat sticking out from between two logs. Calmly, I locked the shed and ran back to the cottage. In the kitchen, Mrs Pietrzyk, tired and worn after the restless night, was busy cooking. Gasping for breath, I told her what I had seen. But she was not surprised: she already knew. Staring full in my face with her ancient, all-knowing eyes, she said, as if quoting from a holy book, 'Whoever comes under my roof seeking shelter, no matter who he is, no matter what he believes in, he will be safe with me.' In a flash I understood. Shocked, I watched her fill a tin bowl with hot dumplings and pour pork fat over it. 'Hold it, child,' she screeched in her usual way. 'Take it to him.' As if mesmerised, I blindly obeyed and went back to the shed. It seemed as deserted as before, even the field-grey flap had disappeared. I stood benumbed, the hot dish burning my fingers and filling the air with a strong smell of food. There was a brief commotion behind the pile of logs and an unkempt head suddenly popped out. I saw the pale face of the German, a boy rather than a man, staring at me in terror. He grabbed the steaming bowl from my hands and fell on the food with unspeakable greed. He was still trembling from hunger and fear. For a long while I watched him blankly. I felt no pity, no hatred, no joy.

The war ended.

Postscript

This is the end of my story and the starting point of a new one. I had not intended to write more in this book. However, my friends who have read the manuscript wanted to know what had happened to some of my relations and friends since the wartime days. It made me think that my unknown readers might like to know, too.

Mother, Sophie and I returned to Warsaw soon after the liberation and lived there for many years. In 1957 Sophie, with her husband and six-month-old daughter, left for Israel. Mother followed soon after to look after the growing family. I stayed in Warsaw much longer, until in June 1968 my husband and I, with our three teenage daughters, had to leave Poland for ever.

In 1971 Sophie died at the age of forty-one, leaving her husband and three young children – a girl and two boys. For some time Mother stayed on with her beloved grandchildren. Then she left Israel and came to England to spend her last years with me and my family. She died in Leeds in 1980.

My father never returned from Russia. Soon after the war, the International Red Cross confirmed his death in the Katyń forest in the spring of 1940.

While Stefan, with hundreds of other Poles, was burning alive during the Warsaw Uprising, Jadwiga was taken by the Germans to a labour camp. She survived and returned to Warsaw after the war, as beautiful as ever but no longer the same. She promptly remarried and left Poland for good.

My grandma Viera disappeared during the Warsaw Uprising. She was never found. The family who sheltered her vanished too. Nobody knew what had happened to them.

Auntie Maria remained a member of our family for as long as she lived. Immediately after the war her loving care was in demand again. Mother's second brother, Jerzy, who had lost his wife and daughter at the beginning of the war, returned with the new Polish Army from Russia, bringing with him a second wife. She was already pregnant. They begged Auntie Maria to move in with them and take care of the baby. So she did and was the heart and soul of the family until she died peacefully at the age of seventy-five.

My second guardian-angel, Staś, whose full name is Stanislaw Chmielewski, still lives in Warsaw. He proved a good, helpful friend again when, in 1968, we had to leave Poland in great haste.

Of my three best friends, only Hanka survived. She is a scientist and lives in Poland. I have already described Zula's tragic end. Renata, too, was killed by the Germans for hiding on the 'Aryan' side, and so was her sister Joanna and their father. The only member of Renata's family who survived the war was her mother.

And now a fairy tale without a happy ending: the first familiar face I saw in the street of the ruined Warsaw after my return in April 1945, was Roman's. We met in the crowd quite by chance. Having lost his parents in the ghetto, he had escaped and joined the resistance away from Warsaw. He grew up and changed almost beyond recognition. And so, certainly, did I. The spell of our early days was gone. We had kept in touch for some time before he disappeared from my sight. He left Poland in the 1950s.

One day in May 1945, wandering through the ruins, climbing the mounds of rubble which had replaced the streets of my town, I found myself in front of the house where, nine months earlier, we had stopped for a short while to wash and dress ourselves before leaving Warsaw. To my great surprise, it remained as it had been – only half-ruined. The once shattered windowpanes of the salvaged wing had now been replaced with fresh plywood boards, which meant someone was living there. I climbed up the ramshackle steps and knocked at the door of the well-remembered flat. A girl of my age let me in. I explained that in that flat, under the rubble of a half-ruined room, I had buried my manuscripts just after the Uprising. Taken aback, she led me to the room which, she said, had never been used by her family. It still looked as I remembered it, one leg of the piano dangling over the precipice. And here they were, all my copybooks and loose sheets covered with my untidy handwriting, hidden safely in a hole in the floor, under a few bricks.

Twenty-three years later I lost them again. But this is another story.

Chronology

This brief chronology lists only the major events relevant to *Winter in the Morning*.

13 March 1938 Annexation of Austria by Nazi Germany
October 1938–March 1939 Annexation of Czechoslovakia by Nazi Germany
23 August 1939 Hitler and Stalin conclude a non-aggression pact between Nazi Germany and Soviet Russia
1 September 1939 Germany invades Poland: the beginning of the Second World War
3 September 1939 Great Britain and France declare war on Germany
8 September 1939 The beginning of the siege of Warsaw
17 September 1939 As a result of the agreement between Hitler and Stalin, Soviet forces enter Poland from the East to meet the German Army advancing from the West
18 September 1939 The Polish government and high command cross the Romanian frontier on their way to exile
27 September 1939 Surrender of Warsaw to the Germans
5 October 1939 Final defeat of Poland
Spring 1940 Katyń Massacre: mass execution of Polish prisoners in Russia
16 November 1940 Sealing of the Jewish ghetto in Warsaw
22 June 1941 Despite the earlier agreement, Germany invades Russia. USSR joins the Allies by entering the war against Germany
22 July–13 September 1942 First mass deportation from the Warsaw ghetto (First *Aktion*)
18–22 January 1943 Second *Aktion* and first acts of resistance by the Jewish Fighting Organisation
19 April–16 May 1943 Uprising in the Warsaw ghetto

Spring–Summer 1943 Nazi reports on the Katyń Massacre are published

6 June 1944 D-Day landing in Normandy; the beginning of the Allied invasion of Western Europe

1 August–3 October 1944 The Warsaw Uprising

January 1945 The Russian Red Army starts its major offensive in Poland, pushing Germans back to the West

17 January 1945 Ruined and deserted Warsaw taken by the Red Army

19 January 1945 Cracow and its vicinity liberated from the Germans by the Red Army

9 May 1945 End of the Second World War

VIRAGO MODERN CLASSICS
&
CLASSIC NON-FICTION

The first Virago Modern Classic, *Frost in May* by Antonia White, was published in 1978. It launched a list dedicated to the celebration of women writers and to the rediscovery and reprinting of their works. Its aim was, and is, to demonstrate the existence of a female tradition in fiction, and to broaden the sometimes narrow definition of a 'classic' which has often led to the neglect of interesting novels and short stories. Published with new introductions by some of today's best writers, the books are chosen for many reasons: they may be great works of fiction; they may be wonderful period pieces; they may reveal particular aspects of women's lives; they may be classics of comedy or storytelling.

The companion series, Virago Classic Non-Fiction, includes diaries, letters, literary criticism, and biographies – often by and about authors published in the Virago Modern Classics.

'Good news for everyone writing and reading today' – *Hilary Mantel*

'A continuingly magnificent imprint' – *Joanna Trollope*

'The Virago Modern Classics have reshaped literary history and enriched the reading of us all. No library is complete without them' – *Margaret Drabble*

VIRAGO MODERN CLASSICS
&
CLASSIC NON-FICTION

Some of the authors included in these two series –

Elizabeth von Arnim, Dorothy Baker, Pat Barker, Nina Bawden,
Nicola Beauman, Sybille Bedford, Jane Bowles, Kay Boyle,
Vera Brittain, Leonora Carrington, Angela Carter, Willa Cather,
Colette, Ivy Compton-Burnett, E.M. Delafield, Maureen Duffy,
Elaine Dundy, Nell Dunn, Emily Eden, George Egerton,
George Eliot, Miles Franklin, Mrs Gaskell,
Charlotte Perkins Gilman, George Gissing,
Victoria Glendinning, Radclyffe Hall, Shirley Hazzard,
Dorothy Hewett, Mary Hocking, Alice Hoffman,
Winifred Holtby, Janette Turner Hospital, Zora Neale Hurston,
Elizabeth Jenkins, F. Tennyson Jesse, Molly Keane,
Margaret Laurence, Maura Laverty, Rosamond Lehmann,
Rose Macaulay, Shena Mackay, Olivia Manning, Paule Marshall,
F.M. Mayor, Anaïs Nin, Kate O'Brien, Olivia, Grace Paley,
Mollie Panter-Downes, Dawn Powell, Dorothy Richardson,
E. Arnot Robertson, Jacqueline Rose, Vita Sackville-West,
Elaine Showalter, May Sinclair, Agnes Smedley, Dodie Smith,
Stevie Smith, Nancy Spain, Christina Stead, Carolyn Steedman,
Gertrude Stein, Jan Struther, Han Suyin, Elizabeth Taylor,
Sylvia Townsend Warner, Mary Webb, Eudora Welty,
Mae West, Rebecca West, Edith Wharton, Antonia White,
Christa Wolf, Virginia Woolf, E.H. Young

A MODEL CHILDHOOD
Christa Wolf

'This is a powerful book, a most extraordinary testament . . .
it is her vision of the fundamental strangeness of what
seemed at the time a fairly ordinary childhood, in the bosom
of a normal Nazi family in Landsberg, which makes Christa
Wolf's narrative so moving, so convincing' – *The Times*

In 1933, Nelly is four years old and lives in Landsberg. Nelly's
family believes in Hitler's new order: her father joins the party, and
she, as a matter of course, joins the Nazi youth organisations. In
school Nelly learns of racial purity and the Jewish threat, and when
the local synagogue burns, she feels not pity, only fear of an alien
race. No voice of objection is raised, not even when the euthanasia
programme dooms Nelly's simple-minded Aunt Dottie. It is only
much later, when her family is fleeing westward before the
advancing Russian army, that Nelly, now in her teens, tries to
come to terms with the shattering of the fundamental values of her
childhood.

Christa Wolf, novelist, short-story writer, essayist, critic, journalist
and film dramatist, born in Landsberg, Warthe, in 1929, lives in
East Berlin. East Germany's most prestigious woman of letters, in
this her fourth novel she explores the experience of Nazism as it
was lived by ordinary people in an ordinary town. In doing so
Christa Wolf has created a great novel which is also a plea to
remember and to learn from the past.

Now you can order superb titles directly from Virago

☐ A Model Childhood	Christa Wolf	£8.99
☐ Joyce's War	Joyce Storey	£4.99
☐ Mrs Miniver	Jan Struther	£5.99
☐ Hearts Undefeated	Jenny Hartley (ed)	£9.99

Please allow for postage and packing: **Free UK delivery.**
Europe; add 25% of retail price; Rest of World; 45% of retail price.

To order any of the above or any other Virago titles, please call our credit card orderline or fill in this coupon and send/fax it to:

Virago, 250 Western Avenue, London, W3 6XZ, UK.
Fax 0181 324 5678   Telephone 0181 324 5516

☐ I enclose a UK bank cheque made payable to Virago for £..............
☐ Please charge £.............. to my Access, Visa, Delta, Switch Card No.

☐☐☐☐☐☐☐☐☐☐☐☐☐☐☐☐☐☐☐

Expiry Date ☐☐☐☐   Switch Issue No.   ☐☐

NAME (Block letters please) ....

ADDRESS ....

....

....

Postcode ....Telephone ....

Signature ....

Please allow 28 days for delivery within the UK. Offer subject to price and availability.

Please do not send any further mailings from companies carefully selected by Virago ☐